Cataloging for
School Librarians

D1533103

Cataloging for School Librarians

Marie Kelsey

ROWMAN & LITTLEFIELD
Lanham • Boulder • New York • Toronto • Plymouth, UK

Published by Rowman & Littlefield
4501 Forbes Boulevard, Suite 200, Lanham, Maryland 20706
www.rowman.com

10 Thornbury Road, Plymouth PL6 7PP, United Kingdom

Copyright © 2014 by Rowman & Littlefield Publishers, Inc.

All rights reserved. No part of this book may be reproduced in any form or by any electronic or mechanical means, including information storage and retrieval systems, without written permission from the publisher, except by a reviewer who may quote passages in a review.

British Library Cataloguing in Publication Information Available

Library of Congress Cataloging-in-Publication Data

Kelsey, Marie Ellen, 1948–
   Cataloging for school librarians / Marie Kelsey.
      pages cm
   Includes bibliographical references and index.
   ISBN 978-1-4422-3245-7 (hardcover : alk. paper) — ISBN 978-1-4422-3246-4 (pbk. : alk. paper) — ISBN 978-1-4422-3247-1 (ebook)
   1. Cataloging—Handbooks, manuals, etc. 2. School libraries—Handbooks, manuals, etc. I. Title.
   Z693.K45 2014
   025.3—dc23
                                                                    2014012391

∞™ The paper used in this publication meets the minimum requirements of American National Standard for Information Sciences—Permanence of Paper for Printed Library Materials, ANSI/NISO Z39.48-1992. Printed in the United States of America

Dedicated to catalogers everywhere.
Without your tireless efforts, there would be no *resource discovery*.

DISCARDED
PASADENA CITY COLLEGE
SHATFORD LIBRARY

MAR   2015

1570 E. Colorado Blvd
Pasadena, CA 91106

Contents

Part IV. Conclusion

Figures

Preface

Cataloging for School Librarians grew out of the cataloging course I taught for many years both in the classroom setting and online for distance students. To students studying to be school librarians, cataloging rules and all the processes involved in classification, subject heading assignment, and creating MARC records can seem overwhelming and something to be avoided, since catalog records can be acquired for a small fee from book vendors. However, I believe it is important for school librarians and professionals in other types of small libraries to understand more than how to transfer MARC records from vendor files to their local OPAC. Without a true understanding of the principles and practicalities of constructing bibliographic records, the catalog will not maintain its integrity or remain functional.

The audience for *Cataloging for School Librarians* is predominantly students wishing to become school librarians, but it also fulfills the needs of any beginning library student or individuals already working in libraries who wish to understand bibliographic control more completely. The K–12 environment is the foundation for the explanations and examples provided here, but the rules and concepts apply universally to cataloging for any type of library. This book does not delve into the intricacies of serials cataloging, complicated corporate author situations, publications resulting from conferences, or how to use Library of Congress Classification or Subject Headings. These are best left to more advanced textbooks. In this book the focus is the catalog record for books and some nonprint items, *Sears List of Subject Headings*, and the *Abridged Dewey Decimal Classification*, all typical of school or other small libraries.

The overarching theme of this book is "resource discovery," a phrase taken from the new cataloging code, *Resource Description and Access* (RDA), in its statement of purpose and scope. The concept of resource discovery is closely related to Charles Ammi Cutter's first objective for the catalog: a person ought to be able to use the catalog to *find* a book if the author, title, or subject is known. In the information age the importance of being able to "discover resources" has become immense. There is more to be discovered than ever before, and a credible catalog is a vital means to that discovery.

ORGANIZATION

Cataloging for School Librarians is arranged in four parts. Part I, "Essential Information," includes chapters 1 through 4. Chapter 1, "Introducing the Library Catalog and Access to Resources," takes the reader from book catalogs to OCLC and introduces the influential individuals who developed bibliographic control into the practice and profession it is today. Chapter 2, "Supporting Resource Discovery: RDA and FRBR," looks at the diverse screen displays in today's OPAC interfaces, all built on catalog records intended to discretely identify single items held in a library. In contrast, RDA and *Functional Requirements for Bibliographic Records* (FRBR), the new catalog code and its underlying conceptual structure, are examined as a means of capitalizing on relationships among records, a new way to maximize resource discovery. Chapter 3, "Obtaining OPAC Bibliographic Records," moves the reader closer to the actual bibliographic product by identifying the various sources for available records, exclusive of original cataloging. Finally, chapter 4, "Understanding Cataloging in Publication (CIP)," provides detailed information about this rich source of bibliographic data, explaining the parts of the CIP record and the contributions made to it by the Children's and Young Adults' Cataloging Program (CYACP). The dilemmas CIP can present for school librarians are also considered.

Part II, "Descriptive Cataloging," comprises chapters 5 through 10. Here the focus shifts from acquiring records from outside sources to understanding and carrying out the process of original cataloging. Chapter 5, "Creating Access Points," distinguishes between main and added entries, gives examples of selecting these elements, and highlights the changes between AACR2 and RDA in assigning them. Chapter 6, "Creating Authorized Forms of Names," covers Library of Congress name authorities and the importance of consistency in forms of names used in the bibliographic record. Chapter 7, "Creating MARC 21 Records," leads the student through the fine points of Machine Readable Cataloging (MARC), the coding system allowing bibliographic data to be manipulated by computers. Chapters 8 and 9, "Cataloging Books" and "Cataloging Nonprint and Electronic Materials," show the student how to synthesize the lessons of chapters 5, 6, and 7 in the creation of bibliographic records. Chapter 10, "Cataloging Books in Series," deals with both nonfiction and fiction series. The fiction series requires special attention to access points because of the myriad ways students ask for these popular publications.

Part III, "Subject Cataloging and Classification," contains chapters 11 through 13. Chapter 11, "Using *Sears List of Subject Headings*," describes both the conceptual foundations of Sears and the mechanics of assigning the subject headings. Chapter 12, "Using *Abridged Dewey Decimal Classification*," relates the biography of Melvil

Dewey, the structure of his classification system, and the fundamentals of number building and applying standard subdivisions. Chapter 13, "Building Dewey Numbers in Three Major Areas," focuses on languages, literature, and history.

Part IV, "Conclusion," consists of chapter 14, "From Resource Discovery to Information Fluency," a reflection piece considering the library catalog and resource discovery in the larger context of information seeking and information fluency among today's students and teachers. The OPAC faces much competition from the unstructured Internet and the thriving social media sites that "catalog" books and offer opportunities for discussion about them, but a newly conceptualized OPAC, the product of RDA and FRBR and based on bibliographic relationships, could make meaningful contributions to the new landscape of information fluency and resource discovery.

Chapters 1–13 contain reinforcement exercises. The book ends with two appendices, a glossary, a key to the exercises, a bibliography, and an index. Appendix A is a table showing the highest profile differences between bibliographic records constructed under the *Anglo-American Cataloguing Rules, Second Edition* (AACR2) and the new RDA. Knowing these few major differences will help the librarian easily identify a new RDA record among the many already existing AACR2 records. Appendix B displays ten OCLC bibliographic records complete with MARC coding, all constructed according to RDA rules. They represent a variety of media types.

It is my intention to present a useful introductory text that elucidates the process and product of cataloging. The degree to which this book gives school librarians the skills and confidence to create a reliable library catalog will be the measure of its success. Resource discovery by all stakeholders depends on these skills.

I

ESSENTIAL INFORMATION

1

Introducing the Library Catalog and Access to Resources

Before you begin learning the cataloging process itself, it is well to know something about how your work continues a tradition begun long ago. You will see how knowledge organizers have pondered both the tangible and intangible aspects of making products of the human mind accessible to potential users. Both the process and the product developed contemporaneously with technology, which advanced from the printing press to the Internet. During this time it became clear that cataloging and digitization were made for each other. Early technology, or the lack of it, kept catalog records static and local, but the move from book and card catalogs to flexible online public access catalogs (OPACs) made information accessible far beyond each individual local community. It also dramatically altered the appearance of catalog records. Before digitization, standard catalog records followed a rigid format. Today, online catalogs display records in a remarkable number of creative ways.

Catalog records are a representation of an actual item. When we cannot put our hands on the book or other product of the information industry, we need a way to learn something about the item so we can decide if we want to see it. The catalog record does that by functioning as a surrogate for the actual item. Another more commonly used name for the surrogate is *bibliographic record*. There are rules and standard procedures for constructing these surrogates, with each record being created through a step-by-step process. You describe the item, you identify access points for it, and you classify it so that it groups with other like items and is physically findable, by assigning it a location. There are millions of books, periodical titles, e-books, and media in existence today. Although you will never have one million items in your school library collection, you will have enough items that, unless they are represented by bibliographic records (surrogates) in your online catalog, you will not be able to access them efficiently. In essence, they will be lost to your users, depriving them of a chance to learn something new. Today's OPACs offer multiple ways of accessing

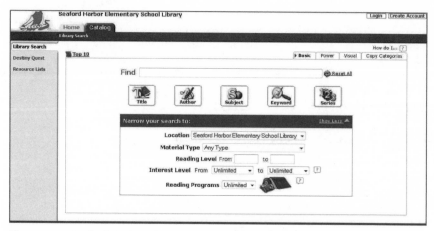

Figure 1.1. Seaford Harbor Elementary School Library Catalog OPAC Search Screen

bibliographic records, ranging from broad searches retrieving large numbers of records to search strategies that narrow results to something more manageable.

Figure 1.1 is an online catalog search screen from the Follett Company of the type used in school libraries. Users can search by author, subject, title, keyword, or series. They can also narrow their searches by type, reading level, interest level, and reading program. These are all useful limiters in a school setting.

The search screen for the Follett OPAC clearly identifies major access points in a catalog record:

- **Keywords are access points.** Depending on the OPAC software, a keyword search can search any number of fields in the catalog record. For example, there are author fields, title fields, publisher fields, notes fields, and subject fields. Each field is given a code. Not all OPACs will search every single field in a record during a *keyword* search. Some limitations may be imposed.
- **Authors and other individuals are access points.** If there are multiple authors, or authors and illustrators, you may or may not have access via every possible name associated with the item. You will make this decision based on cataloging rules and cataloger preference.
- **Titles are access points.** This includes the title proper and any variant titles. For example, the title proper might be *The 500 Hats of Bartholomew Cubbins*, but you may want to provide access via "500" spelled out, so you would provide an extra access point by entering *The Five Hundred Hats of Bartholomew Cubbins*.
- **Subject headings are access points.** These represent what the item is about and are assigned from preestablished lists of subject headings.

Special Tidbit: Entry Points in OPACs and Card Catalogs

- In OPACs, the entry point can be any word in the field. For example, to find *The 500 Hats of Bartholomew Cubbins*, you could enter the OPAC by using the word "hats," and you would more than likely find the book.
- In card catalogs, the entry point was always the first word. In this case you would have gone to the "F" drawers and looked for "Five Hundred Hats of . . ." . If you had tried to find this book in the "H" drawers under "Hats," you would never have found it, because there was no card made for it. You also would never find it under its actual first word, "The." We skip initial articles in alphabetizing: A, AN, and THE. Everything else counts. If the book were titled *And Then There Were Five Hundred Hats*, the first word "And" would be used to alphabetize, and you would look in the "A" drawer or start your OPAC browse for the title using the word "And."

ACCESS POINTS IN CARD CATALOGS

When we used card catalogs, each access point had to have a separate card. If there were 100,000 titles in the collection and each one needed an average of four cards (one author, possibly one illustrator, one title, and one to three subject headings), that would be 400,000 cards representing those items and providing access to them. Additionally, there was a shelflist card, which was filed in the cataloging department in classification, or shelf, order. These were used for inventory and other purposes. Card catalogs took up a lot of space and were expensive to build and maintain.

ACCESS POINTS IN OPACS

Today, with OPACs, one master catalog record is made, and software used to access these records can search in that one record for authors, titles, subject headings, the ISBN, and so forth. In many OPACs there are little drop down boxes revealing all the various searchable fields. This potential to provide multiple access points puts the OPAC light years ahead of the old catalog cards, which were limited in how many access points they could reasonably provide for the users. Besides broadening searches, terms also may be combined in OPACs, which has the effect of narrowing the search results, a handy feature that permits more precise results.

The OPAC was an immense improvement over the card catalog. The elimination of paper cards and the drawers they were filed in made the information more accessible to many people with disabilities, such as the visually impaired and wheelchair users. It also revolutionized the daily work of the cataloger and led to the development of the integrated library system (ILS), in which circulation, cataloging, the OPAC, and other library functions interface with one another.

HISTORICAL BACKGROUND

Before we get down to the nuts and bolts of current-day cataloging, we need to look at a little cataloging history and theory. How was cataloging done in the past, and how does that differ from what we do today?

Book Catalogs

The earliest form of library catalog was in a book format, not cards. The oldest of these that we know of was in the ancient Alexandrian Library in Egypt. Catalog records were displayed in a list on each page and were quite inflexible. The librarian constructed an individual entry for each book as it arrived in the library, but this did not make a useful catalog. It had no particular order other than accession and no space to add anything new between entries already permanently listed on the pages. This was the predominant form of library catalog until the late nineteenth century, when cards began to enter the picture, making library catalogs more flexible and much easier to update than book catalogs.

Antonio Panizzi

In the nineteenth century, library catalogs were not standardized, but rather were community based and therefore varied in their construction and conventions. As long as collections remained small, this was tolerable. Then there was the British Museum and its vast collection. In 1819 it had a book catalog organized alphabetically by author with no subject access. By the 1830s cataloging for the British Museum was in disarray (as was the museum itself). The museum administration hired Antonio Panizzi (an Italian lawyer) to upgrade the catalog. The board of trustees gave him the task to "standardize the format of the bibliographic records and . . . assure that enough detail was included to differentiate one from another" (Hufford, 1991). Panizzi went to work with a committee of librarians and created *Rules for the Compilation of the Catalogue* (a compendium of ninety-one rules), which was approved by the board in 1839. The first volume of catalog records constructed according to these rules was published in 1841. Its main goal was to create an alphabetical arrangement within a book catalog. The vestiges of Panizzi's rules are with us today.

Charles Coffin Jewett

Across the Atlantic Ocean, in the United States, Charles Coffin Jewett was a librarian's assistant while in graduate school at Andover Theological Seminary. His boss was preparing a catalog for the seminary's library, which made an excellent training ground for Jewett. In 1841 he was appointed librarian and professor of modern languages at Brown University. The small library collection had been cataloged only twice. Jewett completed the third book catalog in 1843. He eventually moved on, and after serving as librarian at the new Smithsonian Institution, he became the cataloger at the Boston Public Library. Here he devised a new type of book catalog, titled *Index to a Catalogue of a Portion of the Public Library of the City of Boston*, with each book listed in three separate places (by author, subject, and title) within one overall alphabetical listing. Since any individual book has several characteristics (number of pages, size, the existence of illustrations, etc.) that information was also recorded. All that information consumed a lot of space (always a problem), so he decided to put the complete information at one entry only, the author entry. The other entries had abbreviated information.

This was a prodigious task, creating yet another inflexible product. Once the book catalog was made, nothing new could be interfiled in it. To update this catalog, the librarian had to start all over or create a supplemental volume. To use such a catalog, it was necessary to page through a large tome or tomes.

Jewett also constructed a cataloging code based on Panizzi's for the Smithsonian Institution titled *On the Construction of Catalogues of Libraries, and Their Publication by Means of Separate, Stereotyped Titles*. Stereotyping was a method of printing using a metal copy of the typeset image that allowed the record to be retained indefinitely. If another library needed cataloging for the same book, it could be ordered from these plates. Again, this wasn't cards, but it was a way of producing a book catalog. The plan was not implemented at that time; however, years later this is what the Library of Congress (LC) ultimately did, producing master bibliographic records and using them to make cards that were sold to American libraries (Taylor & Joudrey, 2009).

Charles Ammi Cutter

Jewett's subordinate in the Boston Public Library cataloging department was Charles Ammi Cutter. In 1868 Cutter became librarian at the private Boston Athenaeum, the third largest library in the United States. Here he created a book catalog, some aspects of which showed marked improvement over earlier book catalogs. For one thing, words in the titles were no longer used as de facto subject headings. The content of each book was analyzed and subject headings assigned accordingly. When this catalog (*Catalogue of the Library of the Boston Athenæum 1807–1871*) was published it propelled Cutter to fame in the library profession. Cutter used what he had learned to construct his famous *Rules for a Dictionary Catalog* (1876), a new cataloging code. In it he outlined what he believed to be the objectives of the catalog, a concept still relevant today. Cutter's first objective for the catalog is that a person ought to be able to use it to find book if the author, title, or subject is known. Second, a catalog ought to show what the library has by any given author, on any given subject, and in a given kind of literature. Last, the catalog ought to facilitate choosing a book according to its edition and its character (whether it is literary or topical). Today these objectives are invoked as one predecessor of the catalog's latest conceptual framework, the *Functional Requirements for Bibliographic Records* (FRBR), covered in chapter 2.

It is not altogether clear just when someone hit upon the idea of displaying the information on cards and making several cards for each book, each card being a different access point (author, title, subject). In 1890 Melvil Dewey published his 3rd edition of *Library School Card Catalog Rules*, in which he showed examples of cards. They were not, however, exactly like the cards that were developed in the twentieth century.

The First to Use Card Catalogs

"In its more modern form, it [the card catalog] began to make its appearance in British and American libraries round about 1876, in which year the well-known firm of Library Bureau was established, with Melvil Dewey at its head" (Sharp, 1935, 26). However, as early as 1871 the Boston Public Library had begun its own card catalog, getting a head start on other U.S. libraries (*Annual Report of the Trustees* 1899).

Special Tidbit: The Library of Congress

What is the Library of Congress? Following is a definition directly from its website:

> The Library of Congress is the nation's oldest federal cultural institution and serves as the research arm of Congress. It is also the largest library in the world, with millions of books, recordings, photographs, maps and manuscripts in its collections.
> The Library's mission is to support the Congress in fulfilling its constitutional duties and to further the progress of knowledge and creativity for the benefit of the American people.

The LOC is not the official national library of the United States, but it certainly serves as one. James C. Billington is the current Librarian of Congress (2014).

Library employees handwrote cards in the days before the invention of typewriters. Melvil Dewey and Thomas Edison developed and perfected the approved library hand to be taught in library schools and used in all libraries. Furthermore, even though the Library of Congress began distributing printed typeset catalog cards, handwritten library cards were still preferred for years by many library directors (*History of the Card Catalog* 2011, June 8).

"Card catalogs were popularized in the United states by Library of Congress (LC) cards, first made available for sale in 1901, and by H. W. Wilson cards, which began production in 1938 in response to the needs of small libraries" (Taylor & Joudrey, 2009, 48). The Library of Congress had actually begun an early card catalog around 1865, consisting of 4 1/2-by-7-inch cards with clippings from earlier book catalogs pasted onto them. In 1898 the LC initiated a new catalog on standard-sized cards of 7 1/2 by 12 1/2 cm. Cutter's rules and some earlier rules from the American Library

Association formed the basis of this new catalog. At this point, cataloging practice was well on its way to becoming standardized across the United States (*Rules for Descriptive Cataloging in the Library of Congress*, 1949). For an interesting history of the evolution of the card catalog, see The Library History Buff at http://www .libraryhistorybuff.org/cardcatalog-evolution.htm.

Card Catalogs and Modern Cataloging Codes

As the physical format of cards came to be accepted and widely used, cataloging rules evolved steadily, while the modern publishing industry constantly increased its output. The challenges of building a catalog record by describing an item precisely and rendering it findable through various access points (always constrained by space limitations in the card environment) fueled the cataloging profession. From the LC to the library community across the country, librarians were advancing toward standardization and uniformity, setting the stage for cooperative and shared catalog records. *Catalog Rules, Author and Title Entries* was published by the American Library Association in 1908. In 1949, the ALA published two rule books, one for name headings, or access points (*A.L.A. Cataloging Rules for Author and Title Entries*), and one for description, or the body of the record (*Rules for Descriptive Cataloging in the Library of Congress*). These new codes were developed by committees rather than individuals, as had been the practice in the nineteenth century.

The *A.L.A. Rules* were replaced by the 1st edition of the *Anglo-American Cataloging Rules* (AACR) in 1967. Working together, American, British, and Canadian catalog librarians developed this set of rules, which has been continuously revised and republished until the publishing of the current code, *Resource Description and Access* (RDA). Note that the important term "access" is rightfully now part of the actual title of the cataloging rules.

Three Influential Twentieth-Century Librarians and the Library Catalog

The twentieth century had its own stars of bibliographic control. First is the Library of Congress cataloger and theorist Seymour Lubetzky, who at midcentury articulated what he believed to be the two main functions of descriptive cataloging (the body of the record). The first is to describe the significant features of a book in order to distinguish it from other books and other editions of the book and characterize its contents, scope, and bibliographic relations. The second is to present data in an entry that will fit well with the entries of other books and other editions in the catalog and respond best to the interests of the majority of readers. Lubetzky's concept of cataloging complemented Cutter's 1876 theory of the objectives of the catalog (which actually focused more on access than description). Providing the groundwork for the 1961 International Conference on Cataloguing held in Paris, Lubetzky's concept was integrated into the resulting *Paris Principles*, becoming the basis for all forthcoming editions of the *Anglo-American Catalogu-*

ing Rules (Chan, 2007). Lubetzky, who lived to be 104 years old, has been hailed as both a major catalog theorist and an effective practicing cataloger who offered many commonsense solutions to typical cataloging dilemmas.

For the second star, we must look to the life and career of the only female in this discussion of the movers and shakers of the cataloging world. Rather than a theorist, she was practical in ways that completely revolutionized how bibliographic records were created and disseminated. Catalog cards were used in most libraries until about the mid-1970s, when digitized catalogs began to appear because a coding system was developed at the Library of Congress by Henriette Avram, who was not educated as a librarian. A bright, inventive person with a background in computer programming, she went to work at the LC in 1965, eventually heading the Processing Department. There she began to develop a way for computers to format, manipulate, and exchange bibliographic information, which came to be called by its acronym, MARC (for Machine Readable Cataloging). Since 1968 the LC has been putting its catalog records into this format and making them available internationally. MARC is not a cataloging code, however. It is a framework for bibliographic data that renders it understandable by a computer. With the MARC format, the library world was on the cutting edge of organizing information and providing flexible access to it. It took about a hundred years to go from awkward and quickly dated book catalogs, to labor-intensive card catalogs, to the speed and flexibility of the OPAC.

Special Tidbit: The Online Catalog

Do not refer to the online catalog as the "online card catalog" or any other phrase that uses the word "card." It is no longer card based, so it is not a card catalog.

Our third influential twentieth-century librarian is Fred Kilgour. Once catalog records were available in machine readable form, it was possible to envision OPACs, but someone had to take the first steps toward fulfilling this vision. Fred Kilgour seized upon the opportunity to use Library of Congress MARC records in a shared cataloging environment. After joining the Ohio College Association in 1967, he initiated the creation and development of OCLC (originally Ohio College Library Center), a library network that today links 72,000 institutions in 170 countries. Originally housed at Ohio State University, Columbus, today it is located in Dublin, Ohio, a suburb of Columbus. It houses the mainframe computer that holds over 300 million machine readable catalog records. Libraries pay a fee to belong to OCLC, which gives their catalogers access to the database. They can use records exactly as they find them, or they can edit them for their own use, and they can add new records for items not in the database. These additions are then available for all the other subscribers to use. This shared cataloging network, this vast opportunity for access, would not be possible were it not for the MARC format, a standard that, when adhered to, makes the records in the OCLC database compatible with one another.

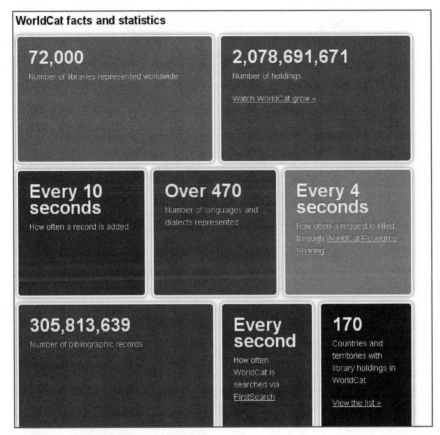

Figure 1.2. WorldCat Facts and Statistics

The OCLC records also have symbols of holding libraries attached to them. For example, the Wisconsin Historical Society's holding symbol is WIH. The holding symbol for the Hennepin County (Minnesota) Public Library System is HCO. The bibliographic record for any item these libraries own will have their holding symbol attached to it. All member libraries can see what items everyone owns, a feature that facilitates interlibrary loan among these libraries. As catalogers use the OCLC database, each bibliographic record is electronically delivered to the purchasing library or library consortium for its online catalog.

Figure 1.2 is a screen print of an OCLC statistics page.

Number of Holdings

This means the number of holding symbols attached to OCLCs bibliographic records. Hundreds of library holding symbols could be attached to any one record, indicating that each of these libraries owns the item. Notice that there are well over a billion!

Number of Bibliographic Records

This means the number of separately cataloged items in the OCLC database. Each item may have multiple holding symbols attached to it. The number of items in the OCLC database is over 300 million and growing daily.

The information provided here about OCLC is not meant to imply that OCLC is the best vendor for the K–12 library environment. School librarians have other vendors to choose from, most notably book vendors that can supply MARC bibliographic records for the items purchased.

As libraries digitized their bibliographic records and began using them in their own local OPACS, this paved the way for the creation of union catalogs. Union catalogs show the holdings of more than one library. OCLC is a gigantic union catalog. A school district might be part of a district-wide union catalog showing the holdings of all the schools and possibly of local public libraries. Examples of statewide union catalogs are I-Share in Illinois and Iowa's Iowa Locator. A union catalog vastly expands access to library materials through its scope and reach.

SUMMARY

Methods for creating and storing bibliographic records have been evolving for decades, as have the rules for the content of the records. In the past century we have gone from the book catalog to the card catalog to the OPAC. Necessity, several visionary individuals, and modern technology were the driving forces behind these developments. Today's catalogs are not rigid like book catalogs nor as cumbersome to create and maintain as card catalogs. Because of digitized bibliographic records, today we have enormous flexibility in searching for published information and wider access to it than ever before in the history of libraries and information dissemination. The next chapter explores twenty-first-century bibliographic control developments in RDA and its foundational theory, FRBR.

TEST YOUR CRITICAL THINKING

1. Describe what is meant by entry or access points into the catalog and how these points have evolved and changed, from book catalogs to card catalogs to OPACs.
2. Resistance to change and to new developments within any profession is a common occurrence. What objections do you think were raised when book catalogs gave way to "library hand" written cards and in turn when those cards gave way to printed cards? What about when printed cards gave way to OCLC and OPACs? Were any of these changes greeted favorably rather than with dismay?

RESOURCES

Annual report of the trustees of the public library of the City of Boston, 1898. (1899). Boston: Municipal Printing Office.

Chan, L. M. (2007). *Cataloging and classification: An introduction.* Lanham, MD: Scarecrow Press.

Cutter, C. A. (1869, January). The new catalogue of the Harvard College Library. *North American Review, 108,* 96–129.

Fred Kilgour (n.d.). In *Wikipedia.* Retrieved February 25, 2012, from: http://en.wikipedia.org/wiki/Fred_Kilgour.

History of the card catalog (2011, June 8). In *LIS Wiki.* Retrieved from: http://liswiki.org/wiki/History_of_the_card_catalog.

Hufford, J. R. (1991). The pragmatic basis of catalog codes: Has the user been ignored? *Cataloging & Classification Quarterly, 14*(1), 27–38.

Jewett, C. C. (1853). *Smithsonian report on the construction of catalogues of libraries and their publication by means of separate stereotyped titles with rules and examples* (2nd ed.). Washington, DC: Smithsonian Institution.

Library catalog (n.d.). In *Wikipedia.* Retrieved December 9, 2013, from: http://en.wikipedia.org/wiki/Library_catalog.

Rules for descriptive cataloging in the Library of Congress. (1949). Washington, DC: Library of Congress, Descriptive Cataloging Division.

Sharp, H. A. (1935). *Cataloguing, a textbook for use in libraries.* London: Grafton.

Spicher, K. M. (1996). The development of the MARC Format. *Cataloging & Classification Quarterly, 21*(3–4), 75–90.

Taylor, A. G., & Joudrey, D. N. (2009). *The organization of information* (3rd ed.). Westport, CT: Libraries Unlimited.

2

Supporting Resource Discovery: RDA and FRBR

The introductory chapter to RDA declares its purpose and scope as follows: "RDA provides a set of guidelines and instructions for formulating data to *support resource discovery*, with the resources having all types of content and delivered in all types of media."

"Supporting resource discovery" is a contemporary version of Cutter's first and second objectives for the catalog, both of which focus on the catalog as a finding tool. Whether the term used is *find*, *discover*, or *access*, the meaning is the same. The title *Resource Description and Access* divides its scope between description of bibliographic items (Lubetzky's focus) and access to them, but when it comes down to it, no amount of description is useful if the record cannot be found in the catalog and consequently in the collection. "The primary goal of RDA is to facilitate resource discovery within catalogues in a *more consistent and powerful way* that started with the various cataloguing standards many decades ago" (HLWIKI International, 2013). This is a worthy goal, because the world of bibliographic control transitioned many years ago from card catalogs to OPACs, while the ongoing editions of the *Anglo-American Cataloguing Rules* failed to fully adapt to this new physical format. Features that were not possible in a card catalog (limitless access points, diverse displays of bibliographic information, and numerous linkages among bibliographic records) became quite possible in the digital catalog, but the code remained firmly fixed in the age of cardstock. RDA and its theoretical underpinning, FRBR, have been conceived to exploit the potential of the digital age and move cataloging into the twenty-first century.

Much ink has been spilled in the last several years by individuals and committees creating, justifying, and describing RDA and FRBR, but for most catalogers the changes between RDA and AACR are minimal. For school librarians, who receive most of their cataloging from vendors and other agencies, it will hardly cause a

Table 2.1.   Comparison of AACR and RDA

Anglo-American Cataloging Rules (AACR)	*Resource Description and Access* (RDA)
Part 1 is Description. It consists of general rules for description of all kinds of media and a series of chapters, each on a different format, such as music, maps, motion pictures, and electronic resources. The bibliographic record is conceptualized as one piece.	**Section 1** is Recording Attributes of the Manifestation and Item. This is in essence the same as Description, but the bibliographic record is conceptualized in FRBR as four distinct parts, two of which are Manifestation and Item. RDA provides the rules for the data used in the four parts.
Part 2 is Choice of Access Points, Headings for Persons, Geographic Names and Corporate Bodies.	**Section 2** is Recording Attributes of the Work and Expression as conceptualized through FRBR. Again, in essence this is the same as Description.
	Section 3 is Recording Attributes of Person, Family, and Corporate Body. This is the same as Headings for Persons, Geographic Names and Corporate Bodies in AACR and specifies how to create an authorized form of a name.
	Section 4 is Recording Attributes of Concept, Object, Event, and Place and is not yet developed.
	Sections 5–10 are all on Recording Relationships, much of which involves assigning relationship designators to creators and contributors. In the long run, relationships will be crucial to the design of newly conceptualized OPACS.

ripple in their daily work. Table 2.1 displays a comparison of the basic structure of the two cataloging codes.

The actual form and structure of bibliographic information as now specified in RDA does not differ greatly from its immediate predecessor, the *Anglo-American Cataloguing Rules, Second Edition* (AACR2). What is more difficult to grasp is the multilayered conceptualization of a bibliographic record (Work, Expression, Manifestation, and Item) when compared with the one-dimensional record that is more familiar to us. For the mechanics of cataloging, there are a manageable number of individual rule changes between AACR2 and RDA. These are covered in the chapters on cataloging books and nonprint items.

ACCESS IN THE AGE OF THE ELECTRONIC RECORD

Resource discovery is accessing any particular given item from among any number of other items. With cards, there were space constraints. If more than three people authored a book, the rules said to provide access through only the first three individuals' names. A card had to be made for each access point. If the cataloger were to provide an access point for every name and every other possible access point, the card catalog would have filled up much too quickly, because *each access point required a separate card.* These cards were sold in sets, usually consisting of five to seven cards per set. The first card of the set was called the *main entry* and the last card the *shelflist card.* In between were cards for *added entries* of additional authors or editors, the title, and a number of subject headings. Today a bibliographic record is just one tiny digitized record, not a set of multiple cards, so saving space or time is not an issue. With this constraint a thing of the past, access opportunities have expanded dramatically. One digitized record is constructed, and the OPAC software can theoretically search anywhere in that record, depending on the indexing programmers provide for accessing fields in the MARC record. That means it should be possible, for example, to retrieve all items published by Capstone Press, an access point not in traditional card catalogs. In today's electronic catalogs, not only is searching by publisher possible, but this kind of indexing is actually being done in some OPACs. We now have great potential for resource discovery through the OPAC and its multiple access points, flexible digitized records, and creatively designed interfaces.

DISPLAY OPTIONS AND THE MARC 21 FORMAT

Once a catalog record is in the MARC format, the information in the record can be rearranged and enhanced in any manner. The resulting "look" is called the display interface or the graphical user interface. For catalog records, this can mean the search screen *or* the display results. In the display, the title can be the first information showing at the top of the screen. Just as easily, the location of the item (the call number) can be displayed first, or the author. Summaries can be hidden, and subject headings may be displayed anywhere, instead of in their traditional location at the bottom of the record. Whatever the designers want to do is possible. Consequently, there are many varieties of search and screen displays today. This is a significant departure from the days when every library catalog displayed cards all appearing in the same format. If the user learned to read a card in one library, it was easy to read and understand the cards in any library. In some ways, this consistency in description display made resource discovery easier than the current trend toward displaying bibliographic records in widely divergent ways.

Do any online catalogs these days mimic the layout on catalog cards? Or have they all taken the basic information and rearranged it in new, creative ways? Classic MnPALS (in Minnesota) presents a screen display closely mimicking the card display, and there are probably others that do the same. Mostly, however, screen displays today are highly creative. Even MnPALS offers an alternative interface to its standard traditional format. But no matter what the interface looks like, the basic catalog record coded in the MARC format is the same, OPAC to OPAC. It is only what the user sees on the screen that changes. For comparison, figures 2.1–2.3 show a catalog record conforming to the old card format and two displaying the information in a creative new way.

Figure 2.1 is from classic MnPALS. *Under Siege: Three Children at the Civil War Battle for Vicksburg* by Andrea Warren mimics a catalog card in the order of the display of the bibliographic information. Note the labels of each part down the left side of the screen.

Figure 2.2 is Hennepin County (Minn.) Public Library's record for the same book in a creative interface display.

Take note of the following differences:

1. The first thing at the top of the record display is the title at HCPL but the location in MnPALS.

You are searching: MSU Library Catalog

	Add to Your Bookbag	ILL Request	Save/Mail

Choose view: Full View | Brief View | MARC Names | MARC Tags

Record 1 out of 1   ◀ Previous Record ▶

Location/Available	MSU,M Memorial Library --ERC Juvenile Collection--Lower Level Call #: E475.27 .W37 2009 ⓘ
Author	●Warren, Andrea.
Title	●Under siege! : three children at the Civil War battle for Vicksburg / by Andrea Warren.
Portion of Title	Three children at the Civil War battle for Vicksburg
Edition	1st ed.
Publisher	New York : Melanie Kroupa Books, c2009.
Physical Details	166 p. : ill., maps ; 25 cm.
Bibliography	Includes bibliographical references (p. [143]-146) and index.
Contents Note	War comes to Vicksburg : December 1862 -- The Christmas Eve Ball : December 24, 1862 -- The general's boy goes to war : spring 1863 -- Burying the family silver : late spring 1863 -- At the battle front : late spring 1863 -- The Yankees are coming! : May 1863 -- The road to Vicksburg : May 15-18, 1863 -- Enemy at the gates : May 17-25, 1863 -- Into the caves : late May and early June 1863 -- Dangerous days : early June 1863 -- Growing desperation : middle June 1863 -- Empty stomachs : late June 1863 -- Surrender! : July 4, 1863 -- The unfinished war : July 1863 and beyond -- Postscripts -- Other information about the war -- Facts about the war -- Children orphaned by war -- Women and the war -- Reconstruction.
Subject	●Children -- Mississippi -- Vicksburg -- History -- 19th century -- Juvenile literature.
	●Children -- Mississippi -- Vicksburg -- History -- 19th century.
Subject	●Vicksburg (Miss.) -- History -- Siege, 1863 -- Juvenile literature.
	●United States -- History -- Civil War, 1861-1865 -- Children -- Juvenile literature.
	●Vicksburg (Miss.) -- History -- Siege, 1863.
	●United States -- History -- Civil War, 1861-1865 -- Children.
Author	●Farrar, Straus, and Giroux.
Browse Call Number	●E475.27 .W37 2009
ISBN	9780374312558

Figure 2.1.   MnPALS Screen Display for *Under Siege*

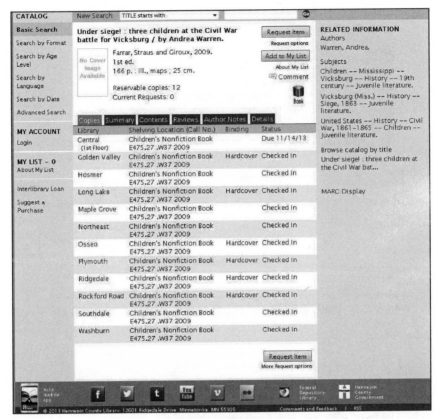

Figure 2.2.   Hennepin County Public Library Screen Display for *Under Siege*

2. The author has her own labeled line in MnPALS. In HCPL, one must look in the box on the right for the author's name.
3. There is a contents note displayed in the MnPALS record. In HCPL, one must click on a tab to see the contents. This is an extra step.
4. The summary note is displayed in MnPALS. One must click on the Summary tab in HCPL to see the summary. Again, this is an extra step.
5. The subject headings are on the right in HCPL. In MnPALS, the subject headings are below the contents note.
6. The tab for Reviews in HCPL takes one to reviews from journals such as *Booklist* and *School Library Journal*. There is no equivalent to this in the MnPALS record.
7. HCPL has an icon indicating this is a book. MnPALS does not have an equivalent.

Figure 2.3 is from the Boise, Idaho Public Library.

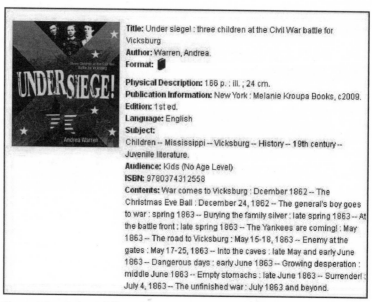

Title: Under siegel : three children at the Civil War battle for Vicksburg
Author: Warren, Andrea.
Format:

Physical Description: 166 p. : ill. ; 24 cm.
Publication Information: New York : Melanie Kroupa Books, c2009.
Edition: 1st ed.
Language: English
Subject:
Children -- Mississippi -- Vicksburg -- History -- 19th century -- Juvenile literature.
Audience: Kids (No Age Level)
ISBN: 9780374312558
Contents: War comes to Vicksburg : Dcember 1862 -- The Christmas Eve Ball : December 24, 1862 -- The general's boy goes to war : spring 1863 -- Burying the family silver : late spring 1863 -- At the battle front : late spring 1863 -- The Yankees are coming! : May 1863 -- The road to Vicksburg : May 15-18, 1863 -- Enemy at the gates : May 17-25, 1863 -- Into the caves : late May and early June 1863 -- Dangerous days : early June 1863 -- Growing desperation : middle June 1863 -- Empty stomachs : late June 1863 -- Surrender! : July 4, 1863 -- The unfinished war : July 1863 and beyond.

Figure 2.3. Boise, Idaho Public Library Screen Display for *Under Siege*

Take note of the following:

1. The record mimics a card format to some degree.
2. The title is the first thing at the top of the record.
3. It has a format icon for a book.
4. The subject heading appears in the middle of the record.
5. It does not have as many subject headings as the first two records do.
6. It has no summary and no reviews in this display. Further down in this record, below holdings information, are windows for a summary and reviews, but each takes an extra click to reveal the information.
7. It has a language note that the other two records do not have.

FUNCTIONAL REQUIREMENTS FOR BIBLIOGRAPHIC RECORDS (FRBR)

What we have seen in the foregoing catalog record examples is access and description based upon earlier AACR catalog codes, demonstrating a continued reliance on the concept of bibliographic records as discrete items. The most current code is RDA, the elements of which are based on FRBR, a model conceptualized in terms of relationships among records. The potential for enhanced resource discovery lies within these new standards. While the actual appearance of bibliographic records has not changed much with RDA, the emphasis on relationships in FRBR's conceptual framework greatly increases the likelihood that the users will find what they seek

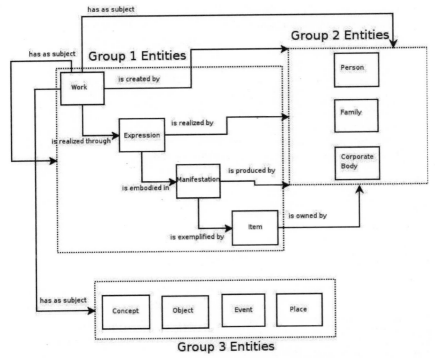

Figure 2.4. Schematic Representing FRBR. *Source:* FRBR Blog, http://www.frbr .org/2006/02

and will also find all materials in the catalog related to it in one way or another. What follows is a brief discussion of FRBR to give you an elemental appreciation of its precepts so you will not feel lost when library catalogs begin to truly exploit its potential. Although FRBR can be slippery to grasp, if you concentrate on its parts, that should make it easier. One way catalogers represent FRBR is through the use of a schematic, such as the one in figure 2.4.

Think carefully about what the letters FRBR mean. *Functional* (F) here means *how the elements will work in a practical sense.* In this context, *requirements* (R) means *how the elements will work in the way we need them to, the way we must require them to.* "For Bibliographic Records" (B and R) needs no definition. FRBR is a combination of the elements needed to create functional bibliographic records according to a contemporary conceptualization of OPACs and a new definition of user tasks, although these user tasks sound much like Cutter's objectives for the catalog.

According to FRBR's theorists, user tasks are behaviors library users perform to meet their information needs. These tasks are to

- find (locate a resource),
- identify (ensure that the found resource is the one the user really wants and not some other similar resource),

- select (if there are a number of possible resources, choose the one most useful to the user's information need), and
- obtain (get the selected resource to a location where it can be used).

Table 2.2.

Group 1	Group 2	Group 3
Primary Entities: Products of intellectual or artistic endeavor, such as books, films, and so forth, conceptualized in four ways: • The work • The expression • The manifestation • The item Taken together, these have come to be known as WEMI	**Responsibility Entities:** Those involved in creating, producing, or disseminating the products listed in Group 1 • People • Corporate bodies	**Subject Entities:** Subject headings • Concept • Object • Event • Place • Any Group 1 or 2 entity

The question then becomes, what data and data structures will help a user perform these tasks? To accomplish this, FRBR authors developed an "entity-relationship" model. Three groups of entities were defined. These groups are designated in figure 2.4, a schematic meant to demonstrate FRBR's vision of relationships among entities, and outlined in table 2.2.

The information in the table is nothing new. To varying degrees, it is the same bibliographic information catalogers have been creating for years. Group 1 is more abstract than Groups 2 and 3. To be sure, many people have struggled with understanding Group 1, Primary Entities.

What FRBR has done is conceptualize a bibliographic record for any product of human creativity into three separate groups. Each group is defined as consisting of entities. Group 1 has the primary entities. Primary entities are actually perceived sections of each catalog record, the work, the expression, the manifestation, and the item (WEMI categories). Think of the entire bibliographic record as made up of various pieces of information. Each piece of information is assigned to a WEMI category. With this we are being more three-dimensional in our thinking instead of conceiving of a bibliographic record as a flat representation with no categorizing of its parts. Following is a discussion of how FRBR might deal with *Little House on the Prairie*, by Laura Ingalls Wilder, in terms of its four primary entities. Each one is defined here along with possible attributes (characteristics).

Group 1, Primary Entities and Their Attributes

The Work. Abstract. The story of the Ingalls family's homesteading in Kansas in the mid-nineteenth century is the work. It is not an actual physical book, but is more like an ideal form of a creative endeavor as it existed in its creator's mind.

Wilder recalled her childhood and conceptualized a written work about it. A work is realized through:

The Expression. Abstract. This is the intellectual or artistic realization of a work as an alphanumeric form, a musical form, sound, image, or any other form. One expression would be Wilder's handwritten manuscript. Another would be a French translation of the story. These are not the actual items, but the conceptualization of possible forms of the work. The expression is embodied in:

The Manifestation. Concrete. We capture the expression of a work in some kind of "container," be it a book, a DVD, or a CD. This is the physical embodiment of an expression of the work. Its attributes correspond to the elements of a bibliographic record. The manifestation level attributes are the title as found on the title page, statement of responsibility, edition statement, place of publication, and publisher, among others. For a film of *Little House on the Prairie*, the manifestation would include the actors portraying the characters, the director, and the form (DVD) and extent of the carrier (2 DVDs). The manifestation is exemplified by:

The Item. Concrete. This is an individual copy of a particular manifestation. We shelve the item in our library. Its barcode, call number, autograph of the author, color of the cover, condition of the binding, and the fact that it is held by our specific library are all attributes of the individual item.

Figure 2.5 is a hierarchical display of the WEMI concept for *Little House on the Prairie*.

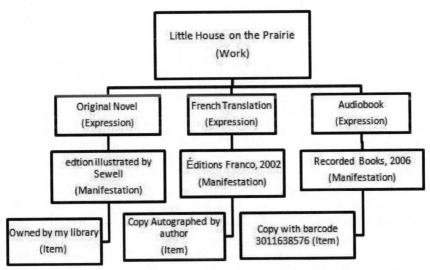

Figure 2.5. Hierarchical Display of the WEMI Concept for *Little House on the Prairie*

Group 2, Responsibility Entities

> **Concrete.** These are the people or corporate bodies that had something to do with the intellectual or creative product. They should be in the record in their authorized forms.

Group 3: Subject Entities

> **Concrete.** These are subject headings. They have been given some new refinements in how they are named. FRBR calls them Content, Object, Event, and Place.

Relationships

The idea behind FRBR is that a bibliographic record is built on *relationships between and among entities*. Again, this is conceptual and in a way, librarians already know about these relationships. A book has a relationship to a movie made from the book. A title has a relationship to an author. A piece of music can have a relationship to a CD compilation of many pieces of music.

Why does this matter? Theorists are hoping these relationships will be exploited in a revolutionary new OPAC. The OPAC built on FRBR will exhibit the myriad relationships among the multiple bibliographic records in its database. A FRBR-ized catalog will make it easier to see different expressions of a single work, to find all manifestations of any work, and to find any related works or expressions. What could be a better way to support resource discovery?

Has anyone attempted this yet? Several OPAC providers have constructed prototypes, but VTLS stands out as the leader, with its Virtua Integrated Library System. Figure 2.6 is the screen display of linked Hamlet records as they might appear in Virtua.

FRBR AND RDA

RDA rules are available only through online access to the *RDA Toolkit* (http://www .rdatoolkit.org/). Its organization concretely reflects all three groups, their entities, and their relationships that FRBR laid out conceptually. Following is the table of contents for RDA, with title words taken from FRBR emphasized in boldface print.

> Introduction
> Section 1: Recording **Attributes** of **Manifestation & Item**
> Section 2: Recording **Attributes** of **Work & Expression**
> Section 3: Recording **Attributes** of Person, Family, & Corporate Body
> Section 4: Recording **Attributes** of Concept, Object, Event & Place
> Section 5: Recording Primary **Relationships** Between Work, Expression, Manifestation, & Item

Section 6: Recording **Relationships** to Persons, Families, & Corporate Bodies

Section 7: Recording **Relationships** to Concepts, Objects, Events, & Places

Section 8: Recording **Relationships** Between Works, Expressions, Manifestations, & Items

Section 9: Recording **Relationships** Between Persons, Families, & Corporate Bodies

Section 10: Recording **Relationships** Between Concepts, Objects, Events, & Places

Appendices

Glossary

Index

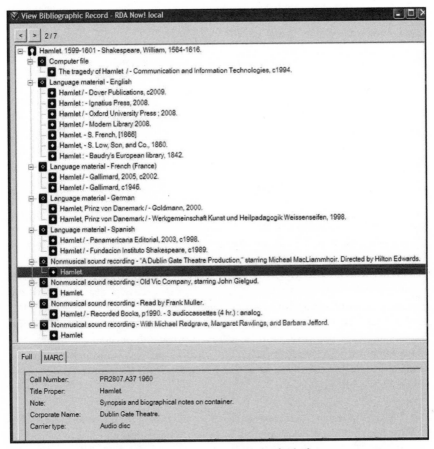

Figure 2.6. Virtua Integrated Library System FRBR-ized Display

The RDA-based bibliographic record in Table 2.3 shows the WEMI entities in the right-hand column. The parts labeled Manifestation and Item are more concrete and

Table 2.3.   RDA Bibliographic Record Showing WEMI Entities

020	|a 9780810993136 (paper over board) : |c $12.95	Manifestation
050 00	|a PZ7.K6232 |b Dia 2007	Item
100 1	|a Kinney, Jeff.	Work
240 10	|a Diary of a wimpy kid	Work
245 10	|a Diary of a wimpy kid : |b Greg Heffley's journal / |c by Jeff Kinney.	Manifestation
260	|a New York : |b Amulet Books, |c c2007.	Manifestation
300	|a 217 p. : |b ill. ; |c 22 cm.	Manifestation
336	|a text |b txt |2 rdacontent	Expression
337	|a unmediated |b n |2 rdamedia	
338	|a volume |b nc |2 rdacarrier	Manifestation
520	|a Greg records his sixth grade experiences in a middle school where he and his best friend, Rowley, undersized weaklings amid boys who need to shave twice daily, hope just to survive, but when Rowley grows more popular, Greg must take drastic measures to save their friendship.	Manifestation
650 0	|a Middle schools |v Juvenile fiction.	
650 0	|a Friendship |v Juvenile fiction.	
650 0	|a Schools |v Juvenile fiction.	
650 0	|a Diaries |v Juvenile fiction.	
949	|a 30116003545123 (barcode)	Item

easier to understand than are Work and Expression. Each is matched with the part of the record it represents. Parts of the bibliographic record not identified are not part of WEMI. Do not be concerned if you do not fully understand the labeling of the information in this record; it is enough to know that a bibliographic record built on FRBR and RDA is conceptualized within this multilayered overlay, a departure from the previous practice of focusing only on describing an item and providing access points to it in the catalog through a one-dimensional record. The numbers in the left-hand column are part of the MARC format, as are other codes throughout this record.

Resource discovery is facilitated by all three of the following important components. It remains to be seen what the future holds for their application to new conceptions of the catalog.

- FRBR (*Functional Requirements for Bibliographic Records*) is a conceptual model for describing and organizing bibliographic information.
- RDA (*Resource Description and Access*) is a content standard defining what information is recorded and how.
- MARC (Machine Readable Cataloging) is a communication format, or the computer code necessary to handle the data.

SUMMARY

Supporting resource discovery is the purpose of the new cataloging code, *Resource Description and Access*. The earlier *Anglo-American Cataloging Rules* (AACR) were also meant to create a finding tool, but they remained card focused, failing to fully adapt to the developing digital environment and the capabilities of the OPAC. RDA and AACR are similar and will not necessitate a major shift in the actual work of bibliographic control for school librarians. Catalog search and display interfaces facilitate resource discovery, with today's OPACs offering myriad searching functions and many creative displays of bibliographic information. It is anticipated that RDA and its conceptual framework, FRBR, will lead to a more robust OPAC through the use of both FRBR entities and their attributes and the relationships among them. The next chapter provides an overview of how school librarians can obtain OPAC bibliographic records.

TEST YOUR CRITICAL THINKING

1. Analyze the three OPAC bibliographic displays for *Under Siege* and determine which you think would work better with elementary and secondary students. If you have access to a Follett OPAC, compare that display with the three in this chapter.
2. Choose any written work that has appeared in various manifestations and identify and describe it in terms of WEMI, as was done in this chapter for *Little House on the Prairie*.

RESOURCE

HLWIKI International. (2013). *Resource description and access (RDA)*. Retrieved from: http://hlwiki.slais.ubc.ca/index.php/Resource_Description_and_Access_%28RDA%29.

3

Obtaining OPAC Bibliographic Records

No librarian has to manually construct a full bibliographic record for each item in the OPAC. For school librarians to do this would be a very poor use of time, particularly when students and teachers need their services far more than the OPAC needs original cataloging. MARC records may be obtained in several ways. You may use them just as you find them through various sources, or in a process called copy cataloging. Copy cataloging involves editing a preexisting record for local use.

BOOK VENDORS

Book vendors are the first and best source for acquiring bibliographic records. Order them along with your books. Mackin and Follett are well-known companies. When setting up an account with them, tell them how to process the books, what kind of subject headings you want, and other specifications concerning the records for your library. These vendors should be using Library of Congress (LC) catalog records modified to your specifications. It will cost something to have the vendor supply these customized bibliographic records, but it is worth the small extra expense. The librarian's time is better spent with the students and teachers.

CATALOGING IN PUBLICATION (CIP)

Another good method is to use the Cataloging in Publication (CIP) information in the book. It is an incomplete catalog record, because the LC cataloger does not have the completed book in hand when it is initially cataloged.

The CIP record may be used by manually copying it into the OPAC. School librarians may want to modify it to some degree, because it will show Library of Congress subject headings, but school libraries usually use Sears subject headings. Missing information will have to be filled in. Also, the cataloger needs to be alert to changes made to the book after the CIP information is printed in it. It is not unusual to find changes, particularly in the title, so the title in the CIP data may not be exactly the same as the title on the printed title page. The name authority work has been done in the CIP record, so for the most part, the forms of the names appearing in the records are reliable.

The overall format of a CIP record can vary from book to book. Some CIP information is set in a left-justified print block, some mimics a catalog card, and some is centered, with no left or right justification.

LIBRARY OF CONGRESS ONLINE CATALOG

Another good source for catalog records is the Library of Congress OPAC (catalog .loc.gov; see figure 3.1). MARC records may be imported directly from the LC catalog to a file on your computer. In other words, it is not necessary to manually copy the records into the OPAC. However, to assist with manual copying, the actual MARC coding is also available to users via a tab with the record.

Once records are imported, they may need to be edited before being exported to the OPAC. Two companies providing both editing and exporting services are Mitinet Library Solutions (MARC Magician) and Book Systems (eZcat).

LIBRARY OF CONGRESS ONLINE CATALOG

Figure 3.1.   Library of Congress Online Catalog Logo

WORLDCAT

Another source for catalog records is OCLC's WorldCat (figure 3.2).

Records can be printed out and then manually copied and modified as needed. Many states fund a subscription to WorldCat for all their citizens, so librarians should check for this and make full use of it, if it is available. Unfortunately, World-Cat records do not have a button for displaying the MARC format. Librarians will

Figure 3.2. OCLC WorldCat Logo

have to know and understand the format in order to use WorldCat data as a basis for records in a local OPAC. WorldCat is actually the OCLC database, but because it is used by the public, records look different than they do to catalogers, who use a different interface and access mode. In the cataloging mode, MARC coding is displayed, a format the general public would not find useful.

ACCESS PENNSYLVANIA

Access Pennsylvania (http://www.accesspa.state.pa.us/) is a database containing exportable MARC records for more than 22 million titles for a variety of library items, including books, e-books, and DVDs. More than 1,800 of the participating libraries are from the K–12 environment.

COMMERCIALLY AVAILABLE MARC RECORDS

BookWhere from WebClarity Software is a commercially available product that allows the user to search more than 2,800 libraries to locate bibliographic records that are rated and scored for the user based on their completeness. Records can be exported. BestMARC from Mitinet and eZCat from Book Systems are two other sources for purchasing MARC records.

Because errors do creep into even the most conscientiously prepared MARC records, a number of companies, such as Marcive and MARC Magician, can execute global changes to bibliographic databases and carry out MARC cleanup.

Special Tidbit: Google Books and the WorldCat

Google Books interfaces with WorldCat. To use this interface, enter a search for a publication at http://books.google.com/. Click on the record. Look on the left side of the screen for the link "Find in a Library." This takes you to the WorldCat record and presents a list of some of the holding libraries.

COPYRIGHT ISSUES

With all the importing and copying of MARC records that can be done, you might wonder if copyright laws are being violated through these practices. MARC records from the Library of Congress are created by employees of the federal government and thus are in the public domain within the United States. As for OCLC, although it claims copyright rights to WorldCat as a compilation, it does not claim copyright ownership of individual records. Nevertheless, it does protect its biggest asset, the OCLC bibliographic database, by continuing to require membership fees from libraries wishing to use its various features and functions to their greatest advantage (WorldCat rights and responsibilities, 2013). Finally, factual data cannot be copyrighted, and some argue that catalog data fall into that area. However, if a library signs a licensure agreement with a vendor of MARC records, it may be constrained from sharing records (Simpson, 2011).

At least one academic library is encouraging use of its original cataloging by other libraries. In 2011 the University of Florida began adding the following Creative Commons note to all its original cataloging submitted to OCLC: "This bibliographic record is available under the Creative Commons CC0 public domain dedication. The University of Florida Libraries, as creator of this bibliographic record, has waived all rights to it worldwide under copyright law, including all related and neighboring rights, to the extent allowed by law" (University of Florida, George A. Smathers Libraries, 2013). By invoking the Creative Commons Zero claim, the library gave up its rights to its original cataloging and offered it to be freely used by anyone.

In 2012 Harvard University also made its more than 12 million bibliographic records freely available under the Creative Commons CC0 license. Seeking to encourage innovative uses and future developments, the university permits bulk download of these released records (Millions of Harvard Library catalog records, 2012).

It remains to be seen just how widespread open access to cataloging metadata will be. *Metadata*, now a ubiquitous term, is loosely defined as "data about data." In the library cataloging context metadata is the bibliographic data for any cataloged item as placed in a "container" known as the MARC format. Open access means openly licensed and freely accessible. It is a current trend and an issue that is not going away. A particularly insightful and lucid article on this topic is freely available online from the *Journal of Academic Librarianship* (Flynn, 2013).

COPY AND ORIGINAL CATALOGING

Another option is to edit previously existing catalog records to create a new record for a unique item. This is called copy cataloging and is frequently done in public and academic libraries by both professional catalogers and paraprofessionals or assistants. The last choice is to provide all the bibliographic information yourself, otherwise known as original cataloging, an option that will not often be necessary.

KNOWING AND UNDERSTANDING CATALOGING

Why is it necessary to know cataloging if there are so many sources from which to acquire the records? This skill is part of the professional knowledge base and is vital to information access. If librarians do not understand how catalog records are constructed, what their underlying structure is, and what rules govern their construction, they will not know if their records meet the national standard. They may create records that cannot be shared because they do not conform. Errors in bibliographic records may mask the existence of an item in the library. One consequence is that duplicate materials may be purchased, because it was not possible to accurately determine that a copy already existed in the library. Worse yet, students and teachers might fail to locate needed materials at a crucial moment. The literature of library science includes articles on types of barriers between users and materials. A poorly constructed catalog can be one of these barriers.

SUMMARY

There are a number of ways to acquire MARC records, the best of which is to purchase them from a book vendor as books are purchased. Set up a profile with the vendor so the MARC records can be customized to your users' needs. If the library has items not acquired through a vendor, there are several other sources for acquiring MARC records, such as the Library of Congress catalog and WorldCat. Original and copy cataloging are other options.

Understanding and applying cataloging rules and procedures is essential to accurately integrating new records with those already existing in the catalog and to making any item findable. In the larger picture, if catalog records do not conform to national standards, they cannot be part of a union catalog. The next chapter explains CIP records, a resource for cataloging data, in more detail.

TEST YOUR CRITICAL THINKING

1. Your principal has discovered WorldCat and believes this would be an excellent source for catalog records for the library's OPAC. How do you respond?
2. You have several unique gift books you wish to place in your collection. Since you did not purchase them through a vendor, you do not have MARC records for them. There is no CIP data on the verso of the title pages of any of them. Enumerate and prioritize the other choices you have for finding and acquiring OPAC records. Defend your first choice and explain why it is better than the others.
3. To see various options for MARC records and materials processing, go to the Mackin website and download the form at the link titled "Specifications" (http://www.mackin.com/PROCESSING/MAIN.aspx). Determine which options you consider essential and how much they would cost per item cataloged.

RESOURCES

Flynn, E. A. (2013). Open access metadata catalogers and vendors: The future of cataloging records. *Journal of Academic Librarianship, 39*(1), 29–31.

Millions of Harvard Library catalog records publicly available (2012, April 24). Retrieved from: http://archive.is/sSaex.

Simpson, C. (2011). *Copyright catechism II: Practical answers to everyday school dilemmas.* Santa Barbara, CA: Linworth.

University of Florida, George A. Smathers Libraries. (Dec. 10, 2013). *Creative Commons CC0.* Retrieved from: http://www.uflib.ufl.edu/catmet/creativecommons.html.

WorldCat rights and responsibilities for the OCLC cooperative frequently asked questions (n.d.). Retrieved from: http://rlin21.rlg.org/worldcat/recorduse/policy/questions/default.htm.

4

Understanding Cataloging in Publication (CIP)

Cataloging in Publication (CIP) data is usually printed on the back of the title page of the book (on the verso, or left-hand, page) and is incomplete because catalogers at the Library of Congress do not see the completed book when they create these preliminary catalog records. It is nevertheless extremely useful information for the school librarian looking for a good, usable bibliographic record. This chapter covers the fine points of CIP. An overview of the purpose of the CIP program at the Library of Congress may be found at http://www.loc.gov/publish/cip/about.

The process of creating the CIP data, from the publisher, to the LC, back to the publisher, goes like this:

1. Publishers transmit the required application form and the text of the item in electronic format to the CIP office at the LC.
2. CIP Division staff review the application and text for completeness and eligibility, assign the work a Library of Congress control number, and forward the application and the accompanying electronic galley proof of the book to the cataloging division that has the appropriate subject expertise (subject area of the book).
3. Catalogers construct *incomplete* descriptive cataloging, assign subject headings, name access points, and LC and Dewey Decimal classification numbers. Because the catalogers see only a proof, they do not know the final pagination or the full extent of illustrations. They also do not know the final size of the book. Also omitted are the publisher and place of publication.
4. The CIP record is then transmitted to the publisher, who prints it on the back of the title page in the final form of the book for publication. At the same time,

a machine readable version of the record (MARC) is distributed to large libraries, bibliographic utilities, and book vendors around the world.

5. The CIP process is complete when the publisher sends a copy of the published book to the CIP Division. Upon receipt of the book, LC staff members add other data elements to the catalog record (such as pagination and size) and ensure that the data elements in the record accurately describe the published work. Changes in title, subtitle, series, author, or subject may be made at this time. After this verification process, the machine readable version of the catalog record is again distributed.

CIP records used to look like small catalog cards, but today the format varies. Figures 4.1 through 4.3 are examples of recent CIP records. Figure 4.3 shows a centered layout that is a little bit different from the one shown in figure 4.1.

In the first CIP example, notice the letters AC in the lower right corner. AC stands for the Annotated Card Program at the Library of Congress. This program provided audience-specific bibliographic information for children's and young adults' fiction and nonfiction books for decades. In September 2010 it was renamed the Children's and Young Adults' Cataloging Program (CYACP) and dropped nonfiction from its purview. The examples here are from nonfiction published before 2010.

The following discussion looks at a CIP record in detail and then addresses the implications of CYACP practices for the school library catalog. The record being examined is the one in figure 4.2.

- **Aronson, Marc.** This is the author's last and first name. The name authority work for this name has been done by this point, and for the most part, you can trust the integrity of this name heading. However, it is still a good idea to verify it. The Library of Congress authority files and establishing the correct forms for names associated with any particular work are covered in more depth later in this text. This authority file can be used to verify names in CIP.

Library of Congress Cataloging-in-Publication Data
Kirk, David, 1955-
Miss Spider's Wedding / paintings and verse by David Kirk
p. cm.
Summary: Miss Spider proves that her heart knows best when it comes to choosing a husband.

ISBN 0-590-56866-3
[1. Spiders—Fiction. 2. Insects—Fiction. 3. Marriage—Fiction. 4. Stories in rhyme.]
I. Title.
PZ83.3.K6554MW · 1995
[E]—dc20 94-42096
CIP AC

Figure 4.1. CIP for *Miss Spider's Wedding*, by David Kirk. Centered layout.

Library of Congress Cataloging-in-Publication Data

Aronson, Marc.
Sir Walter Ralegh and the quest for El Dorado / by Marc Aronson.
p. cm
Includes bibliographical references and index.
Summary: Recounts the adventurous life of the English explorer and courtier who spelled his name "Ralegh" and led many expeditions to the New World.
ISBN 0-395-84827-X
1. Ralegh, Walter, Sir, 1554?–1618—Juvenile literature.   2. Great Britain—Court and courtiers—Biography—Juvenile literature.
3. Guiana—Discovery and exploration—Juvenile literature.
4. Explorers—England—Biography—Juvenile literature.
[1. Raleigh, Walter, Sir, 1554?–1618.   2. Explorers.]   I. Title.
DA86.22.R2   A76   2000
942.05'5'092—dc21
[B]   99-043096

Figure 4.2.   CIP for *Sir Walter Ralegh and the Quest for El Dorado,* by Marc Aronson. Traditional card format layout with left justification.

Library of Congress Cataloging-in-Publication Data
Kuklin, Susan. How my family lives in America / Susan Kuklin. — 1st ed.   p.   ̄cm.
Summary: African-American, Asian-American, and Hispanic-American
children describe their families' cultural traditions.
ISBN 0-02-751239-8
1. Minorities—United States—Social life and customs—Juvenile literature.
2. Afro-Americans—Social life and customs—Juvenile literature.
3. Asian Americans—Social life and customs—Juvenile literature.
4. Hispanic Americans—Social life and customs—Juvenile literature.
5. United States—Social life and customs—1971—Juvenile literature.
[1. Afro-Americans—Social life and customs. 2. Asian Americans—Social life and customs.
3. Hispanic Americans—Social life and customs.] I. Title.
E184.A1K85 1992   305.8'00973—dc20 91-22949

Figure 4.3.   CIP for *How My Family Lives in America,* by Susan Kuklin. An alternative centered layout.

Special Tidbit – CIP Gone Wrong

Sometimes a *completely wrong* CIP record is printed in the book. For example, if a publisher has published two books with similar titles, the CIP for each may be switched between the two books. (Weihs & Intner, 2009)

- *Sir Walter Ralegh and the Quest for El Dorado* / **by Marc Aronson.** This is the title of the book as found on the title page, followed by the authorship statement, also as found on the title page. This also should be verified by comparing the title page to the CIP, because it is not unusual to find differences between them due to decisions about the title and order of the authors on the page made after the CIP record is created.
- **Publisher/place of publication.** There is no publisher or place of publication information, because publishers want to have the most current and accurate information about their companies in the final catalog record, as taken from the actual published volume of the book.
- **p. cm.** These abbreviations signify missing information. Imagine an empty space in front of the "p." The "p" stands for "pages." Since the cataloger does not have the completed book in hand, only an electronic galley proof, it is not possible to determine the paging at the time the CIP record is created. This information is filled in later. The abbreviation "cm." stands for "centimeters" and indicates the height of the book. Again, this is information not available at the time of CIP construction. When the book is published, this information can be filled in. It might say: 237 p. ; 28 cm.
- **Includes bibliographical references and index.** This is a "note" that will not often appear in a CIP record and usually must be constructed after the book is published.
- **Summary: Recounts the . . . to the New World.** This is a summary of the content of the book, in this case a work of nonfiction. Today, bibliographic records for children's nonfiction do not have summaries written by LC catalogers, although they do at times include summaries provided by the publisher.
- **ISBN.** This is a unique International Standard Book Number assigned to this book.
- **Four LC subject headings.** This serves as an example of a CIP record with an error. The name Ralegh in the first subject heading is misspelled and should have been "Raleigh" even though the alternative spelling was used in the title. No two books will have the same ISBN. Notice the subdivisions within each subject heading. For example, subject heading number 2 is Great Britain -- Courts and courtiers -- Biography -- Juvenile literature. Each of those subdivisions identifies the narrower scope of the book. It's not just about "Great Britain"; more specifically, it is about Great Britain's courts and courtiers. Then, to refine it more, we are told that it is a Biography. Last, we are told it is Juvenile literature.
- **CYACP subject headings.** Notice how the last two subject headings start the numbering over again. We have 1. Raleigh, Walter, Sir, 1552?-1816. 2. Explorers. Both of these are short and to the point, unlike the first four, which are longer with more subdivisions. Notice that the last two are enclosed in square brackets. [1. Subject heading. 2. Subject heading]. Those brackets indicate children's subject headings. In other words, the first four subject headings are for adults and the last two are for children. The subject headings in brackets are CYACP subject headings, not Sears. This creates a dilemma when ordering MARC records. Should the vendor include Sears subject headings as well as CYACP headings?

- **Title.** Following the subject headings, see a Roman numeral I. Title. This is evidence of one of those rules left over from the days of cards. The fact that it says "I. Title" means that you would have created a card for the title and filed it in the "S" drawers under Sir Walter Ralegh. In a computer catalog a title is an automatic access point. You won't see the equivalent of "I. Title" in an OPAC record. The capability to look up this book by title is provided in the MARC coding.
- **DA86.R2 A76 2000.** This is a Library of Congress classification number. You will not have to be concerned about this at all. School libraries classify according to the *Abridged Dewey Decimal System* (one volume).
- **942.05'5'5092 – dc21.** This is a Dewey Decimal Classification number assigned from the 21st edition of the unabridged *Dewey Decimal Classification* (multiple volumes).
- **[B].** This "B" means the book is a biography. You have the option of using that as a classification category. For example, you could have this: B Ral meaning the book is a biography and the first three letters of the biographee's name are Ral (for Raleigh). This means you would shelve the book in the Biography section of your collection, in alphabetical order by the name of the biographee.
- **99-043096.** This is the Library of Congress control number, a unique number assigned by the Library of Congress. There is a simple explanation of LCCNs here at http://en.wikipedia.org/wiki/Library_of_Congress_Control_Number, and a more complicated explanation from OCLC at http://www.oclc.org/bibformats/es/0xx/010.html.

Special Tidbit: MARC and CIP

The MARC records you receive from your vendor may be CIP records. In other words, the book is so new that the catalog record is still incomplete. You should fill in the missing information; otherwise it may never get filled in. The original MARC record will eventually be updated by the Library of Congress, but unless you are checking for this through the various access points to LC records, you will not know what information the Library of Congress eventually put in the MARC record to complete the record. The Follett Company's catalogers fill in the missing information needed in any CIP record before they send the catalog records to libraries.

UNIQUE QUALITIES OF CYACP RECORDS

Some elements of CYACP records distinguish them from LC bibliographic records for adult materials. A CYACP catalog record for fiction includes summaries written by LC catalogers. The CYACP used to provide summaries for children's nonfiction, but does not do so any more. Any summaries in the catalog records for children's nonfiction are taken from information supplied by publishers. Because of the ONIX program, it is becoming increasingly common for summaries from publishers to appear in non-CYACP catalog records. ONIX is a metadata standard developed by publishers to provide a framework for data about their publications. The LC catalogers who create CIP copy have access to this information, and if it includes a summary that conforms to LC standards for brevity and unbiased content, that summary will be used in LC's CIP record. To distinguish these descriptions from summaries provided by LC catalogers, they are concluded by the phrase "Provided by publisher" or something similar. The only summaries written today by LC catalogers are for fiction for children and young adults. The CYACP website provides guidelines for writing these summaries.

Summary notes, while creating opportunities for keyword searching, will not be consistent in their application and usage. It will always be a hit and miss situation for the searcher. Subject headings, on the other hand, provide preformatted terms which, due to their consistency in terminology and in the guidelines for assigning them, help ensure that the user will locate everything the library has on the topic.

Today, children's nonfiction is given only regular LC subject headings, followed by -- Juvenile literature. A work of fiction, if it is based on real events, people, or other topical areas, could receive a subject heading reflecting these areas followed by -- Juvenile fiction.

Other rules were in effect for the older nonfiction records used as examples in this chapter. These records were created at a time when both adult LC subject headings and children's subject headings from LC were applied. The unbracketed subject headings are from the regular *Library of Congress Subject Headings* (LCSH). Notice how they have " -- Juvenile literature" as the last element in them. This subdivision of the subject heading tells the adult user to be aware that this is a catalog record for a book delivering its content at a child's level. The subject headings within the brackets do not have -- Juvenile literature in them because their assumed audience is children, so by default, an alert would be superfluous. The CYACP uses child-friendly subject headings from either the LCSH or its complementary specialized list, *Children's Subject Headings* (CSH). This list is only fifteen pages long, because catalogers choose children's subject headings first from the main LCSH. If the terminology is deemed not child-friendly, the catalogers select from the children's subject headings or create a new one for this list. This list may be accessed at http://www.loc.gov/aba/publications/FreeLCSH/CHILDRENS.pdf.

A word about MARC and subject headings is in order here. *In a MARC record there are no brackets to indicate the presence of CSH.* The differentiation between adult and children's subject headings lies in the MARC coding, which is covered later in this book. It is possible to also add Sears subject headings and give them appropriate MARC codes.

Children's nonfiction today will have only adult LCSH subject headings with -- Juvenile literature as the subdivision. Children's fiction may have both LCSH and CSH. For example, the book by Margi Preus, titled *Shadow on the Mountain*, received the following as two of its children's subject headings:

World War, 1939-1945 -- Underground movements -- Norway -- Fiction
Spies -- Fiction.

Its two regular LCSH subject headings are:

World War, 1939-1945 -- Underground movements -- Norway -- Juvenile fiction
Spies -- Juvenile fiction.

Notice how the regular LC subject headings here have the subdivision -- Juvenile fiction, alerting the adult user to the fact that the content is fiction, not fact, at a child's level. The two sets of subject headings are identical in this case, except for the last element. This will not always be the case. Wording used in children's subject headings may be different from the wording used in regular LC subject headings. One example is this set of subject headings for a book titled *The Impossible Knife of Memory*, by Laurie Halse Anderson. In this case, both the number of subject headings and the vocabulary used differ markedly between LC regular and LC children's subject headings.

Adult: Fathers and daughters -- Juvenile fiction
Adult: Post-traumatic stress disorder -- Juvenile fiction
Adult: Dysfunctional families -- Juvenile fiction
Adult: Veterans -- Juvenile fiction
Children's: Family problems -- Fiction

To learn more about current CYACP subject heading practice, check the website at http://www.loc.gov/aba/cyac/childsubjechead.html.

WHY LIBRARY OF CONGRESS SUBJECT HEADINGS MATTER TO THE SCHOOL LIBRARIAN

There is a good reason that it is important for the school librarian to understand LC subject heading practice for juvenile materials. Most school libraries use Sears subject headings, which can be added to MARC records by the vendor or the school librarian. For children's fiction the MARC records received from the vendor will have both types of subject headings in them, children's and adults'. It is possible to insert Sears subject headings as well. This will mean there could be three different subject authorities shaping the subject access to the library's materials. These subject headings may not all express the same subject in the same way. For example, the Library of Congress labels the medical condition depression as "Depression, Mental," and Sears calls it "Depression (Psychology)." If you use Sears and "Depression (Psychology)" and you already have some "Depression, Mental" subject headings in your catalog, you now have inconsistency. If students who want something on "depression" search for the precise subject heading "Depression, Mental," they may miss the records for "Depression (Psychology)." The students may not find *everything* you have on the topic.

In cases where the school librarian must construct the entire MARC record, a determination must be made about subject headings. If Library of Congress regular and children's subject headings are the choice, the librarian must consult the online version of these subject lists to select the needed headings. On the other hand, in the past the librarian may have used Sears and a copy will probably be available. If assigned locally from Sears, there is no guarantee that the terminology will be the same as in subject headings from the Library of Congress. In addition, Sears is much shorter and less complex than LC subject headings, perhaps making it the more attractive choice. Time constraints are a reality in school libraries, and the terminology used in Sears might be perceived as quicker to use as well as having a more child-friendly vocabulary.

School librarians might well prefer Sears, yet in today's school library environment, because of the demands of timeliness and economic pressures, no doubt librarians are accepting both the CYACP and the LC subject headings. Depending on their software, OPACs can allow nearly any word to be an access point, so if students do a keyword search for "Depression," they should find everything the library has on that mental condition. They will probably also find things on economic depressions, but they can just ignore those. This is not much of a problem in small files, but it could be quite significant in large catalogs.

This practice of using subject headings from various subject heading sources goes against what catalogers have always stood for. Consistency in subject retrieval terms guarantees that you will find everything on the topic in one place in the catalog. Inconsistency means you run the risk of missing things. While the constraints school librarians face today are very real, they still need to consider the long-range implications of these inconsistencies for retrieval. Using CYACP CIP records without considering the issues of subject access will result in a less-than-optimal tool for resource discovery.

Special Tidbit: AASL Website and CIP

The American Association of School Librarians maintains an excellent explanation of CIP and how to make use of it in a school library at http://www.ala.org/aasl/aasl archive/pubsarchive/kqarchives/added/ciptutor.

SUMMARY

CIP information is in nearly every new book published today and can be very useful for creating OPAC records. Because the CIP record is created before a book is published in its final format, selected pieces of information are missing from it. Once the book is in hand, the missing information can be filled in and a full MARC record created.

Library of Congress MARC records for children's materials contain LC subject headings, both regular and children's. This can lead to inconsistencies in the catalog, because these are not Sears subject headings, the usual subject headings of choice in the school library environment. Inconsistencies in subject heading treatment will without a doubt lead to less-than-optimal retrieval.

The next chapter focuses on the process of creating a catalog record, beginning with decisions about access points.

TEST YOUR CRITICAL THINKING

1. What two characteristics of the following CIP record tell you that it does not conform to current practices?

    Axelrod-Contrada, Joan
       Pesky critters! : squirrels, raccoons, and other furry invaders / by Joan Axelrod-Contrada.
       p. cm.
       A look at squirrels, raccoons, and other pesky critters, as well as the ways to prevent unwanted visitors from invading your home.
       Includes bibliographic references and index.
       1. Pests -- Juvenile literature. 2. Pests -- Control -- Juvenile literature. 3. Animal behavior -- Juvenile literature. [1. Animals -- Habits and behavior. 2. Pest control.]
       SB603.3 .A94 2014 591.6 2013005606

2. You have purchased some new books from the local Barnes and Noble for your library collection, but then realize you will not be receiving MARC records for them because you did not purchase them through your vendor. You decide to use the CIP record as a basis for your MARC records and to have your aide transcribe the data from the CIP record to the OPAC. What guidelines might you give the aide before starting this project?

RESOURCES

Children's subject headings (CSH) list (n.d.). Retrieved from: http://www.loc.gov/aba/cyac/childsubjhead.html.

Library of Congress control number (n.d.-a). In *Wikipedia*. Retrieved from: http://en.wikipedia.org/wiki/Library_of_Congress_Control_Number.

Library of Congress control number (n.d.-b). Retrieved from: http://www.oclc.org/bibformats/es/0xx/010.shtm.

McCroskey, M., & Turvey, M. R. (2003). What is CIP and how does it benefit the school library media specialist? *Knowledge Quest, 32*(2), 45–46.

McCroskey, M., & Turvey, M. R. (2013). *Using CIP to create the local catalog record: The nuts and bolts.* Retrieved from: http://www.ala.org/aasl/aaslarchive/pubsarchive/kqarchives/added/ciptutor.

Purpose of the CIP program. (n.d.). Retrieved from: http://www.loc.gov/publish/cip/about/.

Weihs, J., & Intner, S. S. (2009). *Beginning cataloging.* Santa Barbara, CA: Libraries Unlimited.

II

DESCRIPTIVE CATALOGING

5

Creating Access Points

There are two fundamental parts to creating a bibliographic record: constructing the description of the item being cataloged and establishing authorized entries or access points for the record. This chapter covers main and added entries as access points and leaves subject access for later chapters. MARC coding for main and added entries is also described, with more extensive coverage of the entire bibliographic record appearing in chapter 7.

It was once believed that every catalog record had to start with some piece of information in the "first slot" in the record. With cards, that first slot was traditionally called the "main entry." It was thought of as being the most important or the main card of a card set. Some items had personal main entries, some had title main entries (they started out with the title), and occasionally items had corporate main entries. As bibliographic records became digitized and OPACs developed, there was no reason to conceptualize the physical bibliographic record as something comprising multiple cards. The record became just one tiny digitized item that was accessible through computer software, not by thumbing through multiple items (cards). With the change in physical format, many catalogers began asking if the concept of one main and several added entries was still valid. The catalog code, *Anglo-American Cataloguing Rules, Second Edition* (AACR2), did not address this issue, and rules for constructing bibliographic records continued as before.

RDA AND THE CONCEPT OF MAIN ENTRY

As the deadline for implementation of RDA at the Library of Congress approached (March 31, 2013), catalogers wondered how the new code would deal with what many consider to be an outmoded concept. In a computer environment, why does any particular access point have to be the main one? RDA itself does not mention the phrase "main entry." Philosophically, if not practically, it is more about "access points" than about determining a main entry or added entries.

There wouldn't necessarily have to be a "main access point" any more. All names and titles associated with the bibliographic item could be access points, with none being the main one. Furthermore, there can be many more access points in an electronic record than space-consuming cards permitted. Yet RDA is largely based on AACR2, and catalogers must still decide upon a main entry and added entries, albeit with a good deal more flexibility than AACR2 allowed.

RDA TERMINOLOGY CHANGE FROM AACR2

- Main entry (AACR2) is now Authorized Access Point, Primary Access Point, Main Access Point (RDA).
- Added entry (AACR2) is now Access Point, or Secondary Access Point (RDA).

MARC FORMAT

More important than labeling something a main entry and something else an added entry is how entries are coded in the MARC record. Catalog users need to feel assured that if they do an author search, the computer looks for authors, not titles or subjects. If an author's name is entered in an area defined and coded for subject headings, no amount of author searching will retrieve it. Putting each name access point of the bibliographic record in its correct field will help ensure that it is retrievable.

HOW TO CHOOSE ACCESS POINTS (MAIN ENTRY, ADDED ENTRIES) ACCORDING TO AACR2, WITH RDA MODIFICATIONS, AND APPLY MARC 21 CODES

Main Entry

In most cases with children's books, the main entry is a personal author. In the MARC format, this is the 100 field or 100 tag. Because there are other types of main entries than a person's name, the 100 field is often referred to generically as the 1XX field. A personal main entry goes in the 100 tag, a corporate main entry goes in a 110 tag, and conference main entry goes in a 111 tag.

Added Entries

Added entries are for other people or groups of people having something to do with the intellectual or artistic content of the item. In the MARC format, this is the

700 field or 700 tag. As with the 1XX codes, the 7XX can be used for personal added entries, corporate added entries, or other types such as conferences and meetings and title added entries that are not the main title of the item.

Indicators

All tags are followed by two indicators in MARC coding. These can be numbers (0, 1, 2, etc.) or blank spaces, or a combination of numbers and blanks. an example is 100 1b (the "b" stands for "blank."); another is 700 0b. The indicators signify meanings, but it is an inefficient use of space to spell out the meanings, so codes of numbers and blank spaces are used instead. They are a shortcut for defining something about the information within the entire tag. Any instructional manual or guide to the MARC format will tell you what the indicator codes mean for each tag. Indicators have unique meanings per tag. Indicators are displayed in MARC records in varying ways, depending on the cataloging system used.

Trace

To "trace" something in a catalog means to provide an access point by that "something." We trace a subject or a particular person such as the illustrator. If we provide an access point by the name of someone other than the main entry, we say we are tracing that name in the catalog, and it will go in a 7XX field.

WHERE TO BEGIN

To determine the main and added entry access points, start with the title page of a book (not its cover). For projected audiovisual materials, start with the title screen. These areas (page and screen) were called the *Chief Source of Information* in AACR2. RDA calls them the *Preferred Source of Information*. RDA is less rigid about the source of information than was AACR2. Preferred sources for various types of resources are listed in RDA. If the preferred source does not yield sufficient information, RDA allows catalogers to use information from outside the resource.

School librarians should know the following rules and examples, which represent the vast majority of the main entry/added entry circumstances encountered in bibliographic records for K–12 materials. Rule numbers from AACR2 and explanations of rule changes due to RDA are included.

Common Combinations of Authors and Illustrators

- One author
- One author, one illustrator who is not also the author
- Two authors/illustrators whose surnames are identical

- Author and illustrator are the same person
- Two or three authors
- Two authors, one editor, one illustrator
- Three authors
- More than three authors
- Editors, up to three
- Editors, more than three
- Other books with editor(s)
- Poets and poetry
- Art and artists
- Photography and photographers
- Corporate authors

One Author

If the item has one author, that person is the "main entry" or the authorized access point (RDA).

- AACR2 Rule 21.4A1: Enter a work . . . by one personal author under the heading for that person.

Title: *The Secret Garden,* by Frances Hodgson Burnett (figure 5.1)

The author, Frances Hodgson Burnett, is the main entry.
MARC coding for the author main entry:

- The author main entry goes in the 100 MARC tag.
- It is followed by the indicators "1" and a "blank."
- Following the indicators is a delimiter (a dollar sign, but any other symbol could be used) and a subfield code "a".
- Following the author's name are her established years of birth and death, preceded by a delimiter and subfield "d".

MARC Coding: 100 1b $a Burnett, Frances Hodgson, $d 1849-1924

One Author, One Illustrator Who Is Not Also the Author

If the item is a children's picture book and has both an author and an illustrator (different people), the author is the personal main entry and the illustrator is a personal added entry. (Catalog records for illustrated adult books will not often have the artist/photographer traced.)

- AACR2 Rule 21.11A1: Enter a work that consists of a text for which an artist has provided illustrations under the heading appropriate to the text. Make

THE SECRET GARDEN

BY FRANCES · · · · ·
HODGSON BURNETT
ILLUSTRATED BY· · ·
CHARLES ROBINSON

WILLIAM HEINEMANN ·
21 BEDFORD STREET · ·
LONDON · W·C· 1912 · ·

Figure 5.1.   Title Page for *The Secret Garden*, by Frances Hodgson Burnett

    an added entry under the heading for the illustrator if appropriate under the provisions of 21.30K2.

- AACR2 Rule 21.30K2: Illustrators. Make an added entry under the heading for an illustrator if a) the illustrator's name is given prominence in the chief source of information of the item being cataloged equal to or greater than that of the person or corporate body named in the main entry heading; b) the illustrations occupy half or more of the item; or c) the illustrations are considered to be an important feature of the book.

LIBRARY LIL

by SUZANNE WILLIAMS

illustrated by STEVEN KELLOGG

Dial Books for Young Readers New York

Figure 5.2. Title Page for *Library Lil*, by Susan Williams. Illustrated by Steven Kellogg. Text copyright © 1997 Suzanne Williams. Illustrations copyright © 1997 by Steven Kellogg. Used by permission of Dial Books for Young Readers, a division of Penguin Group (USA) LLC.

Title: *Library Lil*, by Suzanne Williams. Illustrated by Steven Kellogg. (figure 5.2)

MARC coding for the author main entry (Williams), with an illustrator added entry (Kellogg):

- The author main entry goes in the 100 MARC tag (or field). The illustrator goes in the 700 MARC tag.

MARC Coding: 100 1b $a Williams, Suzanne.
MARC Coding: 700 1b $a Kellogg, Steven, $e ill.

The illustrator goes in the 700 MARC tag (or field). Notice the use of the designator "ill.," which is preceded by delimiter and subfield code "e."

RDA CHANGE: ill. is spelled out as

$e illustrator

Special Tidbit: MARC Relators vs. RDA Relationship Designators

In MARC (not AACR2), $e is called a relator code. It is here that you will find ill. and ed. There are many more relators than ill. and ed., and they are used extensively in RDA, where they are called relationship designators. They are part of the actual catalog code (RDA). They play a large role because RDA is all about bibliographic relationships.

Two Authors/Illustrators Whose Surnames Are Identical

On the title page for *Mother Goose, Numbers on the Loose*, note how the authors' names are not individually displayed with each given name and surname. This does not mean their names can be combined in the main or added entry. Each person must have a full entry and be placed in the appropriate MARC field.

Title: *Mother Goose: Numbers on the Loose*, by Leo & Diane Dillon. (figure 5.3)

MARC coding for the author main entry (Dillon) with an illustrator added entry (Dillon):

100 1b $a Dillon, Leo.
700 1b $a Dillon, Diane, $e ill.

Author and Illustrator Are the Same Person

If the author is also the illustrator, make that person the main entry and do not repeat that person as an added entry. For example, look up in any OPAC the title

LEO & DIANE DILLON

HARCOURT, INC.
Orlando   Austin   New York
San Diego   Toronto   London
MANUFACTURED IN CHINA

Figure 5.3.   Title Page for *Mother Goose, Numbers on the Loose*, by Leo Dillon and Diane Dillon. Copyright © 2007 by Houghton Mifflin Harcourt Publishing Company. Used by permission of Houghton Mifflin Harcourt Publishing Company. All rights reserved.

Where the Wild Things Are, by Maurice Sendak. He both wrote and illustrated this book. He is main entry only, with no added entry.

Two or Three Authors

AACR2 calls these works of shared responsibility. If an item has two or three authors, the first one on the title page is the main entry, or the authorized access point (RDA). The second and third persons on the title page are personal added entries, or the secondary access point (RDA).

- AACR2 Rule 21.6C1. Works of Shared Responsibility. If responsibility is shared between two or three persons or bodies and principal responsibility is not attributed to any of them by wording or layout, enter under the heading for the one named first. Make added entries under the headings for the others.

FIRST HOUSES

Native American Homes and Sacred Structures

Jean Guard Monroe and Ray A. Williamson

Illustrated by Susan Johnston Carlson

Houghton Mifflin Company
Boston

Figure 5.4. Title Page for *First Houses*, by Jean Guard Monroe and Ray A. Williamson. Copyright © 1993 by Houghton Mifflin Harcourt Publishing Company. Used by permission of Houghton Mifflin Harcourt Publishing Company. All rights reserved.

Title: *First Houses: Native American Homes and Sacred Structures,* by Jean Guard Monroe and Ray A. Williamson. Illustrated by Susan Johnston Carlson. (figure 5.4)

The first author is the main entry.
MARC coding for *First Houses*:

100 1b $a Monroe, Jean Guard
700 1b $a Williamson, Ray A.

Option: Trace illustrators also, if it is a children's book. The illustrators do not count toward the "two or three authors." They have a separate function from authors.

700 1b $a Carlson, Susan Johnston, $e illustrator (RDA form)

Two Authors, One Editor, One Illustrator

Title: *Respect, a Girl's Guide to Getting Respect and Dealing When Your Line Is Crossed,* by Courtney Macavinta and Andrea Vander Pluym. Edited by Elizabeth Verdick, illustrated by Catherine Lepage. (figure 5.5)

The main entry is Macavinta, Courtney (100 field). There is an added entry for Vander Pluym, Andrea R. (700 field) and one for the editor, Verdick, Elizabeth. Included here is an added entry for the illustrator as well, an optional addition. MARC coding for *Respect*:

100 1b $a Macavinta, Courtney
245 10 $a Respect, a girl's guide
700 1b $a Vander Pluym, Andrea R.
700 1b $a Verdick, Elizabeth, $e editor
700 1b $a Lepage, Catherine, $e illustrator

Three Authors

Title: *Tuberculosis Update,* by Alvin Silverstein, Virginia Silverstein, and Laura Silverstein Nunn. (figure 5.6)

MARC coding for the author main entry and the second and third named authors on the title page:

100 1b $a Silverstein, Alvin
245 10 $a Tuberculosis update
700 1b $a Silverstein, Virginia B.
700 1b $a Nunn, Laura Silverstein

Respect

A Girl's Guide to Getting Respect and Dealing When Your Line Is Crossed

by Courtney Macavinta and Andrea Vander Pluym

edited by Elizabeth Verdick

illustrated by Catherine Lepage

free spirit
PUBLiSHiNG®

Helping kids
help themselves™
since 1983

Figure 5.5. Title Page for *Respect, a Girl's Guide to Getting Respect and Dealing When Your Line Is Crossed*, by Courtney Macavinta and Andrea Vander Pluym. Copyright © 2005. Used with permission of Free Spirit Publishing Inc., Minneapolis, MN; 800-735-7323; www.freespirit.com. All rights reserved.

Figure 5.6. Title Page for *Tuberculosis Update*, by Alvin Silverstein, Virginia Silverstein, and Laura Silverstein Nunn. Courtesy
of Enslow Publishers.

More Than Three Authors

This explanation is in the past tense because RDA is now the official cataloging
code and treats items written by multiple authors differently than AACR2 did. If an
item had more than three authors, the item received a title main entry, and only the
first author on the title page received a personal added entry or tracing.

- AACR2 Rule 21.6C2. If responsibility is shared among more than three persons or corporate bodies and principal responsibility is not attributed to any
one, two or three, enter under the title. Make an added entry under the heading
for the first person . . . named . . . in the item.

RDA CHANGE: The main entry, or the authorized access point, is *the first named person, not the title* in the case of more than *three authors*. This is a major departure from AACR2. By RDA guidelines, *any or none* of the other authors may be traced. This decision is up to the cataloger.

In the AACR2 catalog record for *Children's Literature in the Elementary School* (figure 5.7), it is not possible to tell just exactly how many people worked on this book, because in the description area it says only: Charlotte S. Huck . . . [et al.]

Note the phrase [et al.]. This is Latin for "and others." That was the wording used in the description of the item when there were more than three authors or editors all carrying out the same function. In this situation, only the first name on the title page was used in the description.

RDA CHANGE: There is no need for [et al.]. All names associated with the item may be recorded in the description, or all but the first named individual may be omitted, but do not use [et al.]. Instead, you may record the statement of responsibility in this way: Charlotte S. Huck [and three others] or [and other authors].

Another title, *Power Up Your Library: Creating the New Elementary School Library Program*, by Sheila Salmon, Elizabeth K. Goldfarb, Melinda Greenblatt, and Anita Phillips Strauss, illustrates the same concept (figure 5.8). The four individuals were all

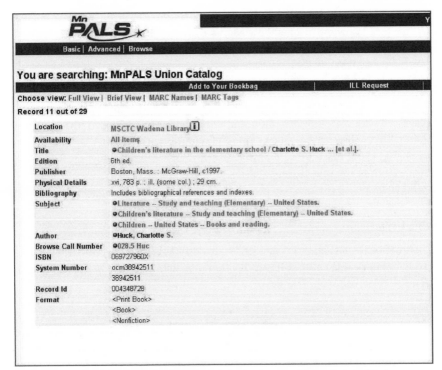

Figure 5.7.   OPAC Record for *Children's Literature in the Elementary School*

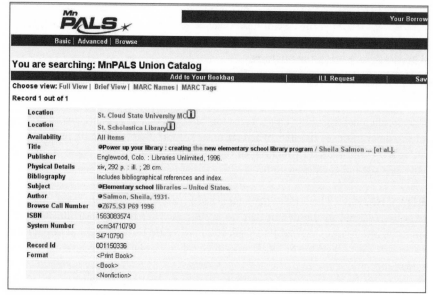

Figure 5.8.   OPAC Record for *Power Up Your Library*

contributing authors. Because there were more than three of them, a title main entry was used, and only the first author would have been traced under AACR2 rules.

245 00 $a Power up your library
700 1b $a Salmon, Sheila

RDA CHANGE: Besides having a personal main entry for this book, every name associated with this item may be traced but does not have to be. This is a radical shift in accessibility via the names of multiple contributors. Under AACR2 and older cataloging codes based on cards, space was always an issue, a situation that forced the creation of the rule of three and the limited number of accessibility points that could be used.

Editors, Up to Three

If an item has an editor, it gets a title main entry. Editors collect the material written by other people and put it together, often including some editorial comments. Trace all three editors in 700 fields.

Special Tidbit: Three Authors or More

You will not often encounter a "more than three authors" situation in the K–12 collection.

- AACR2 Rule 21.7B1. Collections of works by different persons . . . enter it under its title . . . make added entries under the headings for the compilers or editors if there are not more than three.
- If there are more than three compilers/editors . . . make an added entry under the one named first.

Editors, More Than Three

The [et al.] (RDA requires "and others" to be used) situation in the description applies. Trace only the first editor.

RDA CHANGE: There is no change for the main entry. For works produced under editorial direction, the authorized access point is still the title. The statement of responsibility is treated the same as explained for *Children's Literature in the Elementary School.* Include an access point for the first editor in the tracings, but tracing the other editors is optional.

Other Books with Editor(s)

See OPAC records for:

- *With Their Eyes, September 11th: The View From a High School at Ground Zero.* This is a collection by various students, with an editor. This would have a title main entry, and the editor is traced in the 700 field.
- *You're On! Seven Plays in English and Spanish.* This is a collection of plays with an editor. Again, this would have a title main entry, with the editor traced in the 700 field.

Title: *Teens Talk About Alcohol and Alcoholism,* written by students from the Mount Anthony Union Junior High School in Bennington, Vermont. Edited by Paul Dolmetsch and Gail Mauricette. (figure 5.9)

Here we have two editors. Use a title main entry and trace both editors and the name of the school.

MARC coding for book with two editors:

245 00 $a Teens talk about alcohol and alcoholism
700 1b $a Dolmetsch, Paul, $e editor
700 1b $a Mauricette, Gail, $e editor
710 2b $a Mount Anthony Union Junior High School (Bennington, Vt.)

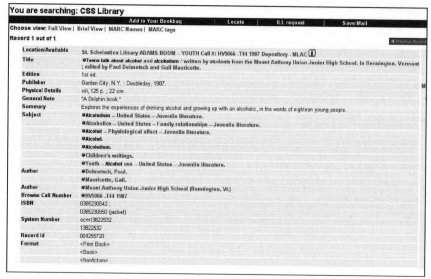

Figure 5.9. OPAC Record for *Teens Talk about Alcohol and Alcoholism*

Poets and Poetry

There are two types of poetry books:

- A book of several or many poems contributed by several or many authors. These books are edited by someone and so are assigned a title main entry. The editor(s) is/are traced following the rules for editors.

Title: *The Cambridge Book of Poetry for Children.* Selected and edited by Kenneth Grahame. (figure 5.10)

The title is the main entry. Trace the selector (i.e., editor).
MARC coding for book of poetry by many poets:

245 04 $a The Cambridge book of poetry for children
700 1b $a Grahame, Kenneth, $d 1859-1932.

In this case, Grahame's entry consists of the years of his birth and death. Those years are preceded by the delimiter and subfield code "d."

700 1b $a Petersham, Maud Fuller, $d 1890-1971, $e illustrator

The Cambridge Book of Poetry for Children

Selected and Edited by
KENNETH GRAHAME
Author of The Golden Age. Dream Days
The Wind in the Willows, etc.

Decorations by
MAUD FULLER

New York: G.P. Putnam's Sons
Cambridge, England: University Press

Figure 5.10. Title Page for *The Cambridge Book of Poetry for Children*, Selected and Edited by Kenneth Grahame

- A book of poems by a single author. The author of the poetry is the main entry.

In the case of Jack Prelutsky, well-known children's poet, he sometimes gathers other people's poetry and sometimes writes entire books of poetry himself. For examples, go to any OPAC and search for Prelutsky, Jack as an author. You will retrieve a list of books with his name attached to them.

- When he is the author of all the poems in the book, he is the main entry.
- When he is the selector, the title is the main entry, and Prelutsky is an added entry.
- Prelutsky is not traced as a subject. The book is not about him.

Title: *A Pizza the Size of the Sun*. Poems by Jack Prelutsky.

MARC coding for book of poetry by Jack Prelutsky:

100 1b $a Prelutsky, Jack
245 12 $a A pizza the size of the sun
700 1b $a Stevenson, James, $d 1929- $e illustrator

Art and Artists

Deciding on the main and added entries for books containing reproductions of visual arts presents a special situation. The cataloger must decide which makes up the bulk of the book, the artwork or any accompanying text.

- AACR2 Rule 21.17 A (Art work without text, or very little text). The artist is the main entry.
- AACR2 Rule 21.17 B (Art work with text). The author of the text is the main entry.

Art Book Situation One: Main Entry Assigned to Artist

An example of reproductions of art with more art than text is *Robert Lawson, Illustrator: A Selection of His Characteristic Illustrations*, with introduction and comment by Helen L. Jones. (figure 5.11)
MARC coding for the artist as the main entry:

100 1b $a Lawson, Robert, $d 1892-1957
245 10 $a Robert Lawson, illustrator : a selection of his characteristic illustrations
600 10 $a Lawson, Robert, $d 1892-1957
700 1b $a Jones, Helen L.

ROBERT LAWSON

Illustrator

A Selection of His
Characteristic Illustrations

With Introduction and Comment by
HELEN L. JONES

☆ ☆ ☆ ☆ ☆ ☆ ☆ ☆

LITTLE, BROWN AND COMPANY

BOSTON   TORONTO

Figure 5.11.   Title Page for *Robert Lawson, Illustrator*, with Introduction and Comment by Helen L. Jones. Courtesy of Little, Brown, & Company.

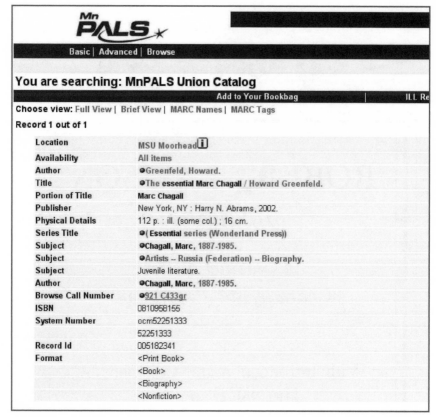

Figure 5.12.   OPAC Record for *The Essential Marc Chagall*, **by Howard Greenfeld**

Art Book Situation Two: Main Entry Assigned to Compiler/Author

Title: *The Essential Marc Chagall*, by Howard Greenfeld. (figure 5.12)

Because there is more text than reproductions of Chagall's paintings in it, the book gets a main entry for the author of the text, Howard Greenfeld.

Chagall should get both an added entry (so people can find this book with him as the "author,") and a subject heading. The title, The essential *Marc Chagall*, would also be an access point. The alternative title, *Marc Chagall*, could be traced as well.

MARC coding for compiler/author as the main entry:

100 1b $a Greenfeld, Howard
245 14 $a The essential Marc Chagall
246 30 $a Marc Chagall
600 10 $a Chagall, Marc, $d 1887-1985
700 1b $a Chagall, Marc, $d 1887-1985

OPAC users will find this book if they search by either Greenfeld or Chagall as authors and Chagall as a subject. An exact title search for *The Essential Marc Chagall* would retrieve this title, as would a keyword search on only the word Marc or only the word Chagall. If there were more paintings by the artist than text by Greenfeld, Chagall, Marc, 1887-1985 would be the main entry.

Photography and Photographers

Books that display or discuss works of photography and photographers are treated the same as art books. The cataloger must decide if there is more photography than text, or more text than photography, and assign the main and added entries accordingly.

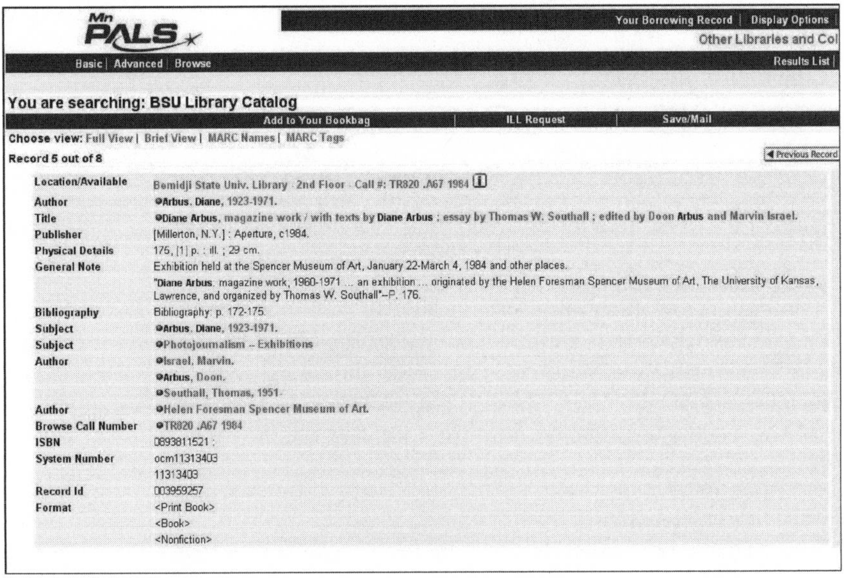

MnPALS

Your Borrowing Record | Display Options |

Other Libraries and Col

Basic | Advanced | Browse

Results List |

You are searching: BSU Library Catalog

Add to Your Bookbag | ILL Request | Save/Mail

Choose view: Full View | Brief View | MARC Names | MARC Tags

Record 5 out of 8

Previous Record

Location/Available	Bemidji State Univ. Library 2nd Floor Call #: TR820 .A67 1984
Author	Arbus, Diane, 1923-1971.
Title	Diane Arbus, magazine work / with texts by Diane Arbus ; essay by Thomas W. Southall ; edited by Doon Arbus and Marvin Israel.
Publisher	[Millerton, N.Y.] : Aperture, c1984.
Physical Details	175, [1] p. : ill. ; 29 cm.
General Note	Exhibition held at the Spencer Museum of Art, January 22-March 4, 1984 and other places.
	"Diane Arbus: magazine work, 1960-1971 ... an exhibition ... originated by the Helen Foresman Spencer Museum of Art, The University of Kansas, Lawrence, and organized by Thomas W. Southall"--P. 176.
Bibliography	Bibliography: p. 172-175.
Subject	Arbus, Diane, 1923-1971.
Subject	Photojournalism -- Exhibitions
Author	Israel, Marvin.
	Arbus, Doon.
	Southall, Thomas, 1951-
Author	Helen Foresman Spencer Museum of Art.
Browse Call Number	TR820 .A67 1984
ISBN	0893811521 :
System Number	ocm11313403
	11313403
Record Id	003959257
Format	<Print Book>
	<Book>
	<Nonfiction>

Figure 5.13. OPAC Record for *Diane Arbus: Magazine Work*, by Diane Arbus

A book titled *Diane Arbus: Magazine Work [exhibition]* is devoted mostly to reproductions of Arbus's photography (figure 5.13). It is edited by Doon Arbus and Marvin Israel.

MARC coding for photographer as the main entry:

100 1b $a Arbus, Diane, $d 1923-1971
245 10 $a Diane Arbus : $b magazine work
600 10 $a Arbus, Diane, $d 1923-1971
700 1b $a Arbus, Doon
700 1b $a Israel, Marvin
700 1b $a Southall, Thomas, $d 1951-

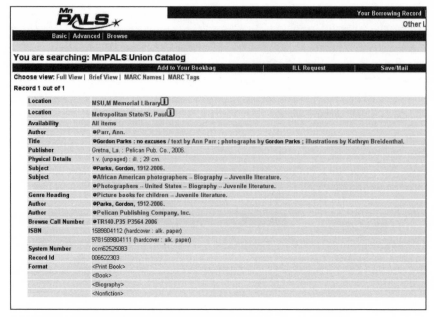

Figure 5.14.   OPAC Record for *Gordon Parks: No Excuses,* **by Ann Parr**

The opposite situation exists with the book titled *Gordon Parks: No Excuses* (figure 5.14). This book consists of more text by Ann Parr than reproductions of photography by Gordon Parks. It also contains other illustrations by Kathryn Breidenthal. The following MARC coding shows the access points.

MARC coding for author as main entry for photography book:

100 1b $a Parr, Ann
245 10 $a Gordon Parks : $b no excuses
600 10 $a Parks, Gordon, $d 1912-2006
700 1b $a Parks, Gordon, $d 1912-2006
700 1b $a Breidenthal, Kathryn.

Corporate Authors

There are also "Corporate Headings" or "Corporate Authors." They are organizations the names of which are searchable entries in the catalog. Sometimes they are main entries, but these days they are mostly added entries. We will not go into the reasons for this differentiation. Two types of corporate entries, one for a government agency and one for a company, are discussed here.

A government agency. These start either with the governmental jurisdiction (such as United States or California) or directly with the name of the agency. If the agency has a fairly distinctive name, the heading starts with that name.

Distinctive Name: Library of Congress.

The Library of Congress probably will not be confused with any other governmental agency worldwide, so its heading is simply

710 2b $a Library of Congress.

An agency may have a nondistinctive name, such as Office of Adolescent Health. There could be many such offices all over the world, so for something like this, start with the name of the governmental jurisdiction:

710 1b $a United States. $b Office of Adolescent Health.

Special Tidbit: Periods after Segments of a Heading

710 1b $a United States. $b Office of Adolescent Health.

Notice the periods after each segment of this heading. It is not

United States Office of Adolescent Health

It is

United States PERIOD. Office of Adolescent Health PERIOD

Another jurisdiction example is

Pennsylvania. Department of Agriculture.

A company name. This also includes institutions of higher education:

The corporate heading for The College of Jewish Studies in Chicago is:

710 2b $a College of Jewish Studies (Chicago, Ill.)

The corporate heading for Films for the Humanities & Sciences is:

710 2b $a Films for the Humanities & Sciences (Firm)

MARC coding for corporate headings goes in a 710 field with various indicators, depending on what kind of corporate heading it is.

UNIFORM TITLES

A uniform title is a device to bring together in the catalog all manifestations of the same work. As a school librarian, you will not encounter a large number of uniform title situations, but you may occasionally do so in relation to Mother Goose tales or other folktales. The Bible is also represented by uniform title entries in the catalog.

Think of how many different Mother Goose variations there are: *The Inner City Mother Goose*, *Mary Engelbreit's Mother Goose Favorites*, *Mother Goose: Numbers on the Loose*, and *Favorite Nursery Rhymes from Mother Goose* are only a few among hundreds.

Notice that "Mother Goose" is not the first word in three of the four titles. In the card catalog, these titles would have been lost to people looking in the "M" title drawers for all Mother Goose books in the library. That is where uniform titles came to the rescue. Catalogers would add either a uniform title main entry or an added entry to these records for "Mother Goose." Those cards would have filed in the title "M" drawers, thereby making the items accessible under Mother Goose. There could be an individual Mother Goose rhyme published all by itself in a small illustrated volume, such as *Hey Diddle, Diddle*. If "Mother Goose" is not somewhere in that record, it will not be retrievable by people looking for Mother Goose items.

Two types of uniform titles are uniform title main entry (MARC field 130, followed by the specific title of the item in the title, or 245, field) and uniform title added entries (MARC field 730). Here are two examples for Mother Goose:

130 0b $a Mother Goose
245 10 $a Inner city Mother Goose

100 1b $a Caldecott, Randolph, $d 1846-1886
245 10 $a Hey diddle diddle and Baby bunting
730 0b $a Mother Goose

For the Bible, if the library has these titles in its collection—*Good News for Modern Man: The New Testament in Today's English Version*, *The Early Reader's Bible*, or *The Miracles of Jesus*—they would not have been accessible in the card catalog, because the first word of these books is not "Bible." Use of uniform titles assured that users could go to the "B" title drawers, look up Bible, and thumb their way through all the various manifestations represented in this catalog. The Bible in a uniform title also makes it possible to locate the same items in the OPAC.

These are typical uniform titles for the Bible and its books:

Bible. N.T. English. Today's English. 1966.
Bible. English. New Revised Standard. 2005.
Bible. N.T. Gospels.

Here is how *The Miracles of Jesus*, retold from the Bible by Tomie dePaola, would be coded:

100 1b $a DePaola, Tomie, $d 1934-
245 14 $a The miracles of Jesus, retold from the Bible
730 0b $a Bible. $p N.T. $p Gospels.

RDA CHANGE: O.T. and N.T. will no longer be used in headings for specific books of the Bible. For example, a book about Genesis will now have the authorized access point Bible. Genesis. If the item needs the testament name in the access point, it will be spelled out: Bible. New Testament.

OPAC INTERFACES AND DETERMINING MAIN AND ADDED ENTRIES

Remember that you cannot rely on the screen display to help you determine which access point is the main entry and which access points are added entries unless the display it is adhering to a card format. In most OPACs, authors, editors, titles, added authors, and so forth can be anywhere on the screen, giving you access and information but not verification for access point function (main vs. added entry).

SUMMARY

Access points are the way we find bibliographic records in the catalog. During the era of card catalogs, the *first word* of the authors' names, titles, etc., was the access point of entry in the catalog. In today's OPACs, any word that is indexed by the OPAC software can be an entry point. Even though the manual card catalog transitioned to the more versatile OPAC, rules for constructing bibliographic records did not change very much. We still must decide which name associated with the item will be the main entry and which names will be added entries. We must decide if the item should have a title main entry rather than a personal entry. AACR2 set limitations on the number of access points in each bibliographic record, but this limitation was due more to the realities of catalog cards than for philosophical reasons.

With today's OPACs, we do not have this constraint. The new cataloging code, RDA, recognizes this freedom and allows for more names to be traced. If you learn the rules in AACR2, you will have no difficulty altering your practice a little to take advantage of this new increase in access points. You will, however, still need to decide on a main entry and its accompanying added entries.

The next chapter considers the next step after selecting access points, that of determining the form of the entry points.

TEST YOUR KNOWLEDGE

Indicate the appropriate main and added entries for the following abbreviated title pages and give the reason for your choice.

Show the correct order of the name and the MARC tags, delimiters, and subfield codes for it. Label the main entry ME and any added entries AE. For example:

Title Page: Giggle, giggle, quack, by Doreen Cronin & Pictures by Betsy Lewin
ME: 100 1b Cronin, Betsy
AE: 245 10 Giggle, giggle, quack
AE: 700 1b Lewin, Betsy, $e illustrator

Reason: AACR2 Rule 21.11A1: Enter a work that consists of a text for which an artist has provided illustrations under the heading appropriate to the text. Make an added entry under the heading for the illustrator.

Title Page 1. Best Shot in the West: The Adventures of Nat Love
By Patricia and Fredrick McKissack, Jr.
Illustrated by Randy DuBurke

Title Page 2. Summer Reading for Teens: How to Close the Achievement Gap
Edited by Richard L Allington, Anne McGill, & Lynn Bigelman

Title Page 3. Encyclopedia of World War II
By Dwight D. Eisenhower, George Patton, Omar Bradley and Douglas MacArthur.
Do this one according to RDA, not AACR2.

Title Page 4. The Beauty of the Beast: Poems From the Animal Kingdom
Selected by Jack Prelutsky. Illustrated by Meilo So.

Title Page 5. Nightmares! Poems to Trouble Your Sleep, by Jack Prelutsky. Illustrated by Arnold Lobel.

Title Page 6. Georgia O'Keeffe: One Hundred Flowers. Edited by Nicholas Callaway

Title Page 7. Will You Be Mine? A Nursery Rhyme Romance. Compiled and Illustrated by Phyllis Limbacher Tildes

TEST YOUR CRITICAL THINKING

Given what you have learned in this chapter about the various decisions and interpretations that must be made when determining a main and any number of added entries for a bibliographic record, formulate an argument against this decision-making practice. Postulate what a catalog record might look like if these decisions were not necessary.

RESOURCES

Anglo American Cataloguing Rules (2nd ed.). (2005). Chicago: American Library Association.

Nicholson, J. (n.d.). *RDA in MARC*. Retrieved from: http://www.llaonline.org/ne/lla2011/RDApreconference.pdf.

6

Creating Authorized Forms of Names

Once main and added entries are chosen, it is necessary to determine what *form* these names will be in. A cardinal rule of catalog building is that each person or group represented in the catalog as an access point should be entered consistently under one form of the name. For example, it would be incorrect to enter books by Wells, H. G. and Wells, Herbert George under both names. Choose *one form* and use it consistently.

Why is this consistency important? If a name is not entered in the same format each time it is used, the collocating function of the catalog will be compromised. To *collocate* means to bring together all like items in one place. This is especially important in a computer environment that requires accuracy for precise and thorough retrieval, because an unforgiving machine is doing the searching, not an individual who can make judgments and allowances for errors. Without consistency in the access points, the user will never be certain that what is retrieved is everything the library has by or about a particular person. Inconsistency in forms of names leads to a breakdown in resource discovery.

Fortunately the Library of Congress has developed an extensive Name Authority File, a controlled vocabulary of names in which LC has recorded "correct" and acceptable forms of entries for people, corporate bodies (such as Library of Congress or Medtronic, Inc.), and geographic names (any country, body of water, political jurisdiction, etc.). In bibliographic records, use of names in their established forms assures accurate collocation. (figure 6.1)

If it is necessary to do original cataloging for an item, be aware of how to locate the correct form of entry for any individual. You can usually find the correct form of entry for the author in the CIP data, WorldCat, the Library of Congress catalog, or the LC Authority Files.

Figure 6.1. Library of Congress Authorities Home Screen

OPACS AND AUTHORITY CONTROL

One of the largest vendors of automated catalogs is Follett. Its Cataloging Module includes an authority structure for both names and subjects, so if a search is done for a name heading that is not "correct," or is in an incorrect form, it often will take the user to the heading that is correct. Granted, most of the time name searching will not present any problems. For most people, the names they use as authors are the same names most people know them by. But fifty years ago a search for "Twain, Mark" would have rerouted the user from the pseudonym to the real name "Clemens, Samuel." Today pseudonyms are acceptable forms of entry and a more effective access point in the catalog for users.

Similarly, fifty years ago J. K. Rowling probably would not have been the famous author's form of entry (Rowling, J. K.). The librarians at the Library of Congress would have researched her full, exact name and established an entry for her under that full name, like this: Rowling, Joanne K.

When investigating and purchasing a new OPAC system, be certain to ask the vendor about the system's authority control and structure.

DETERMINING FORMS OF NAMES

There are many rules in AACR2 for determining forms of names, but a school librarian does not need to know all of them. Here we cover just the types the school librarian would encounter.

Commonly Known Name

Simply put, enter the person under the name by which he or she is most commonly known (AACR2 Rule 22.1A). This may sound self-evident, but in the history of cataloging this is a relatively new way of forming names.

- For decades the rule was to determine the fullest form of the person's name and use that. The current rule is "most commonly known," which may or may not be the "fullest form."

Example: Two Presidents: Clinton and Carter

Former President Clinton's name serves as an example. His full given name is William Jefferson Clinton. In the past he would have been entered in the catalog this way:

Clinton, William Jefferson, 1946-

- He was born in 1946. The hyphen means "to"; someday, when he has gone to that great Oval Office in the sky, the year of his demise will be entered after it.
- But how is he commonly known? "Bill Clinton." He signed official documents using the name "Bill Clinton." Hence, his entry in the name authority file and online catalogs is Clinton, Bill, 1946-
- President James Earl Carter signed documents under the name "Jimmy Carter," and that is the form (Carter, Jimmy, 1924-) under which his name is established in the Library of Congress Name Authority File.

Commonly Known by First and Middle Initials and Last Name

Now consider H. G. Wells, the famous writer of science fiction.

- He did not spell out his entire first and middle names on the title pages of his books. Title pages are the Preferred Source of Information for deciding on choice of entry and form of entry. He was commonly known as H. G. Wells.
- In earlier times, the form of his name in the catalog was Wells, Herbert George, 1866-1946, even though he did not commonly use this full form of his name on the title pages of his books. The rule at that time was "fullest form of the name." Today it is "commonest form of the name," but if the fullest form of the name is needed to distinguish between two otherwise identical names, you may use it in parentheses, such as Wells, H. G. (Herbert George), 1866-1946 (AARC2R Rule 22.18A). In practice, the use of parentheses around full forms of names is not limited solely to distinguishing between identical names; it is often done when the full form is known but is not necessarily used by the in-

dividual. This convention was adopted by the Library of Congress in 1981 and is prevalent in OPACs today. There is a space between the H. and the G. This is important in a computer catalog. If you don't have a space between the two letters, you have turned initials into a name: "H.G."

- Another name like this in the Authority File is the second President Bush. His full name is George Walker Bush, and he was born in 1946, but he is known mostly as George W. Bush. The established form of his name is Bush, George W. (George Walker), 1946-

People Writing Under a Variety of Names, Including Their Own Given Names and Pseudonyms

In 1988 AACR2 recognized that individuals may have "separate bibliographic identities," and all of these identities may receive a different form of name in the name authority file. These names may be linked in the catalog through the use of cross-references (AACR2 Rule 22.2B2).

If authors write under pseudonyms, those are the names used for their catalog entries (AACR2 Rule 22.2B1). This is a major departure from the early days of cataloging (1900–1966), when people were entered in the catalog under their real names (Samuel Clemens, for example, for Mark Twain) rather than their pseudonyms. There would have been a cross-reference in the catalog leading users from Twain, Mark to Clemens, Samuel. Today the entry will be under the pseudonym, Twain, Mark.

On occasion, people write under more than one pseudonym (Victoria Holt, aka Jean Plaidy and others) or under their real names and pseudonyms (Charles Lutwidge Dodgson and Lewis Carroll). In these cases, any of these names may be used for their entries in the catalog, depending upon which work is being identified (AACR2 Rule 22.2B3).

People Writing Under a Forename (Given Name, Single Name, or First Name) such as Cher, Madonna, or Avi

- Musicians are considered to be "authors." The catalog record for a CD recording of Cher's music gets "Cher" as the main entry in the record: Cher, 1946- Sting is entered as Sting (Musician) (AACR2 Rule 22.8).
- The author Avi is entered as Avi, 1937-

People Having Small Variations in Their Name Among Different Title Pages for Different Publications

- For example: Paul J. Jones could have several forms of his name on title pages for different books he has written. One might be Paul Jones, another Paul John Jones, another P. J. Jones. Maybe he has not thought about consistency in the way his name is presented to the public and does not realize that some of his works will be lost to the user who knows only one form of his name.

- The Library of Congress is very concerned about consistency for retrievability and identification. They want to make sure that in the future any books by this individual are credited to the right individual in the name authority file. What happens when LC receives the electronic proof of a new book in the CIP Division, and the book has the name *Paul John Jones* on the title page?

  - First the catalogers check the name authority file to see if the name is already there.
  - If they find the name, then they must make sure it is the same person as the person indicated on the new title page.
  - If the name on the title page is a little bit different than the one in the authority file, but they determine he is indeed one and the same person, they will use the previously established heading for that person. So, originally the name could have been established from the first title page as Jones, Paul John. Then the second book might have Paul J. Jones on the title page. Nevertheless, for the access point, the established name that will be used for the main entry will be Jones, Paul John.
  - The Library of Congress does change the form of an entry because of small variations in names over the course of time, but the name authority staff must consider the ripple effect of a name change and how it will affect other libraries across the country. There are no definitive rules for changing the form of someone's entry. It is a matter of cataloger judgment (D. Williamson, personal communication, September 15, 2011).

THERE'S MORE!

There are many more rules for forms of names in AACR2, but they are not all that necessary for the school librarian to know about. They deal with such things as hyphenated surnames, non-American names, names of royal persons, names in the form of a phrase (Malcolm X, for example), and entries for the office of president of the United States, among others.

CROSS-REFERENCES

- Cross-references provide us with a link from one form of the name to another form.
- The Library of Congress Name Authority File has cross-references in it.
- Cross-references are present in OPACs in all kinds of libraries.

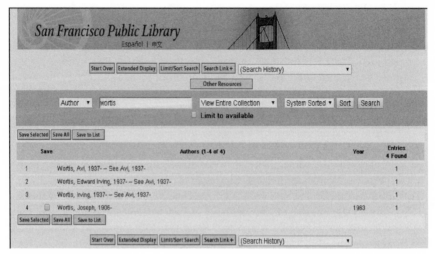

Figure 6.2. San Francisco Public Library's Cross-References for Avi

If you were to look up the children's author Avi under his real name, Wortis, Edward, you would retrieve the information shown in figure 6.2, a SEE reference in the San Francisco Public Library OPAC.

- The famous children's author Avi's *real name* is Edward Irving Wortis. But since he is *commonly known* as Avi, his pseudonym, and because the Library of Congress catalogers investigated until they found his year of birth, his form of entry is: Avi, 1937-
- A cross-reference from his real name to his pseudonym is indicated by the word SEE.

Example of a "SEE ALSO" Cross-Reference (or, "SEARCH ALSO UNDER")

SEE ALSO references are used for people who write under more than one name and are commonly known under each or all (depending upon the number) of them. Figure 6.3 is an example, using the names for Richard Bachman (pseudonym) and Stephen King (real name), who are the same person.

- A search for the author Richard Bachman brings up a display referring the user to his alter ego, Stephen King.
- The See Also cross-reference tells the user that Richard Bachman also writes under the name Stephen King.
- Item number 2 in the list is a hotlink to bibliographic records for the items the library owns written by Richard Bachman.
- Item number 3 is a See reference referring from a form of the name Bachman that includes his year of birth to his authorized name, which does not include that year.

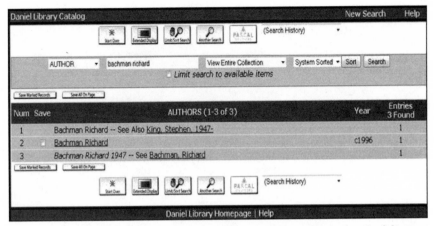

Figure 6.3. Cross-References for Richard Bachman/Stephen King in the Citadel's Daniel Library

- If there is nothing by Richard Bachman in the library, do not have a cross reference involving that name. A person searching for him should simply get no hits. If searching for King, Stephen, the person should retrieve records for those items (assuming the library owns some), but there should be no cross-reference to Bachman.

Another example of this situation is Lewis Carroll, the author of *Alice's Adventures in Wonderland*. He wrote under his pseudonym and under his real name. So there would be SEE ALSO cross-references between the two names if the library had materials by him under both names. Figure 6.4 is an example of a cross-reference from Dodgson, Charles Lutwidge to Carroll, Lewis from the Milwaukee Public Library.

HISTORICAL INFORMATION ON NAME CHANGES IN THE LIBRARY OF CONGRESS NAME AUTHORITIES

Besides keeping track of the authorized access form for an individual, the Library of Congress Name Authorities (authorities.loc.gov) is also a rich source of information on people's name changes. The singer and actor known as Cher has had a number of other names. Table 6.1 is the name authority record for her with the MARC tags in the Library of Congress Name Authorities online.

Here is what the tags in the LC Authorities mean for a personal authorized name:

The 100 field is for the correct form of the name (Cher).

The 400 field is for the form of name that is NOT USED (a SEE reference) (nine of them for Cher).

The 500 field is for a form of a personal name that is also used, in addition to the form in the 100 field (a SEE ALSO reference, or, as LC labels it: "Search

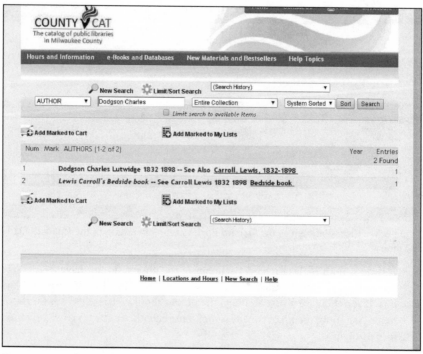

Figure 6.4. Milwaukee County Public Library's Cross-References for Charles Dodgson/ Lewis Carroll

Table 6.1. Library of Congress Name Authorities Record for Cher with MARC Tags

LC control no.:	n 50038010
LCCN permalink:	http://lccn.loc.gov/n50038010
HEADING:	Cher, 1946-
000	02121cz a2200385n 450
001	3265170
005	20130731073651.0
008	800718n| azannaabn |a aaa
010	__ |a n 50038010
035	__ |a (OCoLC)oca00073248
040	__ |a DLC |b eng |e rda |c DLC |d DLC |d WaU |d DLC | d UPB |d WaU
046	__ |f 19460520
100	0_ |a Cher, |d 1946-
370	__ |a El Centro, Calif. |c U.S.
372	__ |a Singing |a Popular music |a Rock music |a Folk music | a Disco music |a Electronica (Music) |a Acting |2 lcsh
374	__ |a Singers |a Actresses |a Actors |2 lcsh
375	__ |a female
377	__ |a eng

```
400    1_   |a Sarkisian, Cherilyn, |d 1946-
400    1_   |a Bono, Cher, |d 1946-
400    1_   |a Allman, Cher, |d 1946-
400    1_   |a Sakesian, Cherilyn, |d 1946-
400    1_   |a Sakisian, Cherilyn, |d 1946-
400    1_   |a La Piere, Cherilyn, |d 1946-
400    1_   |a LaPierre, Cherilyn, |d 1946-
400    0_   |a Cleo, |d 1946-
400    1_   |a Sarkisian, Cheryl, |d 1946-
500    1_   |a Mason, Bonnie Jo
510    2_   |w r |i Group member of: |a Sonny & Cher
670    __   |a Jacobs, L. Cher, 1975: |b t.p. (Cher)
670    __   |a Bronaugh, R.B. Celebrity birthday book, c1981: |b p. 38
            (Cher; singer-actress; b. Cherilyn Sarkisian (or Sakisian) (or
            Cherilyn La Piere) 5/20/1946)
670    __   |a Wikipedia, Apr. 18, 2009 |b (Cher, b. Cherilyn Sarkisian
            on May 20, 1946; also known as: Cherilyn LaPierre; Cleo; Cher
            Bono; in 1979 legally changed her name to: Cher, no surname)
            July 30, 2013 (Cher; birth name: Cherilyn Sarkisian; also known
            as: Cherilyn Sarkisian LaPiere; Cheryl Sarkisian; Bonnie Jo
            Mason; Cleo; Chel r; Cher Bono; born May 20, 1946, El Centro,
            California; Genres: Pop, rock, folk, disco, dance; Occupations:
            Singer, actress, songwriter, music and film producer, film
            director, comedian, television host, model, fashion designer,
            dancer, entrepreneur) Ringo, I Love You ("Ringo, I Love You" is
            a rock song performed by American singer-actress Cher released
            under the pseudonym Bonnie Jo Mason, the name she used at
            the start of her career when based in Los Angeles)
678    0_   |a Cher (1946- ) is an American singer and actress.
```

Also Under"). In this case, Cher recorded as Bonnie Jo Mason and as half of Sonny & Cher is a corporate authorized heading for the name of the singing duo together, so its MARC tag is 510.

The 670 fields (two of them) are used for documenting the sources used for the various names in the record. Notice that the second source is *Wikipedia*.

Figure 6.5 shows what a cross-reference for the singer Cher looks like if someone searches for her under her former husband's surname, Bono.

Table 6.2 shows the Library of Congress authority record for *Twilight* series author Stephenie Meyer. Note the 400 field indicating a form of the name not used, in this case Meyer, Stephanie vs. the form used, Meyer, Stephenie. The difference is in the spelling of her first name.

Next you will see several 670 fields, which cite the sources used and actions taken by catalogers as they established the form of the name.

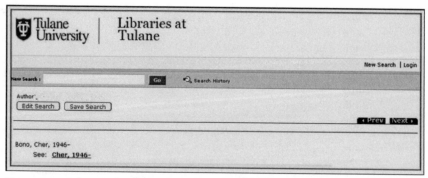

Figure 6.5. Tulane University's Cross-Reference for the Singer Cher

- Look at the first 670 field. It is saying the electronic CIP for this book shows Stephanie, but the title page shows Stephenie.
- The second 670 field tells you that LC called the publisher and established that the correct spelling is with an "e", not an "a".
- The third 670 field tells the user that someone checked the publisher's website and found information directly from the author herself concerning why she spells her name as she does.

Table 6.2. Library of Congress Authority Record for Twilight Series Author Stephenie Meyer

LC control no.:	n 2004030792
LCCN permalink:	http://lccn.loc.gov/n2004030792
HEADING:	Meyer, Stephenie, 1973-
000	00820cz a2200181n 450
001	6375265
005	20130110114934.0
008	041020n| azannaabn |a aaa
010	__ |a n 2004030792
040	__ |a DLC |b eng |e rda |c DLC |d DLC
046	__ |f 1973
053	_0 |a PS3613.E979
100	1_ |a Meyer, Stephenie, |d 1973-
400	1_ |a Meyer, Stephanie, |d 1973-
670	__ |a Meyer, Stephenie. Twilight, 2005: |b ECIP t.p. (Stephanie Meyer) book t.p. (Stephenie Meyer)
670	__ |a Call to pub. 10-20-2004 |b (Stephenie M. Meyer; b. 12-24-73)
670	__ |a WWW site for Time/Warner, Little/Brown, viewed Sept. 20, 2005 |b (Stephenie Meyer; b. 1973; the unusual spelling of my name was a gift from my father, Stephen (+ ie = me); though I have had my name spelled wrong my entire life, it makes it easier to google myself now)
953	__ |a lb17 |b re10

A NAME AS A SUBJECT HEADING

What if the book is *about* a famous person, rather than *by* the famous person? How is the form of the name decided on, and where is it found? The answer is the same as above. Look up the name in the name authority file, whether the item is *by* that person or *about* that person, and use the form as you find it there. If the name is not in the name authority file, try the subject authority file.

Special Tidbit: Access Points vs. Description

This chapter covers access points, not description. When we get to the material on description (all the information in the body of the catalog record that describes the item), the name is transcribed from the title page of the book exactly as it appears on the title page. So if it says "by Laurence P. Pringle" on the title page, it is transcribed that way in the statement of responsibility in the description. The access point must be recorded in its authorized form as either a main entry (100 field) or added entry (700 field). For Pringle, this is: Pringle, Laurence, 1935–.

GEOGRAPHIC NAMES

Believe it or not, geographic names are established in particular "forms" and recorded in the Name Authority File at the Library of Congress. For example, if you had a book about San Francisco, California, you would want to use the correct form of the name of the city as a geographical subject heading. Seems simple enough, right? But think about the choices this involves. How many different ways could you express San Francisco, California?

San Francisco, Calif.
San Francisco, California
San Francisco, CA
San Francisco -- California
San Francisco (California)
San Francisco (Calif.)

That is six different possibilities, but only one of them is correct: San Francisco (Calif.).

NAMES FOR CORPORATE BODIES

This topic was covered briefly in chapter 5. The discussion in that chapter provides examples of forms of entry for corporate entities. That is sufficient coverage for the school librarian.

RDA CHANGES IN FORMS OF ENTRY

1. Before RDA, the use of "Jr." was restricted to situations in which you had two individuals with the same name and needed the distinguisher. With RDA, you may use "Jr." any time:

   100 1b Williams, Hank, $c Jr., $d 1949-

   In that order.

2. Before RDA, dates of birth were recorded as you see in the Hank Williams Jr. entry above. RDA authorizes the following:

   100 1b Williams, Hank, $c Jr., $d born 1949.

   The Library of Congress will not be following this rule, and $d 1949- (the hyphen) will remain.

3. AACR2 stated if you have two people with the same name and no way to distinguish between them (dates of birth/death and/or fullest form of the name), you may add a subfield for the author's field of activity or profession. It is also acceptable to use a term of honor, term of address, title of position or office, initials of an academic degree, or initials denoting membership in an organization. For example:

   Brown, George (Flutist)
   Brown, George, Ph.D.

   RDA concurs with this, but takes it a step further. If no suitable addition is available, use the same access point for all persons with the same name, and use an undifferentiated name indicator to designate the name as one that is undifferentiated:

   Brown, George [undifferentiated]

There are several other changes in RDA relating to forms of various types of names (personal, corporate, conference/proceedings, family names, uniform titles, etc.), but they are beyond the scope of this book. You can find a number of documents on the Internet that cover these changes. A particularly good one is *Changes From AACR2 to RDA: Comparison of Examples*, by Adam L. Schiff of the University of Washington Libraries.

REVIEW OF CHOICE OF ENTRY AND
HOW IT RELATES TO FORM OF ENTRY

Chapter 5 covered choosing both the main entry and added entries for a catalog record. This chapter has covered determining the forms of those names. The form of entry in the Library of Congress Authorities is the form used in the main entry, added entries, and subject headings representing people or groups of people. Choosing authorized access points and establishing the authorized form for access points are two distinct cataloging processes.

SUMMARY

Form of access points refers to authorized headings for use in bibliographic records. This sounds deceptively simple, but in reality there are many things to take into consideration when deciding on the form of a name. Unless names are in a consistent form, there is no assurance the user will retrieve *everything* in the catalog by that person or corporate entity. The Library of Congress has done much of this work for librarians by creating and maintaining authorized forms of names and their cross-references. School librarians should ask their OPAC vendors how the OPAC handles name and subject authority control and purchase a system that does not impede resource discovery.

TEST YOUR KNOWLEDGE

Determine the correct answers to the following multiple choice questions.

1. If names for each individual represented in the OPAC are not in a consistent form, users will:

   A. not be able to find anything in the catalog by them.
   B. not be able to find anything in the catalog about them.
   C. not be able to find everything in the catalog by them.

2. The correct form of entry for an individual is usually in:

   A. the CIP
   B. the CSH
   C. the CYAC

3. Forms of names for authors who prominently used initials (T. S. Eliot or Ulysses S. Grant, for example) sometimes include the full names in:

   A. [ ]
   B. ( )
   C. < >

4. If slight variations occur in the form of the name of any particular individual, the Library of Congress catalogers will consider the _____ effect on the catalog if they change the form of the name in the LC authority file.

   A. management
   B. space

C. ripple

5. An author's name is established in which type of form?

   A. most commonly used
   B. fullest
   C. given at birth

6. Which of the following leads a catalog user from the form of name not used to the form that is used?

   A. See also
   B. See
   C. See other name

7. LC authority files may have several of these fields, used to track actions taken and decisions made during the establishment of a name.

   A. 670
   B. 660
   C. 680

8. This chapter is about access points, not description. In description we transcribe information from the item:

   A. in abbreviated form
   B. per publisher's guidelines
   C. exactly as it is found on the item

9. Established name entries for singers Cher and Adele are:

   A. their given names
   B. their full names
   C. their family names

10. For determining both choice and form of entry, the title page is the:

    A. recommended source
    B. only source
    C. preferred source

Using the Library of Congress Name Authority File or any OPAC with an authority structure, determine the forms of entry for the following individuals:

1. President Richard M. Nixon
2. Grace Hopper, pioneering computer programmer
3. Former first lady Hillary Clinton
4. Violinist Itzhak Perlman
5. Barry Soetoro

6. TV program *American Idol*
7. Senator Ted Kennedy
8. Movie star Brad Cooper
9. Maya Lin, designer of the Vietnam Veterans Memorial
10. Babe Didrikson, one of the greatest all-around athletes

TEST YOUR CRITICAL THINKING

You are soon going to be purchasing a new OPAC system. What questions would you ask the potential vendors about their systems' name authority capabilities?

RESOURCES AND SUPPLEMENTARY READING

Intner, S. S., Fountain, J. F., & Weihs, J. (Eds.). (2011). *Cataloging correctly for kids: An introduction to the tools* (5th ed). Chicago: American Library Association. Chapter 6, "Authority Control and Kids' Cataloging," by Kay E. Lowell, is a very useful supplementary resource to this chapter.

7

Creating MARC 21 Records

Chapter 5 included MARC coding for names used as access points in the catalog record. This chapter covers MARC in more detail. MARC is the acronym for MAchine-Readable Cataloging. It defines a data format that emerged from an initiative led by the Library of Congress beginning in the mid-1960s. It provides the mechanism by which computers use, exchange, and interpret bibliographic information, and its data elements serve as the foundation of most library catalogs used today. MARC became USMARC in the 1980s and MARC 21 in the late 1990s.

INTRODUCTION

MARC was developed at the Library at the Library of Congress by Henriette Avram along with other staff members in the 1960s. Since 1968 the Library of Congress has been distributing its catalog records in this format. Do not confuse MARC with a cataloging code or set of rules for creating bibliographic records. RDA is the current cataloging code, while MARC is a coding system facilitating computer manipulation of bibliographic records.

As online catalogs became increasingly popular in the United States, it became necessary for all catalogers to learn MARC coding in order to create bibliographic records capable of being seamlessly merged into local online catalogs. Often cataloging systems used by school librarians provide a workform into which cataloging information may be entered manually, but is coded automatically as it is entered. Nevertheless, in order to make a catalog record act certain ways, a librarian will need to understand the codes and their application and be able to apply them.

Each element of the catalog record can be coded. There are hundreds of MARC codes, but fortunately only a few of them are used frequently. Those used most frequently are covered in the downloadable document cited in the next paragraph.

Parts VII and VIII of *Understanding MARC Bibliographic: Machine-Readable Cataloging* are indispensable for learning MARC. The entire booklet is downloadable at http://www.loc.gov/marc/umb/. Pages 3, 4, and 5 of Part XI show sample MARC records and what they look like when displayed on a screen or on a card. These examples, however, do not reflect RDA.

BASICS OF UNDERSTANDING FIELDS, TAGS, INDICATORS, DELIMITERS, AND SUBFIELD CODES

- All the elements of a MARC record are grouped in *fields*. For example, the title goes in the "title" field. The edition statement goes in the "edition" field, and so forth.
- These fields are identified in a MARC record by three-digit numbered *tags*. The title goes in the 245 tag. The edition statement goes in the 250 tag, and so forth.
- Immediately after the tag there are two spaces for indicators, which are filled by either numerals or blank spaces. Indicators provide a short hand for a larger meaning, or they are "indicating" something. In Part VII of the MARC booklet blank indicators are symbolized by a number sign (#). In this textbook, the letter "b" indicates a blank.
- Some fields are further defined with *delimiters* and subfield codes. You should note that the dollar sign ($) is the delimiter in this coding book. That $ sign is *not* universally used. Depending on your MARC provider, you will find other signs and symbols that represent a delimiter. Frequently, it is represented as a double cross mark (‡).
- *Subfield codes* come right after delimiters. They are expressed as a, b, c, d, e, q, v, x, y, and z. There are others, but they are not used very often.

DETAILED EXPLANATION OF EACH FIELD AND SUBFIELD THAT SCHOOL LIBRARIANS SHOULD KNOW

All the examples in this section are based on AACR2 (not RDA) and reflect the content of Part VII of *Understanding MARC Bibliographic*, the downloadable booklet.

010 Library of Congress Control Number (LCCN)

This is the identification number assigned to each cataloged item at the Library of Congress. It is based on the year of publication, followed by a unique identifying number. The 010 field has two blank indicators. Other things to know about the LCCN include the following:

- The LCCN appears in the lower right-hand corner of the CIP record, usually on the verso of the title page of all LC-cataloged books. This number may be used to order cataloging from a supplier.
- You can also use this number to search in MARC record databases such as Alliance Plus.
- Catalogers in college libraries use this number to search in the OCLC database for catalog records because most, if not all, academic libraries do not buy their MARC records from their book vendors.

LC Control Numbers have changed over time:

- For 2001 and after, they look like this: 200702743997. That is the year 2007 followed by the unique number. So in this case, the "0" after the 2007 is the first "number" in the unique identifier.
- For 2000 and earlier, they look like this:
  - 00-005968
  - 97-002638
  - 85-038475

020 International Standard Book Number

This is a unique identifier for the item, assigned by the publisher from an internationally agreed upon set of rules, and it should be routinely entered in the 020 with two blank indicators. It is most often displayed with dashes in it, but do not include the dashes when entering it in a MARC record. It, too, may be used for searching in cataloging databases of various sorts. For more than thirty years, the ISBN was ten digits long. In 2007 it was changed to a thirteen-digit format. Read more about the ISBN standard at the Bowker website.

040 The Cataloging Source

As cryptic as this field may seem, it does contain information librarians find useful. Who cataloged the item? ($a Original cataloging agency). Who transcribed it into the MARC format? ($c Transcribing agency). Who modified it or added it to an OPAC? ($d Modifying agency). The $d subfield would have the alphabetical code for the library using it in its own catalog.

In the example on page 2 of the printout, the original cataloging agency and the transcribing agency are both the Library of Congress: DLC. The modifying agency has been assigned an alphabetical code: gwhs. These codes are assigned by the Library of Congress. The codes from LC are not the only organization codes in existence. Various cataloging agencies around the world have created their own, most notably OCLC in the United States, which uses predominantly three-letter codes, such as RRH, which is assigned to the Rush City, Minnesota, public school library, and YWM, which is assigned to the U.S. Military Academy at West Point.

100 Main Entry, Personal Name

The type of name has to be indicated by use of an indicator in the first of the two positions reserved for indicator numbers. As the booklet indicates, there is most often a "1" here because that indicates a single surname (last name):

100 1b Clark, Mary Higgins

Someone like the rock star Cher would get a "0" here, for "forename." She is known only as Cher, her forename, or given name:

100 0b Cher

The second indicator for all types of personal main entries is blank.

Subfields used most often are listed in the MARC document in Part VII in a format that is a little hard to follow, with each subfield listed under the other. Think of it this way instead, with everything on one horizontal line:

100 1b Gregory, Ruth W. $q (Ruth Wilhelme), $d 1910-

The subfields are listed in the order in which they are used, which is not alphabetical.

245 Title Statement and Statement of Responsibility

Whether the record has a title main entry or just a title statement, the title is recorded in the 245, which has two indicators:

- *The first indicator means the title is traced.* Trace a title *only if you have a personal main entry above it.* (This situation had more meaning when we were using card catalogs. To trace a title meant you would make a card that would file under the title in the card catalog). When there is a personal main entry in the 100 field, the first indicator in the title field (the 245) is "1." If the situation is a title main entry, the first indicator is "0."
- *The second indicator is the nonfiling indicator.* Since it is never correct to file or search under the initial article of a title (*a, an,* or *the*), the computer must be told to skip those words and the first space immediately following the article. Thus, a book titled *A DNA Story* would be coded 245 12. A book titled *An Easy Guide to the DNA Story* would be coded 245 13. A book titled *The DNA Story* is coded 245 14 (1 = we trace the title; 4 = the nonfiling characters).

Subtitle

The subtitle of a book is separated from the title following a space colon (:) space and by using a subfield $b. After the end of the title comes the space slash space, followed by a subfield $c.

The example in Part VII is easier to understand looking at it this way:

245 14 The DNA story : $b a documentary history of gene cloning / $c James D. Watson, John Tooze.

Note: If there is a person with subsidiary responsibility (such as an illustrator), add that information on the end of the subfield $c, but insert ISBD punctuation (the ;), like this:

245 14 The DNA story : $b a documentary history of gene cloning / $c James D. Watson, John Tooze ; illustrated by Richard Smith.

There is *no* subfield code in front of "illustrated by Richard Smith." The $c subfield represents all contributors taken together.

246 Varying (or Variant) Form of the Title

Notice the first indicator. There is a choice between "1" and "3." When you choose "1" the following automatically occurs:

- A title note will be generated in a notes field that will indicate what the variant form of the title is.
- The varying form of the title will be traced as a title. In other words, users will be able to look up the item's variant title by using your OPAC's *title* search. The 246 ought to be indexed in the catalog system in the same way the 245 is.

When you choose "3" the following automatically occurs:

- The alternative title is indexed in the OPAC as a title.
- The actual alternative title does not appear in the record on the OPAC screen. A MARC display would reveal it, however.

Notice the second indicator. Using a blank (b), or a "3" (other title), or a "4" (cover title), or an "8" (spine title) will cover most situations in a school library.

- Let's say that the spine title of the book varies from the title on the title page. (Yes, it happens! With cover titles as well.)
- The title from the title page goes in the 245 field, but users should be able to search for the spine title as well.

- Use a 246 field with a second indicator of 8.
- This will automatically generate a "notes field" that reads Spine title: whatever the spine title is, and it also generates a searchable title (just like the 245) with the wording from the spine title. This may sound rather odd. If it's in the "notes field," why do we have to provide an added title field? The answer is that on-line catalogs, when told to do a title search, do not search in notes fields. They search in title fields, so we have to provide one for any alternative titles we want our users to be able to find the item under through a title search.

For example, on the title page it says History and Culture of the Great State of Hawaii. On the spine it says The Great State of Hawaii. Those two titles would be coded as follows:

245 10 History and culture of the great state of Hawaii
246 18 Great state of Hawaii

There is no indicator for nonfiling characters, so do not include the initial article "the" in any 246 fields and do not use a period at the end of the field.

- This will automatically generate a note that says: Spine title: Great state of Hawaii.
- This spine title is then searchable as well. The search is on the 246 field, not the notes field, unless it is a keyword search.

Coding a 246 field for "Other title" (second indicator "3") may be used to provide direct access by the first word in the subtitle, if it is so distinctive that users might search for it as a title. Another good use for the "Other title" designation with a 246 field is to provide access by alternative spellings, such as this:

245 10 St. Albans fire
246 33 Saint Albans fire

245 10 Find it @ your library
246 33 Find it at your library

245 10 10 healthy work habits
246 33 Ten healthy work habits

250 Edition Statement

Both indicators are blank. To indicate the edition, enter whatever it says on the book: Second edition. Special ed. Teacher's edition. Before RDA, the rule was to use abbreviations from Appendices B and C in AACR2. Now we use an abbreviation only if it appears in the item.

260 Publication, Distribution, Etc.

Both indicators are blank. Use subfield $b in front of the publisher name and $c in front of the date of publication, like this:

260 bb New York : $b Chelsea House, $c 1986.

264 Publication, Distribution, Etc.

This is not in the booklet and is a new MARC tag developed for RDA. Expect to see all RDA records from the Library of Congress use the 264 instead of the 260. Most commonly it will look like this:

264 b1 New York : $b Chelsea House, $c 2013.

300 Physical Description

Both indicators are blank. Use $a in front of the extent (paging), $b in front of the illustration statement, and $c in front of the dimensions (size). The following examples are in RDA form:

300 bb iv, 139 pages : $b illustrations ; $c 24 cm

300 bb xiii, 295 pages, 8 unnumbered leaves of plates : $b illustrations (some color), maps ; $c 26 cm

If there are no illustrations, then the example appears like this:

$a 300 bb iv, 139 pages ; $c 24 cm

490 Series Statement

First indicator: 0 = Series not traced, 1 = Series is traced. If a series is to be re-trievable only by keywords, it can go in the 490 field, and it will not matter what indicators are used. If the series title is to be traced as an exact title (will be retrieved in a title search) or as a title keyword, then a first indicator of "1" and an additional field (the 830) are required.

The 830 field is where we put the "uniform title" for the series name. That means the title of the series as it is printed in the book goes in the 490, but if the cataloger feels the need to manipulate that title, or even if it stays exactly the same, it goes in the 830. It is then searchable as an exact title or a title keyword. The 490 field is searchable as a keyword only. Here is an example of the kind of manipulation that might be necessary. The series title on a book is *The Railroads of America*, but perhaps there is already another series with the same title. Catalogers need to differentiate the new Railroads series from the old one, so for the new one (Macmillan), the name of the publisher, is added after the title of the series. This is discussed in the MARC booklet at the point of the 830 field.

Indicators: 1 = blank
                 2 = Nonfiling characters

Subfield $v. This is used to indicate the volume number of the book in the series. For Railroads, it would look like this, if it had a volume (which in the example it does not)—

Railroads of America (Macmillan) ; $v v. 12

—if it actually says "volume" or "v" on the book. If it does not, then it is recorded this way:

Railroads of America (Macmillan) ; $v 12

The ";" semicolon (;) is from the ISBD punctuation rules.

Note Fields. These are in chronologic order, not prescribed AACR2 order.

500 General Note

Both indicators are blank. Use this for general notes not covered in other more specific notes fields. In actuality, there are many more 500 fields than Part VII covers, such as the 511, the 518, and others. They are used in more specialized coding. The 500 fields in Part VII are the most common and those most used for cataloging school library items. If there is no bibliography, but there is an index, it goes in the 500 like this: Includes index. Do not put bibliography notes here. They go in the 504 field.

504 Bibliography Note

Both indicators are blank. Use this for whatever bibliographical situation you may have. Here are some examples:

Includes bibliography (p. 345-346) and index.
Includes bibliographies and index. (There are bibliographies located throughout the text.)
Includes bibliography. (There's only one, and there is no index.)

505 Contents Note

Most often the first indicator will be 0 (meaning "complete contents") and the second indicator will be blank, "b." For example:

505 0b Pride and prejudice -- Emma -- Northanger Abbey

An example of a contents note for a collection of plays by varying authors would look like this:

505 0b The glass menagerie / Tennessee Williams -- Death of a salesman / Arthur Miller -- Long day's journey into night / Eugene O'Neill.

Notice how the punctuation (the space slash space) mimics the punctuation found in the 245 field, where the title statement is separated from the author statement by the space slash space.

This is another example, illustrating chapters of a book (all written by the author of the book, not by individual contributors):

505 0b Ch. 1. Death of a singer -- Ch. 2. What, exactly, is the problem -- Ch. 3. History of the disease -- Ch. 4. Related diseases -- Ch. 5. Causes and special considerations -- Ch. 6. Treatment -- Ch. 7. Recognizing the disease and finding help.

520 bb Summary Note

Both indicators are blank.

CURRICULUM-ENHANCED MARC

The 521, the 526, and the 586 are collectively part of CE-MARC, or "curriculum-enhanced" MARC. These are fields that assist teachers and students alike in selecting materials according to audience, reading levels, and reading motivational program. These three fields are not in the Part VII document. See the article by Adamich (2006) for more information.

521 Target Audience Note

Put grade levels and other audience identifiers here. The first indicator defines various aspects of the target audience and generates a display constant, such as Reading Grade Level or Special audience characteristics . The second indicator for each is blank. The first indicators and their display constants are:

- Reading Grade Level = 0b. For example:

  0b 3.1 generates this display: Reading grade level: 3.1

- Interest Age Level = 1b. For example:

  1b 5-7 generates this display: Interest age level: 5-7

- Interest Grade Level = 2b. For example:

2b 5-8 generates this diplay: Interest grade level: 5-8

- Special audience characteristics = 3b. For example:

3b Vision impaired generates this display: Special audience characteristics. Vision impaired.

- Motivation/interest level = 4b. For example:

4b Highly motived generates this display: Motivation/interest level. Highly motivated.

Another indicator in the 521 field is "8," which means no display constant is generated. Often motion picture ratings are entered in this field.

- MPAA ratings = 521 8b MPAA rating: PG-13.
- Lexile number = 521 8b 800 $b Lexile.

526 Study Program Information Note

The indicators are 0b, which generate the print constant "Reading program." This is where the Accelerated Reader information is coded with subfield codes:

- $a = The name of the program, in this case, Accelerated Reader
- $b = Interest level, or Grades as in the example in the article
- $c = Reading level
- $d = Points possible
- $z = Test number

526 0b $a Accelerated Reader $b grades 3-5 $c 4.4 $d 100 pts. $z No. 47191

586 Awards Note

Both indicators are blank:

586 bb Newbery Award, 2009
586 bb Academy Award for Best Picture, 2010
586 bb National Book Award, 1999

THE 600s: MARC CODING OF SUBJECT HEADINGS

The coding for several types of subject headings is shown in the printed-out booklet. Look at the long list under the second indicator at the 600 and 650 fields. The second indicator identifies the source of the subject heading. LC adult subject headings are "0." LC subject headings for children have a "1" in the second indicator location. Notice what it says for "7": Source specified in subfield 2. That means you can use "7" for Sears and in subfield 2, you would specify: Sears

600 Personal Name Subject Heading

These are such things as:

```
600 10 Woods, Tiger
600 10 Grant, Ulysses S. $q (Ulysses Simpson), $d 1822-1885
```

The form of heading for people as subjects is exactly the same as it is for them as main entries. The first indicator tells us what kind of name it is: 0 = Forename, 1 = Surname (the most common type), and 3 = Family name. The second indicator is blank. The subfields, b, c, q, and d are the same ones used for personal main entries (100s). In addition, the 600 can use subfields $v $x (general subdivision), $y (chronological subdivision), or $z (geographic subdivision). See the complete list in Part VII of the MARC booklet.

650 b0 Topical Subject Heading

These are such things as animals, diseases, or anything that is not geographic or personal.

• The first indicator is always blank.
• The second indicator indicates what authority file it is from: 0 = Library of Congress, 1 = AC, 7 = Sears.
• Note the list of subfields: $v, $x, $y $z.
• 650 b1 is the code and indicator for a children's subject heading.

651 b0 Geographic Subject Heading

These are such things as Duluth (Minn.) or United States or France. Note the list of subfields.

Subdivisions of Subject Headings

Many subject headings have Subdivisions attached to them. Subdivisions are coded with four different subfield codes indicating the subdivision type.

Subfield $v means a form subdivision (What is the "form" of the work?) such as Bibliography, Dictionaries, Chronology, Biography, Encyclopedias, Biography, Juvenile literature, Fiction, etc. Following are examples:

Animal behavior $v Bibliography

"Bibliography" is a "form" subdivision. A bibliography is a specific form or type of literature.

World War, 1939-1945 **$v** Encyclopedias

"Encyclopedias" is a specific form of literature.
The software for your online catalog will translate the $v to "dash dash" and will display it on the computer screen as:

Animal behavior -- Bibliography

World War, 1939-1945 -- Encyclopedias

Subfield **$x** means a general subdivision such as these:

-- Administration, as in Libraries -- Administration
-- Analysis, as in Plants -- Analysis
-- Remodeling, as in Houses -- Remodeling

Following are examples of coding for these:

650 b0 Libraries $x Administration
650 b0 Plants $x Analysis
650 b0 Houses $x Remodeling

They will display as:

Libraries -- Administration
Plants -- Analysis
Houses -- Remodeling

The next subfield is $y. This designates a chronological subfield or subdivision. Here is an example:

651 b0 United States $x History $y Civil War, 1861-1865

• Subfield $x = general subdivision.
• Subfield $y designates a chronological subdivision: (Civil War, 1861-1865).

This displays as:

United States -- History -- Civil War, 1861-1865

You could have this also:

651 b0 United States $x History $y Civil War, 1861-1865 **$v** Fiction (for a novel that takes place during the Civil War).

The next subfield is $z. This designates a geographical subfield or subdivision. Here is an example:

650 b0 Cultivated plants $z Arizona

It displays as:

Cultivated plants -- Arizona

700 Added Authors

This field is for authors other than the main entry. Joint authors, any editors and illustrators, and any other names to be traced go here. These are *not* subject headings. The 700s act like the 100s in their use of indicators. The first indicator is:

0 = Forename, like Cher, or
1 = Surname, like Smith or Jones.

Subfields d ($d) and q ($q) may be added as needed:

700 1b Wells, H. G. $q (Herbert George), $d 1866-1946

You may want to include a subfield e ($e) also, which is used to designate an illustrator. This is not mandatory according to AACR2, but it is useful information to include in a catalog for a school library:

700 1b Tudor, Tasha, $e illustrator

RDA (not MARC) requires the use of the subfield "e" because of its emphasis on relationships.

710 Corporate Added Entries

This is for companies, organizations, societies, and so forth. For example, the book *Making Minnesota Territory, 1849–1858* is closely tied to the Minnesota Historical Society. The Society should be a corporate added entry:

710 2b Minnesota Historical Society

740 Added Titles

This is different from the 246, a variant title, which is for varying forms of the main title. If a book has several short stories or plays in it, it is possible to make these searchable as titles by putting them in 740 fields. They should go in the 505 (Contents) field as well. Most likely they would be searchable there in a keyword search, but suppose the catalog user searched for one of those titles through a title search? If the individual titles are each in their own 740 field, this could help the user considerably.

The first indicator is the nonfiling indicator. The second indicator is 2. The MARC booklet calls it an analytical entry. An analytic provides access to *part* of a total work. In this case, it is access to a play or short story within a larger collection, like this:

740 42 The celebrated jumping frog of Calaveras County

or

740 42 The glass menagerie

Another way of doing this is to have an author/title added entry. The MARC coding booklet does not mention this, but this is what it would look like:

700 12 Williams, Tennessee, $d 1911-1983. $t Glass menagerie

FIXED FIELDS MARC CODES

All the MARC fields covered so far have been variable fields, meaning the number of characters in each is variable. Titles have variable numbers of letters in them, as do authors and the other text elements of the records. Fixed fields are not visible on the OPAC display screen. Each character in the field is a code for some other piece of information, and the number of characters stays the same. There are two main fixed fields.

Leader

First is the Leader (it is right at the front of the MARC record, or in the 001 field) in a MARC record. It contains twenty-four characters that provide computers with information needed for processing the record. A typical Leader could look like this: 01361cam_a2200301_a_450. In this case, some characters are blank. Each of the individual pieces of this string of code add up to twenty-four total characters. Each character tells the computer something (Chan 2007).

008 Field

Second is the 008 field. It has forty positions in it and differs across formats. In other words, the 008 for a book is a bit different from the 008 for a DVD. For a book, positions 18 through 21 are devoted to illustrative information, indicating if it is illustrated and providing codes for individual types of illustrations, such as maps and portraits. Positions 7 through 14 contain the copyright and publication dates. For visual materials, positions 18 through 20 contain the running time of the item, such as 100 (minutes).

Special Tidbit: The End of MARC?

MARC has been around since the 1960s. Change in the cataloging world comes at a snail's pace, but after nearly half a century, a new standard is being considered. It is currently called BibFrame, for "bibliographic framework." It will, of course, be more than a replacement for the current MARC format. The intent is for it to work with interrelationships among the myriad publications we see today, and much of its vocabulary echoes RDA and FRBR terminology.

Information in the 008 can be effectively used for retrieving and sorting bibliographic records. For example, there is a code for "language" in the 008. If you want to limit your search to items in the French language, this is the code the computer would use to retrieve French language materials exclusively. See *Ask Ms. MARC's Tag of the Month* website for more information on the 008 field.

SUMMARY

This concludes MARC coding for monographs (books). School librarians need to know this material because this knowledge will allow fine-tuning of MARC records. It is important to understand how your chosen OPAC software indexes each field in the record in addition to understanding MARC coding. With that combination, it is possible for the media specialist to scrutinize MARC records with a critical eye and create the best OPAC for optimum resource discovery. The next chapter shows you how to put together everything covered so far for cataloging books.

TEST YOUR KNOWLEDGE

Use Part VII of the MARC booklet with the material in this chapter to answer the following questions.

1. MARC stands for Main entry Record, Computer-Readable Format.

   A. True
   B. False

2. Because there are hundreds of tags across several catalog record formats, school librarians generally are not expected to memorize and speak knowledgeably about them.

   A. True
   B. False

3. In the 245 field, the second indicator tells the computer to skip initial articles when sorting alphabetically. Thus, 245 03 means to skip the three letters "The" and the blank space before the first sortable word. For example:

   245 03 The emperor's new clothes.

   A. True
   B. False

4. The 245 field will look like this:

   245 14 The big yellow dog

   if this is representing a title main entry.

   A. True
   B. False

5. Subfield codes have delimiters in front of them. For example, $b ($ = delimiter, b = subfield code). Delimiters can be highly variable. Delimiters in MnPALS may not look the same as delimiters in Follett's Destiny system.

   A. True
   B. False

6. Subfield "q" in the 100 field is for the full form of the name of the individual as established in the Name Authority File at the Library of Congress.

   A. True
   B. False

7. If you see this in the 040:

   DLC $c DLC $d MNS

   you have a record straight from the Library of Congress with no modifications.

   A. True
   B. False

8. A 246 field with indicators 1 and 4 will account for *spine* title/title page variations and will print both a note and a variant title added entry.

   A. True
   B. False

9. For a series to be searchable as an exact title, it must appear in the 490 field.

   A. True
   B. False

10. "Includes index" goes in the 500 field.

    A. True
    B. False

11. Reading motivation program information goes in the 526 and includes a number of subfields.

    A. True
    B. False

12. A book about the singer Michael Jackson should have a subject heading coded this way:

    100 10 Jackson, Michael, $d 1958-2009

    A. True
    B. False

13. The following geographic subject heading is coded correctly for its indicators and subfield.

    651 b0 Minnesota $v Dictionaries

    A. True
    B. False

14. The following subject heading is coded correctly:

    651 b0 France $x History $y 1789-1799, Revolution $x Fiction.

    A. True
    B. False

15. Stanford University, as an added entry, would be tagged:

    A. 700
    B. 710
    C. 711
    D. 740

16. To trace the title of the short story "The Lottery," by Shirley Jackson (in a collection), you could do the following with the displayed coding:

    700 12 Jackson, Shirley. $t The lottery.

    A. True
    B. False

17. If this has a personal main entry, it is coded correctly:

    245 14 The DNA story : $b a documentary history of gene cloning / $c James D. Watson, John Tooze ; illustrated by Richard Smith.

    A. True
    B. False

18. Find the correct form of entry for Nelson Mandela. Show the tag and all coding for him as a main entry.

19. Find the correct form of entry for the children's author Avi and show the tag and all coding for him as a main entry.

20. Find the correct form of entry for Maurice Sendak and show the tag and all coding for him as an illustrator added entry.

21. Find the correct form of entry for Laura Ingalls Wilder as a subject heading, add the subdivisions -- Homes -- Missouri, and show the tag and coding for her as a subject heading.

22. Find the correct form of entry for former president Franklin D. Roosevelt, add the subdivision -- Press relations, and show the tag and coding for him as a subject heading.

23. Show the tag and codes for this subject heading:

    Presidents -- United States -- Portraits.

24. Show the tag and codes for this subject heading:

    France -- History -- 1789-1799, Revolution

25. Show the tag and codes for this subject heading:

    German language -- Dictionaries.

RESOURCES

Adamich, T. (2006). CE–MARC: The educator's library "receipt." *Knowledge Quest, 35*(1), 64–68.

Chan, L. M. (2007). *Cataloging and classification: An introduction.* Lanham, MD: Scarecrow Press.

Follett Software Company. (n.d.). *Tag of the month.* Retrieved from: http://www.follettsoftware.com/tagofthemonth.cfm.

MARC code lists for organizations. (n.d.). Retrieved from: http://www.loc.gov/marc/organizations/orgshome.html.

MARC standards. (n.d.). Retrieved from: http://www.loc.gov/marc/.

MARC 21 format standards for bibliographic data. (n.d.). Retrieved from: http://www.loc.gov/marc/bibliographic/ecbdhome.html.

MARC 21 reference materials. Part VII: A summary of commonly used MARC 21 fields. (n.d.). Retrieved from: http://www.loc.gov/marc/umb/um07to10.html.

8

Cataloging Books

AREAS OF THE CATALOG RECORD

A full catalog record obviously consists of more than name entries, classification numbers, and subject headings. The item being cataloged must be described in terms of its title, author, pagination, etc. AACR2 created a framework for the description consisting of eight areas. RDA does not specifically name these areas, but they are nevertheless part of the structure of the new RDA records. AACR2 areas and their location within the description for a book are shown in table 8.1. Use each area only if you have information to go into it. If there is no information relevant to an area, skip it.

Table 8.1.   AACR2 Areas and Locations in Description for Book

Area	Location (Where to Find the Information)
Area 1: Title and Statement of Responsibility	Title page, also known as the Chief Source of Information in a monograph (book)
Area 2: Edition	Title page and other preliminaries
Area 3: Type of Material. We are not using this area for books. We will use it for nonprint items (DVDs and CDs).	
Area 4: Publication, distribution, etc.	Title page and other preliminaries
Area 5: Physical description	Whole publication
Area 6: Series statement	Whole publication
Area 7: Notes (may consist of several different kinds of notes, each one starting on its own line)	Any source
Area 8: Standard numbers, such as the ISBN	Any source

AACR2 outlines three levels of description the cataloger may choose from, each being increasingly more detailed. Deciding to use Level 1 would mean having less information in each area than required by Level 2. You might think that a school librarian could get by with using Level 1, but that is not advisable. MARC records from the Library of Congress are mostly Level 2, so the bulk of the bibliographic records in the catalog will have that "look" to them. You would not want any original cataloging you do to appear less than up to standard in comparison with the rest of the catalog. Following the guidelines in this chapter will ensure you create standard Level 2 records.

Prescribed Punctuation

There is prescribed punctuation to be used within and between each defined area. Although RDA does not include International Standard Bibliographic Description (ISBD) per se, it does lay out the guidelines in its Appendix D, and the general understanding is that ISBD will continue to be used. ISBD has the following elements:

/ (slash)
: (colon)
; (semi-colon)

Each of these has a *space* before and after it.

This punctuation was developed so that materials in all languages could be described in a way that was understood internationally. If something appears in the Title and Statement of Responsibility Area, it is easily identified as such because it resides in that defined area of the catalog record with predetermined punctuation. This standardization permits records produced in each participating country to be integrated in common files and contributes to conversion of records into machine readable form with minimal editing (Working Group, 1974).

The punctuation seems odd and incomprehensible at first, but with a little practice it will become second nature. Keep in mind that this punctuation protocol has been around since 1971, and it is possible you will have records in your catalog that predate that year, although by now the materials represented by those records should have been weeded. You will not see ISBD punctuation in those records. They are not wrong; they are just old.

Table 8.2 is a display of the fields in a typical bibliographic record with ISBD punctuation and arrangement of descriptive information. This is the MARC coding and data that lie behind the screen display of an OPAC. This is a record for a book published during the AACR2 era, *The Blues of Flats Brown*, by Walter Dean Myers. RDA additions and modifications are included.

Table 8.2. AACR2 Record for *The Blues of Flats Brown,* by Walter Dean Myers, with RDA Modifications

Field Label	MARC Field Tag and Indicators	Catalog Record Information with MARC coding and ISBD Punctuation
ISBN International Standard Book Number	020 bb	9780823416790 : $c $16.95
MARC Code for Organizations/ Cataloging Source Codes	040 bb	DLC $c DLC $d mndueh
Author	100 1b	Myers, Walter Dean, $d 1937- $e author
Title	245 14	The blues of Flats Brown / $c by Walter Dean Myers ; illustrated by Nina Laden.
Edition	250 bb	1st ed.
Edition	250 bb	RDA First edition.
Publisher	260 bb	New York : $b Holiday House, $c 2000.
Physical Description	300 bb	1 v. (unpaged) : $b col. Ill. ; $c 25 cm.
Physical Description RDA Changes	300 bb	RDA 1 volume (unpaged) : $b color illustrations ; $c 25 cm
Content Type (Fundamental form of the communication)	336 bb	RDA text
Media Type (General type of intermediation, or, device required to view it)	337 bb	RDA unmediated
Carrier Type (What it is on)	338 bb	RDA volume
Summary Note	520 bb	To escape an abusive master, a junkyard dog named Flats runs away and makes a name for himself from Mississippi to New York City playing blues on his guitar.
Audience	521 2b	Grades K-1.
Study Program	526 0b	Accelerated Reader $b grades K-3 $c 3.8 $d .5 pts. $z No. 40211.
Adult Library of Congress subject heading	650 b0	Dogs -- Juvenile fiction. The MARC subfield code for Juvenile fiction is: $v Fiction. $v means *form of literature.*

(*continued*)

Table 8.2. *(continued)*

Field Label	MARC Field Tag and Indicators	Catalog Record Information with MARC coding and ISBD Punctuation
		This is important! You will see form subdivisions a lot. "Juvenile fiction" is one form of literature. Remember that "-- Juvenile fiction" is a Library of Congress subject adult subject heading. The coding looks like this: Dogs $v Juvenile fiction. The $v will generate the "dash dash" line on your interface display.
CYACP Library of Congress subject heading	650 b1	Dogs -- Fiction. Code like this: Dogs $v Fiction.
CYACP Library of Congress subject heading	650 b1	Blues (Music) -- Fiction. Code like this: Blues (Music) $v Fiction.
Author	700 1b	Laden, Nina, $e illustrator.

Following are some points to note:

1. The Main Entry (the 100 Field)

Walter Dean Myers is the main entry. He wrote the book.

RDA CHANGE: Author is called the creator in RDA, but **$e** "author" is the relationship designator. RDA's appendices I, J, and K contain the relationship designators and the types of relationships they indicate. Nonprint materials exhibit a large number of relationship designators. Those are covered in chapter 9.

2. Capitalization

The title (the 245 field), *The Blues of Flats Brown*, has a combination of upper- and lowercase letters. In catalog records capitalization is not done in a traditional way. The first word of the title is capitalized, proper nouns are capitalized, and everything else is lowercased. In this title "The" is capitalized (first word of the title), blues is not capitalized because it is not a proper noun, and Flats Brown is capitalized because it is a proper noun or the name of someone (in this case, a dog, personified).

Students often ask why this system of capitalization is used. The definitive historical answer to this question appears to be lost in the mists of time. *Rules for a Printed Dictionary Catalogue*, by Charles Ammi Cutter, states the following:

Capitals are to be avoided, because in the short sentences of a catalog they confuse rather than help the eye. For this reason it is better not to capitalize names in natural history whether English or Latin. It is common now not to use capitals for German nouns. The Boston Public Library formerly went to an extreme in its avoidance of capitals, not using them for such proper names as episcopal, and protestant, royal society, etc. (Department of the Interior, Bureau of Education, 1876)

The title is taken from what AACR2 calls the Chief Source of Information (RDA: Preferred Source of Information), which is almost always the title page of the book.

Notice that the second indicator in this particular 245 field (title) is a "4." That stands for four nonfiling characters: "The" and the blank space before "blues."

3. Statement of Responsibility

First, separate the statement of responsibility from the title with a "space slash space." This is standard ISBD punctuation. Next, from the title page, transcribe "by Walter Dean Myers illustrated by Nina Laden." Note the punctuation and the capitalization. Following the "space slash space," transcribe "by Walter Dean Myers." Use "by" (lowercase) because it is on the title page. If it does not say "by" on the title page, do not use it. If this title page said "The Blues of Flats Brown Walter Dean Myers," then "by" would not be used. It would look like this: The blues of Flats Brown / Walter Dean Myers.

Subsidiary Responsibility

Next there is a "space semicolon space" preceding the statement of subsidiary responsibility, or the illustrator. It says on the title page "illustrated by Nina Laden," so that is how it is transcribed. If it said "pictures by Nina Laden" then it would be transcribed as by Walter Dean Myers ; pictures by Nina Laden.

4. Edition Statement (the 250 Field)

Transcribe this exactly from anywhere in the book, not just from the title page. Many times it will be on the back (the verso) of the title page. Abbreviate the word Edition to "ed." Also abbreviate First edition to 1st ed., Second edition to 2nd ed., and Third edition to 3rd ed. Revised is recorded as "Rev." Transcribe any other words exactly as you find them, such as "Student" in Student edition. This would be transcribed as Student ed.

RDA CHANGE: Transcribe *everything* exactly as you find it in the item. If it says 1st edition, use it that way. If it says First edition, then that is what is used. End the edition statement with a period. RDA is based very much on a "take what you see" approach, in contrast to AACR, which relied more on abbreviations.

5. Publication, Distribution, Etc. Area (the 260 Field)

The place of publication in this case is New York. This means New York City. Transcribe the place of publication (city and state) exactly as you find it in the item. So if it says Minneapolis, MN, that is what you use. If the name of the state is spelled out, use that. If the state is not mentioned anywhere and you feel the place cannot stand alone (it is not famous enough to be readily recognized or needs clarification), add the name of the state in square brackets, as in Rochester, [Minn.]. It is fine to abbreviate the name of the state in these cases. AACR2 recommends abbreviations in its Appendix B. In RDA abbreviations are also in Appendix B. A new tag 264 has been developed for this area of a bibliographic record, but its use is optional. The Library of Congress is opting to use it, so expect to see it in newer records.

If the place of publication is not known, previously it was indicated as S.l., Latin for *sine loco*. In RDA, S.l. is no longer used. Use the following instead: [Place of publication not identified].

If there is more than one place of publication on the title page:

- Use the first place listed or the one set in the largest type. If that one is a foreign place (such as London or Paris) and there is also an American place of publication, then you use both, putting the foreign one first and separating them with a "space semicolon space," like this: London ; New York.
- If there are two places of publication and they are in the opposite order, American first, foreign second, omit the foreign one.
- Separate the place of publication from the publisher by a "space : space". Directly after the colon, insert the subfield b ($b): New York : $b Holiday House.

RDA CHANGE: Record the place of publication names in the order indicated by the sequence on the source of information. Only the first place on the source is required in the catalog record, no matter where the cataloging agency is located.

Name of Publisher (Subfield "b" in the 260 Field)

After the place of publication is the name of the publisher. Record the name of the publisher in the shortest form possible. It must be understandable and identifiable internationally, so the shortest form must be chosen carefully. It should be separated from the place of publication by "space colon space."

Dates (Subfield "c" in the 260 Field)

- Enter a "comma" and the date of publication. Now this gets tricky, because as you probably know, there are often dates all over the place in books.
- The rule of thumb is to choose the date that matches the edition statement. If there is no edition statement, choose the latest date.

- *Copyright date vs. publication date:* Sometimes you will find a copyright date in addition to a publication date in the item being cataloged. Sometimes there is a considerable difference between the two. The copyright date is the first date the content is fixed in a tangible form and the owner is given exclusive rights to offer copies for sale, while the publication date is when it was made available to the public. The book may be a year 2001 paperback reprint of a classic work written in 1980. If that is the case, record the date as 2001 and in the notes area enter *Reprint of the original 1980 edition,* or some other wording that conveys the meaning, such as *Reprint. Originally published: Boston, Mass. : Little Brown, 1985.* This should be done so the user is not misled regarding the currency of the content of the item. Following is an example:

100 10 Nichols, David A. $q (David Allen), $d 1939-
    245 10 Lincoln and the Indians : $b Civil War policy and politics / $c David A. Nichols.
    260 bb Saint Paul : $b Minnesota Historical Society Press, $c 2012.
    ****
    500 bb Originally published: Columbia, MO : University of Missouri Press, 1978.

6. Physical Description Area (the 300 Field)

Here is where the paging, the illustration statement, and the size (in centimeters) of a book go. This was once called the "collation," and occasionally you will still run across that terminology. *The Blues of Flats Brown* is a picture book with unnumbered pages. Consequently the cataloger records this as "1 v. (unpaged)," meaning this book is one volume, with pages that have no numbers printed on them. It does not mean that there are no pages in the book. An alternative is to count the pages and enclose that number in brackets: [25] p.

Following the paging comes the illustration statement. It is separated from the paging by a "space colon space":

1 v. (unpaged) : $b col. ill.

In this case this book has multicolored illustrations, indicated by "col. ill." Other designations you may use in the illustration area are:

1. ill. (for any variety of illustrations)
2. ill., maps, ports. (all in a line like this; used when you have maps and portraits as *some* of the illustrations)
3. ill., photos (AACR2 does not recommend the use of "photos," but we will ignore that because it is significant information, particularly in children's non-fiction. So use "photos" when applicable.)

Next comes the size, measured in centimeters, separated from the illustration statement by "space semicolon space" like this:

1 v. (unpaged) : $b col. ill. ; $c 29 cm.

To measure centimeters, use a regular foot-long ruler with a centimeter edge on it. Set the bottom of the book spine on a table top and line up the centimeter edge of the ruler against the spine, holding both vertically. Round up, so if it is 23 1/2 cm., record that as 24 cm. If the width is less than half the height, or if the width is greater than the height, give both dimensions with the height first and the width second (20 × 25 cm.) For children's picture books, this is not unusual.

RDA CHANGE: Do not use abbreviations in the Physical Description Area. Instead of "1 v.", use "1 volume." Instead of "ill.," use "illustrations." Do not put a period after "cm". The RDA developers have designated "cm" as a metric symbol rather than an abbreviation and for that reason the period is no longer used. However, if the size is followed by a 490 field (series), then include the period.

7. Fields 336, 337, and 338 (New with RDA)

These represent Content Type (336), Media Type (337), and Carrier Type (338). The terms used in these fields are from a controlled vocabulary established in RDA. In other words, the cataloger should not construct the terms for these fields. Use the terms provided in RDA.

- Field 336 Content type is defined as "the fundamental form of communication in which the content is expressed and the human sense through which it is intended to be perceived." Examples are performed music, still image, text.
- Field 337 Media type is defined as "the general type of intermediation device required to view, play, run, etc., the content of a resource." Examples are audio, computer, microform, unmediated.
- Field 338 Carrier Type is defined as "the format of the storage medium and housing of a carrier in combination with the type of intermediation device required." Examples are audio disc, computer disc, volume, videodisc.

8. The Notes Area (a Variety of 500 Fields)

The Order of the Notes

The order of notes fields has become problematic as OPAC software has evolved and as MARC has increasingly provided for additional fields deemed necessary by librarians and users. AACR2 has prescribed an order for notes. Unfortunately, MARC tags are not chronologically in the same order as the prescribed order. Even if the cataloger enters the notes in the AACR2 prescribed order, the OPAC software may very well rearrange them into chronological order. Since this is the reality we are dealing with, *notes are shown throughout this book in MARC field order instead of AACR2 prescribed order.*

MARC 520 Field

Summary note. Bibliographic records for children's fiction receive summary notes. For this work of fiction, it is the only note. Some children's nonfiction works also have summary notes provided by the publisher, not the LC cataloger.

MARC 521 Field

Target audience note. This is not used often in bibliographic description for books. The Library of Congress does not, as a rule, include this note; however, school librarians often need to identify age, grade, and curriculum appropriate materials. For this need a few education-specific elements have been identified by catalogers outside of the Library of Congress. These are referred to as CE-MARC, or, curriculum-enhanced MARC. Some of these elements are actually used regularly in LC cataloging, but for school librarians they can contain information that relates specifically to the school setting. For example, the audience note, the 521, is often used in description for videos (DVDs) to relate movie ratings, but in the illustration of *The Blues of Flats Brown*, it has been applied to the book.

The 521 has these defined meanings identified by its first indicator. The indicator generates a print constant (except for indicator 8), or the wording in the definition phrases below:

b = Audience (simple, generic audience indicator)
0 = Reading grade level
1 = Interest age level
2 = Interest grade level
3 = Special audience characteristics
8 = No display constant

The second indicator is blank (b). For example:

521 0b Reading grade level: 3.1

The "0" should generate the print constant of "Reading grade level."

MARC 526 Field

Study Program Information Note. This note identifies the reading motivation program that contains this book. Using various subfields, different facets of the item and the test can be identified (Adamich, 2006; see Follett, n.d.-b).

See chapter 7 for more details about the 521 and 526 fields.

9. The Subject Headings (600, 650, 651 Tags)

Notice that in this case there are two subject headings, each in its own field of the catalog record and each one labeled Subject. The subject headings include subdivisions separated from the main heading by "dash dash" (--).

Dogs -- Fiction is the first subject heading.
Blues (Music) -- Fiction is the second subject heading.

Those two subject headings are from the *Children's Subject Headings* and the CYAC Program. The second indicator "1" codes it as such. They include the -- Fiction designation with them to alert the child to the fact that this is a story book that includes dogs as the primary focus.

The other subject heading is from the main Library of Congress adult cataloging division. The subdivision -- Juvenile fiction is an alert to the adult user of the catalog that this is a children's book. Its second indicator is 0.

It is entirely possible your school library will be displaying *Sears* subject headings. You would fill out your profile with your cataloging provider, indicating in that profile that you want Sears subject headings. Those would include the "-- Fiction" designation on the fiction books also, just as they are in the CYACP records.

10. Added Entries (the 700 Field)

These include other people who had something to do with the creation of the book. Choice of access rules are applied in the decisions regarding these tracings. You would want to include the illustrator in nearly every case, as you see here:

Laden, Nina, illustrator

Table 8.3 is another example of a bibliographic record with RDA modifications, for *Be Seated, a Book About Chairs*, by James Cross Giblin. Following are some points to note:

1. **Main Entry (the 100 field).** Again, this is a personal main entry. Notice that there are no dates with James Giblin's name. When the LC catalogers established the form for his name, either they did not deem it necessary to have his year of birth or the author did not supply his year of birth to them.
2. **Title (the 245 field).** The title for this one has an element *The Blues of Flats Brown* did not: a subtitle. Notice how the subtitle is separated from the title by "space colon space," no matter what the punctuation is on the title page itself. It is transcribed like this : Be seated: $b a book about chairs.
3. **Statement of Responsibility.** The statement of responsibility has no "by" in it because "by" does not appear on the title page, so it is transcribed as "space slash space": James Cross Giblin. Notice how his middle name (Cross) in

Table 8.3.

Field Label	MARC Field Tag and Indicators	Catalog Record Information with MARC coding and ISBD Punctuation
ISBN International Standard Book Number	020 bb	9780060215378
Location	050 00	NK2715 $b .G46 1993
Author	100 1b	Giblin, James, $e author.
Title	245 10	Be seated : $b a book about chairs / $c James Cross Giblin.
Edition	250 bb	1st ed.
Edition	250 bb	RDA First edition
Publisher	260 bb	New York : $b HarperCollins, $c c1993.
Publisher	260 bb	RDA New York : $b HarperCollins, $c ©1993.
Physical Description	300 bb	ix, 136 p., [8] leaves of plates : $b ill. ; $c 24 cm.
Physical Description	300 bb	RDA lx, 136 pages, 8 unnumbered leaves of plates : $b illustrations ; $c 24 cm.
Series	490 1b	Domestic art and artifacts ; $v 5
Content Type (Fundamental form of the communication)	336 bb	RDA text
Media Type (General type of intermediation, or, device required to view it)	337 bb	RDA unmediated
Carrier Type (What it is on)	338 bb	RDA volume
Bibliographical References Note	504 bb	Includes bibliographical references (p. 123-130) and index.
Summary Note	520 bb	Chronicles the history, technological development, and social significance of chairs in Europe, Africa, Asia, and the United States, from prehistory to the present.
Audience	521 2b	Grades 7-12.
Study Program	526 0b	Accelerated Reader $b grades 7-12 $c 7.3 $d 4 pts. $z No. 11102.
Adult Library of Congress subject heading	650 b0	Chairs $v Juvenile literature. (Chairs -- Juvenile literature)
CYACP Library of Congress subject heading	650 b1	Chairs.
Series Title Stated as Uniform Title	830 b0	Domestic art and artifacts in the 20th century ; $v 5

included in this transcription of the statement of responsibility. Notice also how that middle name is not part of his "form of entry" in the main entry line. Whatever is on the title page is what gets transcribed into the statement of responsibility. In this case, what Mr. Giblin chose to have on the title page is slightly different from what the Library of Congress decided would be his official entry in the catalog.

- ◦ For the main entry, choose what the Name Authority File indicates is his official form of entry.
- ◦ For transcription of the statement of responsibility into the body of the record, copy exactly what is on the title page.

There are no subsidiary statements of responsibility (e.g., illustrator) as there was in *The Blues of Flats Brown*.

4. Edition Statement (the 250 field)

Transcribe the edition as found on the item, but use abbreviations for some words and numerals, as found in Appendices A and B of AACR2.

RDA CHANGE: First edition. Transcribe the edition statement exactly as it is found on the item. Use abbreviations only if they are on the item.

5. Place of Publication, Distribution, Etc. Area (the 260 field)

The place of publication is stated as: New York, NY. That is how it was printed in the chief source of information. For the date here, the copyright date is used, and RDA requires it to be designated by the copyright symbol rather than a lowercase "c."

6. The Physical Description Area (the 300 field)

Pre-paging is indicated by lowercase roman numerals, in this case vi, or "6." *Pre-paging* refers to those pages that come before the main paging of the book and contain various types of introductory material.

To record the pre-paging, find the last numbered pre-page and write it down. Then put a comma right after it and turn to the back of the book to find the last numbered page. Record that after the pre-paging, like this: vi, 136 p.

Next take note of the designation [6] p. of plates. This is a frequent occurrence in catalog records. Many books have plates or pictures in them, often on shiny paper. Their numbering may or may not be within the main numbering sequence of the rest of the book. Often the pages of plates do not have page numbers printed on them. Sometimes plates are printed on both sides of a page, sometimes on one side only. RDA has also revised the *definitions* of *pages* and *leaves*, but there is some discussion taking place currently about the advisability of these changes. Here is what each situation means:

1. [6] p. of plates. This means there are 6 pages of plates, printed on both sides, but page numbers are not printed on the page. That is why the designation is in the brackets. A "page" means something that is printed on both sides.
2. [6] leaves of plates. This means there are 6 leaves, but leaf numbers are not printed on the leaf. A "leaf" means something that is printed on one side only.
3. 6 p. of plates. This means the pages actually have page numbers printed on them. These page numbers can be part of the total sequence of page numbers for the whole book, but they are still recorded separately in the physical description area.
4. 6 leaves of plates. This means the leaves actually have page numbers printed on them. These leaf numbers can be part of the total sequence of page numbers for the whole book, but they are still recorded separately in the physical description area.

Tables 8.4 and 8.5 are two examples.

Even though the plates have been accounted for in the pagination area, indicate that the book is illustrated by using the ill. abbreviation, preceded by "space colon space." Note RDA changes

Table 8.4.

Author	Williams, Tony D.
Title	The penguins : Spheniscidae / Tony D. Williams ; with contributions by Rory P. Wilson, P. Dee Boersma, and D.L. Stokes ; colour plates by J.N. Davies ; drawings by John Busby.
Publisher	Oxford ; New York : Oxford University Press, 1995.
Physical Details	**xiii, 295 p., [8] leaves of plates** : ill. (some col.), maps ; 26 cm. ** **RDA CHANGE:** xiii, 295 pages, 8 unnumbered leaves of plates : illustrations (some color), maps ; 26 cm (if there is a 490 field following, then use a period after cm.)

Table 8.5.

Author	Allen, Arthur, 1959-
Title	Vaccine : the controversial story of medicine's greatest lifesaver / Arthur Allen.
Edition	1st ed.
Publisher	New York : W.W. Norton, c2007.
Physical Details	**523 p., [16] p. of plates** : ill. ; 25 cm. ************************************ **RDA CHANGE:** 523 pages, 16 unnumbered pages of plates : illustrations ; 25 cm (if there is a 490 field following, then use a period after cm.)

7. Series (the 490 field)

Here we have a situation we did not see with *The Blues*. This book is part of a series titled Domestic art and artifacts (to illustrate series statements, this is invented). Notice that it is volume 5 in that series. Some other books on other types of domestic art and artifacts would be topics of the other volumes in the set. Perhaps these would be something like Cooking utensils, or Tables. This one we are looking at is about Chairs.

- Record the series title just as you find it on the item, but change the capitalization so that only the first word and any proper nouns are capitalized.
- Then, if a volume is mentioned on the book, record that by entering "space semicolon space" and the number. If it actually says the word "volume" on the book, record that as "v. 5." If it does not say the word "volume" on the book anywhere, record only the volume number.

A traced series goes in the 490 field. The indicators are 1, which means "the series is traced," and the second indicator is blank. Any time there is a 490 with a first indicator of "1," there must be a matching 830 field or a uniform title added entry for the series name.

In the 490, the series title is transcribed as follows:

Domestic Art and Artifacts, *5* = printed on the book, is transcribed as:

Domestic art and artifacts ; $v 5

Domestic Art and Artifacts, *Volume 5* = printed on the book, is transcribed as:

Domestic art and artifacts ; $v *v. 5*   (abbreviate "volume")

RDA CHANGE: Record the volume numbering in the 490 field exactly as it is printed on the item, but if a uniform title is already established for the series, use the standard abbreviation for the volume in the 830 field (uniform title)

Domestic art and artifacts ; $v *volume 5* (field 490) = printed on the book
Domestic and artifacts ; $v *v. 5* (field 830) = recorded in the uniform title

Or it might say somewhere on the book: *Be Seated* is part of the publisher's series Domestic Art and Artifacts. Other books in that series are:

Lay Down, Best Bet in Beds
Set It Right, Tables That Invite You to Dine

and so forth.

That's a hint that *Be Seated* is part of a series, but the series is not officially numbered, so record it as Domestic art and artifacts with no volume number because there is none indicated on the book itself. Notice the subfield $v. This indicates that a number follows. It does not have to specifically be a "volume" number. If the book says "5", but nothing about "volume 5," use the subfield $v anyway.

Repeat the series information in the 830 field. It is this field that more than likely will be indexed as a title in your OPAC software. The 490 will probably be indexed as a keyword only.

In 2006 there was a major change at the Library of Congress regarding series, the full content of which is beyond the scope of this book. Authority work is no longer being carried out for series titles, a decision at the Library of Congress that has caused misgivings and controversy in the cataloging community.

8. Bibliographical References Note (the 504 field)

These occur frequently in catalog records. Check to see if there is an index or a bibliography or both somewhere in the book. If there is only an index, put it in the general notes field:

Includes index. (500 field)

If there is only a bibliography, put it in the bibliography notes field:

Includes bibliographical references (p. 70-75) (504 field)

If there is both a bibliography and index, put them together in the bibliography notes field:

Includes bibliographical references (p. 70-75) and index. (504 field)

9. Summary Note (the 520 Field)

This is a work of nonfiction, so if it were cataloged today, it would not necessarily have a summary note.

10. Subject Headings (the 650 field)

There are two subject headings with different indicators. The Library of Congress gave this book the adult subject heading **Chairs -- Juvenile literature**. The CYAC Program assigned the subject heading **Chairs** from the adult LCSH. Once again, school librarians may elect to use Sears rather than these subject headings.

11. Series Title (the 830 field)

Here the series is restated in an 830 field (uniform title). The first indicator is blank; the second is the nonfiling indicator.

Table 8.6 is another example, for the book *Anorexia Nervosa: Starving for Attention*, edited by Dan Harmon.

This is a title main entry because the book consists of chapters written by different people, with one person having the responsibility for editorial control. This record has a Contents note (field 505). The second note is a contents note. Notice the two indicators after 505. The "0" will generate a print constant of the word "Contents."

There are abbreviations for "chapter," Ch. 1, followed by the title of chapter, followed by "space slash space" and then the chapter author's name. Then "space dash dash space" appears, followed by Ch. 2. A contents note like this is not always used, but is handy to have if the words in the chapter titles would provide useful keyword access points in a catalog. The other reason to have a contents note is to help users decide if the book would suit their needs. The third note is the summary note.

Next there are the subject headings, the first two from the adult subject headings and the last two from the CYACP. Last there is an added author entry for the editor.

CONTENTS NOTE FOR COLLECTIONS OF PLAYS OR SHORT STORIES

Table 8.7 is an example of a very useful contents note (the contents of a collection of plays) and how to construct it, for *Eight Plays for Children*, edited by Coleman A. Jennings. This record is in AACR2.

Here we have a title main entry. Note that the person who wrote the "foreword" is on the title page, so her name gets transcribed following the "space semicolon space" after the editorship statement.

The contents note here is a little different from the one in the anorexia book, as it does not use the designation "Ch." It has the individual titles and authors of the plays within this book. Again, punctuation is important. Take note of what has been done in this case. The title of the play is separated from the author by "space slash space," just as you find in a title and statement of responsibility area for any book. Following the author's name (in direct order, Constance Congdon, not Congdon, Constance) you have "space dash dash space" followed by the title of the next play. The first word of the title is capitalized and nothing else in the title is, unless it is a proper noun.

Again, both kinds of subject headings have been used in this record. **Children's plays, American** is for the adult catalog. **Plays -- Collections** is for the children's catalog.

Table 8.6. Example of Title Main Entry Record for *Anorexia Nervosa: Starving for Attention*, Edited by Dan Harmon

Field Label	MARC Field Tag and Indicators	Catalog Record Information with MARC Coding and ISBD Punctuation
Location	050 00	RC552.A5 $b H38 1999
ISBN International Standard Book Number	020 bb	978-0936077321
Title	245 00	Anorexia nervosa : $b starving for attention / $c edited by Dan Harmon ; illustrated by Connie Haynes.
Publisher	260 bb	Philadelphia, PA : $b Chelsea House, $c 1999.
Physical description	300 bb	87 p. : $b ill. ; $c 24 cm.
Physical Description	300 bb	RDA 87 pages : $b illustrations ; $c 24 cm.
Series	490 1b	The encyclopedia of psychological disorders
Content Type (Fundamental form of the communication)	336 bb	RDA text
Media Type (General type of intermediation, or, device required to view it)	337 bb	RDA unmediated
Carrier Type (What it is on)	338 bb	RDA volume
Bibliographical References Note	504 bb	Includes bibliographical references (p. 82) and index.
Contents Note	505 0b	Ch. 1. Death of a singer / Mary Bradley -- Ch. 2. What, exactly, is the problem / Lynda Hill -- Ch. 3. History of the disease / Adam Kemp -- Ch. 4. Related diseases / James Abramson -- Ch. 5. Causes and special considerations / Jennifer Deming -- Ch. 6. Treatment / Don Heide -- Ch. 7. Recognizing the disease and finding help / Andrew Moran.
Summary	520 bb	Contributed essays explore the truth and misconceptions regarding anorexia nervosa by examining its history, causes, considerations, treatment, and related eating disorders.
Audience	521 2b	Grades 7-12

(*continued*)

Table 8.6. (continued)

Field Label	MARC Field Tag and Indicators	Catalog Record Information with MARC Coding and ISBD Punctuation
Study Program	526 0b	Accelerated Reader $b grades 7-12 $c 6.1 $d 2 pts. $z No. 42506
Adult Library of Congress subject heading	650 b0	Eating disorders $v Juvenile literature. (-- Juvenile literature)
CYACP Library of Congress subject heading	650 b1	Anorexia nervosa.
CYACP Library of Congress subject heading	650 b1	Eating disorders.
Author	700 1b	Harmon, Dan, $e editor.
Series Stated as Uniform Title	830 b4	The encyclopedia of psychological disorders.

Special Tidbit: Transcribing Obvious Errors

Under AACR2, if there was an obvious error or misrepresentation in the item being cataloged, the cataloger was instructed to correct it in the bibliographic record, like this:

Title: 245 10 Two wolrds [i.e., worlds] / by Matthew Morrison
Alternate Title: 246 3b Two worlds (The indicators mean there will be no note, but there will be title access for Two worlds).

"Take what you see" is a basic tenet of RDA, and catalogers are to *transcribe inaccuracies into the title field as they appear on the source.* The corrected form may be traced in a 246 field, like this:

245 10 Two wolrds / by Matthew Morrison
246 1b $i Corrected title: $a Two worlds (The indicators mean there will be both a note and title access for Two worlds. The subfield code $i means the note will display the initial text saying: "Corrected title:"

This is one of the major changes from AACR2 to RDA, and it has generated many comments from catalogers.

Table 8.7. AACR2 Record Showing Contents Note for *Eight Plays for Children*, Edited by Coleman A. Jennings

Field Label	MARC Field Tag and Indicators	Catalog Record Information with MARC coding and ISBD Punctuation
Location	050 00	PS625.5 $b .E356 1999
ISBN International Standard Book Number	020 bb	9780760340448
Title	245 00	Eight plays for children : $b the new generation play project / $c edited by Coleman A. Jennings ; foreword by Suzan L. Zeder.
Publisher	260 bb	Austin, Tex. : $b University of Texas Press, $c 1999.
Edition	250 bb	1st ed.
Physical description	300 bb	ix, 479 p. : $b ill. ; $c 24 cm.
Contents	505 0b The "0" means Complete Contents. There are other options, but most of the time "0" is what you will need. Use of the "0" may generate a print constant of the word "Contents."	Beauty and the beast / Constance Congdon -- Hula heart / Velina Hasu Houston -- East of the sun and west of the moon / Tina Howe -- The invisible man / Len Jenkin -- Kringle's window / Mark Medoff -- Duke Kahanamoku vs. the surfnappers / Eric Overmyer -- Dogbrain / Michael Weller -- The witch of Blackbird Pond / Y. York.
Adult Library of Congress subject heading	650 b0	Children's plays, American.
CYACP Library of Congress subject heading	650 b1	Plays $v Collections. (Plays -- Collections)
Author/Title Added Entry	700 12	Congdon, Constance. $t Beauty and the beast.
Author/Title Added Entry	700 12	Houston, Velina Hasu. $t Hula heart.
Author/Title Added Entry	700 12	Howe, Tina. $t East of the sun and west of the moon.
Author/Title Added Entry	700 12	Jenkin, Len. $t Invisible man.

(*continued*)

Table 8.7. *(continued)*

Field Label	MARC Field Tag and Indicators	Catalog Record Information with MARC coding and ISBD Punctuation
Author/Title Added Entry	700 12	Medoff, Mark Howard. $t Kringle's window.
Author/Title Added Entry	700 12	Overmyer, Eric. $t Dogbrain
Author/Title Added Entry	700 12	Weller, Michael, $d 1942- . $t Witch of Blackbird Pond.
Author	700 1b	Jennings, Coleman A., $d 1933- $e ed.

Next, each author and title is traced in author/title added entries. These go in a 700 field (for the author) followed by a subfield "t" for the Title. The indicators are 12. The "1" means personal surname (last name first, the most common type of name), added entry. The "2" means analytical entry. That means that the item being represented by this field is *part* of the total book. Analytics are "parts."

The form of entry for the author/title field must be correct according to the Library of Congress Name Authority File. Titles that start with an article should *not* have that article in the subfield "t," because that will make them index under that article (A, An, or The). In other words, the online catalog software should index a 700 subfield "t" as a title, so if the user does an "exact title" search, this field and the 245 would be searched. These author/title added entries give access to a part of a whole, or an analytic.

The editor is traced as an added author.

Another way of doing this is to trace an individual play title in a 740 field (title added entry). If that is done, then there will be no access by the author except via keyword search on the contents note. The title tracing fields would look like this:

740 02 Beauty and the beast
740 02 Hula heart
740 42 The witch of Blackbird Pond

The first indicator represents the nonfiling characters, or the coding necessary to eliminate A, An, and The from the indexing. The second indicator is the type of title, or an analytical title, which gets an indicator of "2."

MORE THAN THREE EDITORS ON THE TITLE PAGE

Table 8.8 is an example showing more than three editors, based on the book *Bird Watcher's Bible*.

Table 8.8.   Record for More Than Three Editors, Based on *Bird Watcher's Bible*

Field Label	MARC Field Tag and Indicators	Catalog Record Information with MARC coding and ISBD Punctuation
Location and Availability	050 bb	QL682 $b .B57 2012
ISBN International Standard Book Number	020 bb	9780385427296
Title	245 00	AACR2 Bird-watcher's bible : $b a complete treasury--science, know-how, beauty, lore / edited by Jonathan Alderfer . . . [et al.].
Title	245 00	RDA Bird-watcher's bible : $b a complete treasury--science, know-how, beauty, lore / edited by Jonathan Alderfer, Roger Tory Peterson, John James Audubon, and Phoebe Snetsinger.
Publisher	260 bb	Washington, D.C. : $b National Geographic, $c 2012.
Physical Description	300 bb	AACR2 vi, 125 p. ; $b ill. ; $c 25 cm.
Physical Description	300 bb	RDA vi, 125 pages ; $b illustrations ; $c 25 cm
Content Type (Fundamental form of the communication)	336 bb	RDA text
Media Type (General type of intermediation, or, device required to view it)	337 bb	RDA unmediated
Carrier Type (What it is on)	338 bb	RDA volume
Subject	650 0b	Bird watching.
Personal Added Entry for first named editor	700 1b	Alderfer, Jonathan K., $e editor.
Personal Added Entry for second named editor	700 1b	Peterson, Roger Tory, $d 1908-1996, $e editor.
Personal Added Entry for third named editor	700 1b	Audubon, John James, $d 1785-1851, $e editor.
Personal Added Entry for fourth named editor	700 1b	Snetsinger, Phoebe, $d 1931-1999, $e editor

This record has a title main entry because the text was done under editorial direction. The second indicator is "4" to account for the first word of the title, "The."

On the title page of this book it says: Edited by Jonathan Alderfer, Roger Tory Peterson, John James Audubon, Phoebe Snetsinger. Under AACR2, this gets transcribed in the statement of responsibility area using only the editor named first on the title page (Jonathan Alderfer), followed by a space and three dots and another space. Then bracket [et al. followed by another bracket. The "et al." is Latin for "and others."

In the Physical Description Area, dimensions, under the RDA rules there is no period after "cm," unless it is followed by a series title. In this case, there is no series. Trace only the first named author or editor, under AACR2 rules.

RDA CHANGE: Record all editors that you wish to in the statement of responsibility and trace as many of them as you want to. If you do not wish to record them all, do it this way:

edited by Jonathan K. Alderfer [and three others]

RDA does not use [et al.].

FOUR AUTHORS

Table 8.9 is an example of an AACR2 record for four authors based on the hypothetical book *Children's Literature: Its Rich History and Enduring Legacy*. Table 8.10 is an example of an RDA record for the same title. These examples illustrate the difference between AACR2 and RDA. This book has four authors.

- Under AACR2 this would have a title main entry and only the first author would be traced.
- Under RDA, this has a personal main entry (the first name on the title page), and optionally all the authors may be named in the statement of responsibility and all may or may not be traced in added entry fields.

PARALLEL TITLES

School librarians need to know a little about parallel titles, because there will no doubt be bilingual materials in the school library. Following is an example of the title and statement of responsibility for a bilingual book (English and Spanish) for the juvenile audience.

245 10 $ Bear at home = $b Oso en casa / $c Stella Blackstone ; [illustrated by] Debbie Harter.

Table 8.9. AACR2 Record for Four Authors for Hypothetical Book *Children's Literature*

Field Label	MARC Field Tag and Indicators	Catalog Record Information with MARC coding and ISBD Punctuation
Title	245 04	Children's literature : $b its rich history and enduring legacy / by Sarah Basswood . . . [et al] **Title main entry when there are more than three authors**
Publisher	260 bb	Chicago : $b Scholarly Press, $c 2012.
Physical Description	300 bb	xlv, 345 p. ; $b ill. ; $c 27 cm.
Subject	650 0b	Children's literature.
Personal Added Entry for first named author	700 1b	Basswood, Sarah. **Trace only the first author**

Table 8.10. RDA Record for Four Authors for Hypothetical Book *Children's Literature*

Field Label	MARC Field Tag and Indicators	Catalog Record Information with MARC coding and ISBD Punctuation
Author	100 1b	Basswood, Sarah, $e author. **The first named author on the title page is the main entry**
Title	245 10	Children's literature : $b its rich history and enduring legacy / by Sarah Basswood, Mary Stein, Gail Fullmer & Karen Johnson. **All authors may be (not mandatory) named in the statement of responsibility.**
Publisher	260 bb	Chicago : $b Scholarly Press, $c 2012.
Physical Description	300 bb	xlv, 345 pages : $b illustrations ; $c 27 cm
Content Type (Fundamental form of the communication)	336 bb	text
Media Type (General type of intermediation, or, device required to view it)	337 bb	unmediated
Carrier Type (What it is on)	338 bb	volume
Personal Added Entry for second named author	700 1b	Stein, Mary, $e author.
Personal Added Entry for third named author	700 1b	Fullmer, Gail, $e author.
Personal Added Entry for fourth named author	700 1b	Johnson, Karen, $e author.

The title page actually has both titles on it, or the Spanish-language title is on the right-hand page facing the English title on the left-hand page.

WHEN DO YOU CREATE A NEW RECORD?

It is not unusual for titles to be published in various editions. Sometimes hardcover and paperback editions are published simultaneously. Sometimes items are designated as special editions, such as Reading Rainbow or Book Club. Catalogers have puzzled over these differences and when to create a new record. This takes on special meaning when contributing to a union catalog, such as OCLC or the local school district union catalog. It is important to indicate precisely what edition or printing each library has for both user information and acquisitions of new materials.

Both OCLC and the American Library Association have issued guidelines to help catalogers determine when a new record is necessary. The OCLC document may be located on the Internet by searching "When to input a new record."

The ALA document *Differences Between, Changes Within: Guidelines on When to Create a New Record* can also be located by searching for that title online. This is a very useful document that makes a distinction between major and minor differences, giving examples and recommendations. In addition, *Library Media Connection* published an article in 2006 differentiating between publications needing a new record and those that do not. Following are some highlights from these documents:

- A reprint of an earlier publication by a new publisher requires a new record with a publication history explanatory note in a 500 field.
- If it says "Second edition" or the like on the item, create a new record.
- If it says "Abridged," create a new record.
- Statements on the item such as "Yearling Book," "Book Club Edition," or "Paperback Edition" are not enough to justify a new record. Check the name of the publisher and the paging. If it is a new publisher, a new record should be made. If the paging is significantly different between the two editions, make a new record. If you do not make a new record, but the ISBN in your current record is for the hardcover and you are holding the paperback with perhaps a different ISBN, enter a second 020 field in the record for the paperback ISBN.
- If the title page has one publisher, but elsewhere in the book there is an indication of a new publisher relating to this particular edition, such as New Scholastic Edition, a new record is not necessary. Record a note about the new publisher in a 500 field and include a different ISBN in a second 020 field.

SUMMARY

This chapter encompasses both bibliographic description per the eight separate areas punctuated in ISBD and RDA changes affecting description and access points.

MARC coding is included as well. All of these elements form an integrated whole when used to build a catalog record. Records for K–12 level materials are relatively straightforward, involving mostly personal main entries and MARC coding that is used repeatedly, so it will all become quite routine for the school librarian after a bit of practice. RDA changes from AACR2 are minimal. It is important to adhere to the ISBD and MARC standards so your records will integrate seamlessly with other records in the existing catalog and reflect the new cataloging code as RDA records become increasingly visible over time.

For sample RDA records from OCLC, see Appendix B.

TEST YOUR KNOWLEDGE

Answer the questions below to solve the quotation puzzle. When you determine the answer (word) for the blank line in each statement, write it on the line. Then find that word in Table 8.11 (for Puzzle 1) and Table 8.12 (for Puzzle 2). Each word is paired with a word for the quotation. Place the paired words in the quotation puzzle on the corresponding numbered lines (e.g., the paired word for the answer to question 1 goes on line 1. in the quotation puzzle). In this way you can answer the questions and fill in the quotation simultaneously.

Puzzle 1

1. The level of description that is best for you to use is level _____.
2. The prescribed punctuation for catalog records is called International Standard _____ _____.
3. ISBD has the following elements: _____, colon, and semicolon.
4. Bibliographic records before 1971 do not exhibit _____ characteristics.
5. In the main entry Myers, Walter Dean, the subfield d indicates the author's year of _____.
6. When transcribing a title, only the first word and all _____ nouns are capitalized.
7. The title is taken from the _____ _____ of information, or the title page.
8. If the first word of a title is "the," the second indicator is _____.
9. *The blues of Flats Brown* / Walter Dean Myers has no _____ on the title page.
10. In the statement of responsibility, a semicolon separates the named person with the main responsibility from the name of the person having _____ responsibility in the work.
11. New RDA rules say to transcribe an Edition Statement _____ as it is on the item. No abbreviations are to be used.
12. In AACR2, if two places of publication, one American and one international, were on the title page in that order, it was correct to show only the _____ site in the description.

13. When an item has more than one date in it, record the date in the $c subfield that matches the _____ statement.
14. Use an _____ _____ note for items with widely differing copyright and publication dates.
15. In the Physical Description Area, _____ means this children's book has no numbers printed on the pages.
16. RDA requires that ill. be spelled out as _____ in the description.
17. If the _____ of the book is greater than the height, record both dimensions in the Physical Description Area.
18. The new MARC 337 field is for a type of _____ device, which for a book is "unmediated."
19. The new MARC 338 is for the physical carrier, or what the item is on. For books, this is "_____."
20. The prescribed order for notes is not the same as the MARC tag _____ order.
21. Because school librarians often must identify age and grade appropriate materials, the MARC 521 field (Target Audience) can be used as a CE (_____ _____) note.
22. In the 521 field, if the first indicator is 2, the display constant will be: _____ _____ _____.
23. "Accelerated Reader, grades 7-12" is in the _____ _____ Information Note, or, the MARC 526 field.
24. In the 6XX fields, a second indicator of "1" means the subject heading is from the _____ Program.
25. In the bibliographic record for *Be seated : a book about chairs*, the established form of entry for the author does not include the author's _____ name or a year of birth.
26. In the Physical Description Area, "lx" is the _____.
27. This particular book is number _____ in the series Domestic art and artifacts.
28. The title and subtitle for *Be seated* are separated by space _____ space.
29. There are no subsidiary statements of _____ on the title page for *Be seated*.
30. A _____ is a "page" in the book that is printed on one side only.

Quotation 1

1. _____	2. _____	3. _____	4. _____
5. _____	6. _____	7. _____	8. _____
9. _____	10. _____	11. _____	
12. _____	13. _____	14. _____	
15. _____	16. _____	17. _____	
18. _____	19. _____	20. _____	
21. _____	22. _____	23. _____	

24. _____ 25. _____ 26. _____
27. _____ 28. _____ 29. _____
30. _____ .

-- Kathryn L. Corcoran, Library Services Director, Munson-Williams-Proctor Arts Institute.

Table 8.11.

American = they	volume = in	Bibliographic Description = users	birth = expect
ISBD = really	CYAC = the	responsibility = your	proper = you
pre-paging = and	2 = Your	exactly = but	subsidiary = cataloging
width = library	middle = shelf	slash = don't	leaf = office
interest grade level = and	chronological = the	by = perfect	edition = probably
illustrations = find	chief (or preferred) source = to	Study Program = on	5 = not
colon = in	1 v. (unpaged) = to	originally published = expect	curriculum enhanced = catalog
4 = do	intermediation = books		

Puzzle 2

1. An RDA change in the physical description area is that ___ _____ ___ _____ will be recorded as 10 unnumbered pages of plates.
2. If you have a 490 field with indicators of 1 and b, you must also have an _____ field.
3. In a series statement, a volume number with "v." or a volume number without "v." is preceded by _____.
4. The note "Includes bibliographical references (p. 235-240) and index" goes in the _____ field.
5. The 520 field (Summary) is identified as a _____ record element.
6. Chairs -- Juvenile literature is not from the _____ Program.
7. & 8. The bibliographic record for *Anorexia nervosa : starving for attention* shows a _____ main entry because the book is a compilation done under _____ .
9. A 505 will give your users _____ access points to chapter content in the book.
10. The first indicator "0" in the 505 field will generate a print _____ of "Contents."

11. The editor's name is an added entry and goes in the ____ field.
12. In the 505 field we capitalize only the _____ word and all proper nouns.
13. In the 505 field we separate combinations of authors and titles from each other with space ____ ____ space.
14. An _____ is an access point to a part of the total book.
15. In an author/title analytic, the author's name must be in the _____ form of the name.
16. Another way to make analytical titles searchable as titles is to put them in the ____ field.
17. The first indicator in the 740 is the _____ indicator.
18. When there are more than three authors or editors, the RDA change in the statement of responsibility is that ____ may be included.
19. Under AACR2, if a book had more than three authors, it was given a _____ main entry, and only the first author on the title page is in the statement of responsibility and is traced.
20. You will find parallel titles on the title pages in _____ books.
21. An _____ edition of a book requires a new record.
22. The presence of a new _____ on a previously published book requires a new record.

Quotation 2

1. _____ 2. _____ 3. _____ 4. _____
5. _____ 6. _____ 7. _____ 8. _____
9. _____ 10. _____ 11. _____
12. _____, 13._____, 14. _____
15. _____. 16. _____. 17. _____
18. _____ 19. _____ 20. _____
21. _____ 22. _____, *Inferno*

Table 8.12.

CYAC = such	editorship = snob	dash dash = he	title = a
authorized = himself	first = books	constant = leather	nonfiling = do
504 = stop	publisher = Brown	keyword = about	bilingual = moments
740 = E-books	analytic = reminded	[10] p. of plates = I've	830 = got
abridged = Dan	$v = to	title = their	all = have
CE MARC = being	700 = bound		

TEST YOUR CRITICAL THINKING

The English teachers and drama coach are constantly doing exact title searches in your OPAC for titles of plays and not finding anything. Consequently, they think the library is inadequate for their needs. As the librarian, you know many of the individual plays are in the collection but not accessible by title because of the way the bibliographic record is constructed. What can you do to increase the school library's credibility with these teachers?

RESOURCES

Adamich, A. (2006). CE-MARC: The library educator's "receipt." *Knowledge Quest, 35*(1), 64–68.

American Library Association, Association for Library Collections and Technical Services. (2007). *Differences between, changes within: Guidelines on when to create a new record.* Chicago: ALCTS/ALA.

Department of the Interior, Bureau of Education. (1876). *Public libraries in the United States of America: Their history, condition, and management. Special report. Part II. Rules for a printed dictionary catalogue, by Charles A. Cutter.* Washington, DC: GPO.

Follett Software Company. (n.d.-a). *Ask Ms. MARC.* Retrieved from: http://www.follettsoftware .com/askmsmarc.cfm.

Follett Software Company (n.d.-b). *Tag of the month.* Retrieved from: http://www.follett software.com/tagofthemonth.cfm.

Hart, A. (2010). *The RDA primer: A guide for the occasional cataloger.* Santa Barbara, CA: Linworth.

Kaplan, A. (2006). Do I have to make a new record? Deciding when you have a new edition and when you have a second copy. *Library Media Connection, 24*(5), 28–29.

Library of Congress (LC) RDA training materials. (n.d.). Retrieved from: http://www.loc.gov/ catworkshop/RDA training materials/LC RDA Training/LC RDA course table.html.

MARC standards. (n.d.). Retrieved from: http://www.loc.gov/marc/.

MARC 21 format standards for bibliographic data. (n.d.). Retrieved from: http://www.loc.gov/ marc/bibliographic/ecbdhome.html.

MARC 21 reference materials. Part VII: A summary of commonly used MARC 21 fields. (n.d.). Retrieved from: http://www.loc.gov/marc/umb/um07to10.html.

Schiff, A. L. (2011). *Changes From AACR2 to RDA: A comparison of examples.* Retrieved from: http://faculty.washington.edu/aschiff/BCLAPresentationWithNotes-RevMay2011.pdf.

Working Group on the International Standard Bibliographic Description. (1974). *ISBD(M): International Standard Bibliographic Description for monographic publications* (1st standard ed.). London: IFLA Committee on Cataloguing.

9

Cataloging Nonprint
and Electronic Materials

Now it is time to leave the domain of traditional print and look at catalog records for nonprint (sometimes referred to as audiovisual, or AV) materials. Theoretically you can catalog any item in the universe using AACR2 or RDA, including art prints, microfilm, kits with a variety of materials, films, sound recordings, and realia. Practically speaking, these are the items that will be housed in a school library most often:

- DVDs (movies, educational videos)
- Books on CD, either alone or in package combinations of a CD and the book
- Children's songs and music on CD

The latest electronic items you may also have are:

- E-books
- Playaways
- Downloadable audiobooks

Nonprint, or audiovisual, cataloging is a mixed bag and can be very frustrating. There aren't always clear-cut "right" or "wrong" rules. The notes fields, especially for commercial movies in video release, can be quite elaborate and problematic at times. Include in the bibliographic record whatever you feel users require, in both description and access points. It is not necessary to include everything that is possible or sanctioned. However, it is extremely important to have bibliographic records for these items in your OPAC. They are every bit as important as books in your collection. Teachers and students both need nonprint materials, because today's students are visually oriented and often the moving image holds their attention better than a textbook. These materials have the potential to improve student learning.

Some students may enjoy and understand written text better if they can hear it. Playaways and downloadable audiobooks fill that need. These devices can be used with a book, with students following along as the narrator reads. With portable reading devices being so popular now, e-books are a new way to get students to read. If there are any of these materials in your library, you owe it to your users to make them accessible through the OPAC.

DVDS

Figures 9.1 through 9.3 show the container and disc of a typical educational DVD, *The Trail of Tears: Cherokee Legacy.*

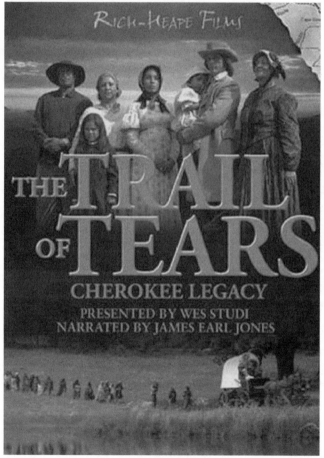

Figure 9.1. Container Cover for DVD *Trail of Tears: Cherokee Legacy.* **Courtesy of Steven R. Heape.**

WES STUDI

AMERICA'S DARKEST PERIOD: JACKSON'S INDIAN REMOVAL ACT
AND THE FORCED RELOCATION OF THE CHEROKEE NATION
TO INDIAN TERRITORY IN 1838

*"Thousands of Cherokees died during the Trail of Tears, nearly a
quarter of the Nation. They suffered beyond imagination...and when
they finally arrived in Indian Territory, they arrived almost without
any children and with very few elders, in a way they arrived with no
past and no future."*

"TRAIL OF TEARS: CHEROKEE LEGACY" PRESENTED BY WES STUDI
NARRATED BY JAMES EARL JONES CELEBRITY VOICES JAMES GARNER,
CRYSTAL GAYLE, JOHN BUTTRAM, GOV. DOUGLAS WILDER
DIRECTOR OF PHOTOGRAPHY ROBERT TULLIER EDITED BY MICHAEL LOSURDO, JR.
MUSIC CONTRIBUTION BY WALELA SCORE BY JAMES NEEL
EXECUTIVE PRODUCER STEVEN R. HEAPE WRITTEN BY DANIEL BLAKE SMITH
PRODUCED BY CHIP RICHIE AND STEVEN R. HEAPE DIRECTED BY CHIP RICHIE

ENDORSED BY THE CHEROKEE NATION AND THE EASTERN BAND OF CHEROKEE INDIANS
DIRECTORS CUT - 115 MINUTES, NOT RATED, CLOSED CAPTIONED

RICH-HEAPE FILMS, INC.

A Native American Owned Corporation

6 52645 68003 3

Copyright MMVI

This DVD video is protected by the copyright laws. It is intended for the private use of
the buyer. Public Performance Rights granted to schools and libraries, all others contact
Rich-Heape Films. Any copy of content is strictly prohibited. All Rights Reserved.
Rich-Heape Films, Inc. • 5952 Royal Lane • Suite 254 • Dallas, Tx 75230
Visit our web site at www.richheape.com • Contact us toll free at 888-600-2922

Figure 9.2. Back of Container Cover for DVD *Trail of Tears: Cherokee Legacy*. Courtesy of Steven R. Heape.

Figure 9.3.   Disc Surface for DVD *The Trail of Tears: Cherokee Legacy*. Courtesy of Steven R. Heape.

Table 9.1 is the RDA catalog record for *The Trail of Tears, Cherokee Legacy.*

1. Title

The title (245) for AV materials used to be followed by brackets [ ] around the general material designator (GMD). The GMD is in all records for nonprint items cataloged before RDA, but with RDA, it is gone. This is a major RDA change, one that has truly shaken the cataloger's world, probably more so than the demise of the rule of three.

The first choice of title source is the *title screen*, not the label on the DVD surface or on its container. RDA permits use of the disc label or container if the title screen is insufficient. Next is "space slash space" and any production or directorial information. This record shows corporate production information with the directorial and

Table 9.1. RDA Record for *The Trail of Tears, Cherokee Legacy*

Field Label	MARC Field Tag and Indicators	Catalog Record Information with MARC Coding and ISBD Punctuation
MARC Code for Organizations/ Cataloging Source Codes	040 bb	DLC $c DLC $d mndueh
Call Number	092 bb	975.004 $b Tra
Title	245 04	The Trail of Tears : $b Cherokee legacy / $c Rich-Heape Films, Inc. in association with the Cherokee Nation and the Eastern Band of Cherokee Indians.
Variant Title	246 30	Cherokee legacy
Edition	250 bb	Director's cut.
Publisher	260 bb	Dallas, TX : $b Rich-Heape Films, $c ©2006.
Physical Description	300 bb	1 DVD (NTSC, 115 min.) : $b sound, color. ; $c 4 3/4 in. + $e 1 guide (5 pages)
Series Title	490 1b	Native American outlook ; $v Number 4
Content Type (Fundamental form of the communication)	336 bb	two-dimensional moving image
Media Type (General type of intermediation, or, device required to view it)	337 bb	video
Carrier Type (What it is on)	338 bb	videodisc
Credits Note	508 1b	Director, Chip Richie ; producers, Chip Richie, Steven R. Heape ; writer, Daniel Blake Smith ; music contributed by Walela.
Performer Note	511 0b	Cast: Narrator, James Earl Jones ; host , Wes Studi ; celebrity voices, James Garner, Crystal Gayle, John Buttrum, Douglas Wilder.
Contents Note	505 0b	Eve of removal - Tradgedy [i.e. tragedy] of removal - Removal camps - Life on the trail - Tradgedy [i.e. tragedy] of the trail - Aftermath.
Summary	520 bb	Summary: Documents the forced removal in 1838 of the Cherokee Nation from the southeastern United States

(continued)

Table 9.1. (*continued*)

Field Label	MARC Field Tag and Indicators	Catalog Record Information with MARC Coding and ISBD Punctuation
		to Oklahoma. Shows the suffering endured by the Cherokees as they lost their land and the difficult conditions they endured on the trail. Describes how thousands of Cherokees died during the Trail of Tears, nearly a quarter of the nation, including most of their children and elders.
Audience Note	**521 bb**	Ages 12-adult. Not rated.
Technical Details	**538 bb**	Region 1
Language Note	**546 bb**	Closed-captioned for the hearing impaired. Primarily in English; some segments in Native American language with English subtitles.
Awards Note	**586 bb**	Winner of the Sun Dance Film Festival Multicultural Film Award, 2006.
Subject	**650 b0**	Trail of Tears, 1838-1839.
Subject	**650 b0**	Cherokee Indians $x History.
Subject	**650 b0**	Cherokee Indians $x Relocation.
Genre Subject Heading	**655 b7**	Films for the hearing impaired. $2 lcgft
Genre Subject Heading	**655 b7**	Documentary films. $2 lcgft
Author	**700 1b**	Richie, Chip, $e director $e film producer.
Author	**700 1b**	Studi, Wes, $e host.
Author	**700 1b**	Heape, Steven R., $e film producer.
Author	**700 1b**	Jones, James Earl, $e narrator.
Author	**700 1b**	Garner, James, $e actor.
Corporate Added Entry for Production Company	**710 2b**	Riche-Heap Films.
Corporate Added Entry for Production Company	**710 2b**	Walela (Musical group), $e performer.
Series Title	**830 b0**	Native American outlook ; $v no. 4

other contributor information in the credits note area (508). If the names of any individuals are included in the statement of responsibility, they should be individuals with major responsibility for the content of the item. The title, *The Trail of Tears, Cherokee Legacy* is all capitalized (with the exception of "legacy") because all the words are proper nouns.

2. Alternate Title (246 Field)

In this instance the cataloger chose to trace the subtitle in a 246. The indicators 30 mean the following: 3 = There will be no note field for this subtitle, but it will be traced as a title, and 0 = its type of title is "portion." Cherokee legacy is a portion of the title. It is actually a subtitle, but there is no provision for "subtitle" in the list of second indicators and their meanings in MARC for the 246 field.

What if the film item has different titles all over it? This happens in real life much too often. It is necessary to make the item accessible by any of the varying titles. Here is where indicators "1" (first indicator) and "b" (second indicator, blank) may be used.

On the title screen the DVD reads: All About Animals and Their Young.
On the DVD surface label it reads: Animals and Their Young in the Wild.
On the DVD container it reads: Animals and their babies.

How you can code these various titles is shown below. (Note that you must provide the text that starts with **Title on**; it is not automatically supplied.)

245 00 All about animals and their young (taken from the title screen)
246 1b $i Title on disc surface: $a Animals and their young in the wild
246 1b $i Title on container: $a Animals and their babies

This will generate notes in the notes field for both 246s that look like this:

Title on disc surface: Animals and their young in the wild
Title on container: Animals and their babies

Each of those varying titles would be searchable as titles.
To review the 246 field, see chapter 7.

3. Publisher (260 Field)

In this field is the place of publication, followed by "space colon space," followed by the name of the publisher, followed by the copyright date.

4. Physical Description Area (300 Field)

The physical description field has changed a little from AACR2. It now includes the NTSC information in the 300 field. In the subfield b ($b), spell out "sound" and "color." DVD and NTSC information were in the 538 field in AACR2. Notice that subfield $a contains the words "1 DVD." This designation does not conform to actual RDA terminology, which is "1 video disc." The Library of Congress recommends "1 DVD" as an acceptable option. The value of using this designation is that it gives users an easily identifiable designation. They will know this is a "DVD" without having to guess what "video disc" means.

With RDA, many libraries are making individual policy decisions about the 300 and the 538 fields and where descriptive information regarding the format of the AV item should go. It appears that many are not adhering closely to exact RDA requirements.

If this were a Blu-ray disc, the 300 field could look like this:

1 DVD (NTSC, 60 min.) : $b Blu-ray, sound, color ; $c 4 3/4 in. + $e 1 guide (5 pages)

Describe the extent and format of the item, in this case, "videodisc."

- Record the running time of the video in parentheses after the specific designator "1 DVD." Running time is extremely important in AV cataloging, because often teachers need to know if an item will fit in their classroom schedule. RDA allows "minutes" to be abbreviated as "min."
- Follow that with "space colon space." Next is information about sound and whether or not the item is in color. These used to be abbreviated as: sd., col.
- Follow that with "space semicolon space" and the size of the video medium. Take note that RDA recommends that the size be recorded in centimeters (CD or DVD, 12 cm.), but it is acceptable to continue to use inches (4 3/4 in.) according to the Library of Congress.
- Frequently there will be a guide with a video, and this is recorded following a plus (+) sign and the number of the items: + 1 guide (5 pages). It is not mandatory to record the number of pages in the guide.

5. Series Title (490 Field)

This is the series of which the video is a part. Nonprint materials are often part of a series. In this case the series title is recorded in both a 490 and an 830. The 490 contains the title as it is on the item. The 830 records it in a uniform title and makes it searchable as a title.

6. 336, 337, and 338 Fields

For more information on these fields, see chapter 8.

Here is a list of the terms used in this chapter for each of the new fields:

Field 336 Content Type

- ○ performed music
- ○ spoken word
- ○ text
- ○ two-dimensional moving image

Field 337 Media Type

- ○ audio
- ○ electronic (as a substitute for the RDA term "computer," which given its context, may confuse the user)
- ○ projected
- ○ unmediated
- ○ video

Field 338 Carrier Type

- ○ audio disc
- ○ online resource
- ○ videodisc
- ○ volume

Notes are next. Nonprint materials catalog records have numerous notes. *The order of the notes is by MARC tag, not AACR2 prescribed order.*

7. Credits Note (508 Field)

If brief enough, this can *instead* (not in addition to) go in the statement of responsibility area after the "space slash space" following the title. This is for directors, musical composers, and so forth. It is more common to see credits information in the 508 field than in the statement of responsibility.

8. Performer Note (511 Field)

Here are recorded the cast, or the presenter, or the narrator, or any other individuals who presented the material. The first indicator "1" will automatically generate the word "Cast."

511 1b Winona Ryder, Gabriel Byrne.

will display as

Cast: Winona Ryder, Gabriel Byrne.

When the first indicator 0 = No print constant, you input whatever label is needed, and that is what will display.

511 0b Narrated by Tom Hanks.

displays as

Narrated by Tom Hanks

The second indicator in the 511 is blank.

9. Summary Note (520 Field)

Always have a summary note on a media bibliographic record, because users cannot browse through videos or other types of nonprint materials the way they can browse books.

10. Audience (521 Field)

In this instance, the audience note is used to designate an age or grade level. For more information on this field, see chapter 8.

11. Technical Details (538 Field)

NTSC is the video system or standard used in North America and most of South America. In NTSC, thirty frames are transmitted each second. The Region 1 designation stems from the commercial DVD player specification requiring that a player to be sold in a given place not play discs encoded for a different region. However, *region-free* DVD players are also commercially available. The contents of this field changed in RDA to include less information because of the more inclusive 300 field. However, current catalog records show the field 538 is still being used to convey many technical details, sometimes duplicating information in the 300 field.

12. Language Note (546 Field)

Closed captioned for the hearing impaired may be here, if this is information that would be useful for your library users. A subtitled version of a foreign-language film could be described in this manner: In Spanish with English subtitles.

Special Tidbit: Using Genre Subject Headings to Assist Teachers

Why would you go to the trouble of adding genre subject headings to the bibliographic records for the video collection? Think of the English teachers who might want to know what movies the library has that are based on novels. The genre subject heading *Film adaptations* would provide a gathering point in the catalog for all such videos. *Documentary films* as a genre might help social studies/history teachers. *Foreign films* could be useful for foreign-language teachers.

13. Award Note (586 Field)

The example in this record is Winner of the Sun Dance Film Festival Multicultural Film Award, 2006. All initial letters are capitalized because the name of the award is a proper noun.

14. Subject Headings (6XX Fields)

Subject headings for nonprint items do not get the format as a subdivision, so *do not* use -- Videorecording or -- DVD as a subdivision following topical subject headings. Topical subject headings may be used along with the form subdivision of $v Drama. For example, Iran hostage crisis, 1979-1981 -- Drama could be applied to the movie *Argo*.

Genre Subject Headings

MARC field 655 is the genre subject heading. Apply this for users who want to be able to access items by what the film *is*, not what it is *about*. This includes such things as feature films, documentary films, horror films, films for the hearing impaired, and so forth. This is a format subject heading rather than a topical one. For years it was permissible for catalogers to use *topical subject headings* in the *Library of Congress Subject Headings* volumes as *genre subject headings*. In other words, the heading's original intent was to be representative of something that is about the topic, not something that is the topic. For example, "Horror films" was meant to identify items about horror films. Librarians have been using such subject headings as genre headings for films.

In June 2010 LC announced plans to formally separate genre/form headings from LCSH to a new, stand-alone thesaurus: *Library of Congress Genre/Form Terms for Library and Archival Materials* (LCGFT). In the 2012 six-volume set of the *Library of Congress Subject Headings*, genre headings are in a volume titled *Supplemental Vocabularies*. The new pdf version of the LCSH available at the LC website also includes the list of the genre headings. Much work is being done in the area of genre headings today, the intricacies of which are beyond the scope of this book. Suffice it to say that it was work that needed to be done because of increased user demands for this type of access. Questions such as "What ghost films do you have?" or "What movies do you have based on historical events?" are representative of those user needs. In the 655 field, the subfield $e lcgft is used to indicate that the term is from the new authority file.

15. Author (700 Field)

This label is a bit misleading, as the individuals traced in this record are not actually authors in the traditional sense, but perform other functions relating to the creative product. The subfield "e" in both this field and the 710 (corporate added entry) is the new RDA relationship designator. All designators are listed in appendices I, J, and K in RDA.

16. Author (710 Field)

In this case note that the added author is the name of the production company. This isn't always necessary, but it can be a handy field to use in some circumstances. Often people are looking for a nonprint item and can't remember the title, but may remember the production company. Films for the Humanities is well-known, as is Weston Woods. If a name is entered in an added author area (corporate author), that will provide access via that name.

17. Classification Numbers for Media Items

For classification, assign a number just as you would for any book in your collection. Put a media designator such as Video or DVD above it. That will tell users the item is shelved in the video collection area of the library. For example:

Video 975.004 $b Tra

or

DVD 975.004 $b Tra

The designator at the head of the call number is up to you; you may use anything you wish. It is not devised according to any authority list.

Table 9.2 is another video record in RDA, for a Blu-ray disc of the 1994 movie *Little Women*.

1. Is this amount of detail mandatory? No, it is not. Time and need dictate the amount of detail included in this kind of catalog record, but the example does demonstrate the possibilities. Maybe your teachers like to look up videos by the name of the actors, so it is advisable to provide added author entries for any of those names. For more RDA records of DVDs, see Appendix B.

Table 9.2. RDA Record for Blu-ray Disc of *Little Women*

Field Label	MARC Field Tag and Indicators	Catalog Record Information with MARC Coding and ISBD Punctuation
MARC Code for Organizations/ Cataloging Source Codes	040 bb	DLC $c DLC $d mndueh
Call Number	092 bb	DVD $a Fic $a Alcott
Title	245 00	Little women / $c Columbia Pictures
Publisher	260 00	Culver City, Calif. : $b Columbia TriStar Home Video, $c 1995, c1994.
Physical Description	300 bb	1 DVD (NTSC, 119 min.) : $b Blu-ray, sound, color ; $c 4 3/4 in.
Content Type (Fundamental form of the communication)	336 bb	two-dimensional moving image
Media Type (General type of intermediation, or, device required to view it)	337 bb	video
Carrier Type (What it is on)	338 bb	videodisc
Edition and History Note	500 bb	Videodisc release of the 1994 motion picture.
Edition and History Note	500 bb	Based on the novel by Louisa May Alcott, published in 1868.
Credits Note	508 bb	Producer, Denise DiNovi ; director Gillian Armstrong
Performer Note	511 1b	Cast: Winona Ryder, Susan Sarandon, Gabriel Byrne, Trini Alvarado, Samantha Mathis, Kirsten Dunst, Claire Danes.
Summary Note	520 bb	Summary: Classic story by Louisa May Alcott about the March family of four daughters, a strong mother and a father away during the Civil War.
Audience Note	521 bb	Rated PG
Technical Details	538 bb	Region 1
Language Note	546 00	Closed-captioned for the hearing impaired.
Language Note	546 00	In English with optional subtitles in French and Spanish.
Award Note	586 bb	Honorable mention at the Women in Movies Film Fair, Seneca Falls, New York, 1995.
Subject	650 b0	March family (Fictitious characters) $v Drama

(continued)

Table 9.2. (*continued*)

Field Label	MARC Field Tag and Indicators	Catalog Record Information with MARC Coding and ISBD Punctuation
Subject	650 b0	Mothers and daughters $v Drama
Genre Subject Heading	655 b7	Film adaptations. $2 lcgft
Genre Subject Heading	655 b7	Video recordings for the hearing impaired. $2 lcgft
Author	700 1b	Ryder, Winona, $d 1971- $e actor.
Author	700 1b	Sarandon, Susan, $d 1946- $e actor.
Author	700 1b	Byrne, Gabriel, $d 1950- $e actor.
Author	700 1b	Alvarado, Trini, $e actor.
Author	700 1b	Mathis, Samantha, $e actor.
Author	700 1b	Dunst, Kirsten, $e actor.
Author	700 1b	Danes, Claire, $e actor.
Author	700 1b	Armstrong, Gillian, $d 1950- $e film director
Author	700 1b	Alcott, Louisa May, $d 1832-1888. $e author.
Author	710 2b	Columbia Pictures.
Author	710 2b	Columbia TriStar Home Video.

2. Dates on the item. This video is a good example of how to handle the dates on DVD or Blu-ray versions of theater movies. In the publisher area, enter the date of the DVD release, followed by a copyright notice for the year the film was released. Then in a note further down in the record, state something like this:

DVD release of the 1994 motion picture.

3. In the Edition and History Note, it is always a good idea to have a note telling the viewer that this is a movie based on a novel by a particular author and then trace that author in the added author field.

4. There are numerous subject headings that would be appropriate here. This example shows only two. Notice the use of the subfield $v for Drama.

To learn more, look at some DVD or videocassette records in OPACs that permit the user to click on the MARC button. You will see some very extensive catalog records along with the MARC codes.

AUDIO CD AND A BOOK

Some libraries have multimedia "kits" made up of a book and an accompanying CD containing an audio reading of the book. The listener can follow along in the book while listening to the CD. These are often stored in multimedia hanging plastic bags (figure 9.4).

An example is the popular children's book *Duck for President*. Figures 9.5 and 9.6 show the cover of the book itself and a CD audio recording.

Table 9.3 is the RDA catalog record for *Duck for President*, by Doreen Cronin.

1. Author (100 Field)

For CDs that are exact readings of a book, use an author main entry. Record the Statement of Responsibility as you find it on the *disc surface*, not on the title page of an accompanying book. Not all audio recordings will have the book with them.

Figure 9.4. Hanging Bags for Book/CD Kits

Figure 9.5. Cover of Book *Duck for President,* by Doreen Cronin. Courtesy of Simon and Schuster, Inc.

Figure 9.6. CD of Audio for *Duck for President*, by Doreen Cronin

Table 9.3. RDA Record for *Duck for President*, by Doreen Cronin

Field Label	MARC Field Tag and Indicators	Catalog Record Information with MARC Coding and ISBD Punctuation
MARC Code for Organizations/ Cataloging Source Codes	040 bb	DLC $c DLC $d mndueh
International Standard Book Number (ISBN)	020 bb	0788205455 (disc) : $c $29.95
International Standard Book Number (ISBN)	020 bb	0689863772 (hardcover book)
Publisher Number	028 00	CD 652 $b Weston Woods
Call Number	099 bb	Cr
Author	100 1b	Cronin, Doreen, $e author.
Title	245 10	Duck for president / $c book by Doreen Cronin & Betsy Lewin.
Publisher	260 bb	[Norwalk, Conn.] : $b Weston Woods/Scholastic, $c ©2004.

(continued)

Table 9.2. *(continued)*

Field Label	MARC Field Tag and Indicators	Catalog Record Information with MARC Coding and ISBD Punctuation
Physical Description	300 bb	1 CD (11 min.) : $b digital ; $c 4 3/4 in. + $e 1 book (unpaged : illustrations. ; 26 cm.)
Content Type (Fundamental form of the communication) – RDA	336 bb	spoken word
Content Type (Fundamental form of the communication) – RDA	336 bb	text
Media Type (General type of intermediation, or, device required to view it) – RDA	337 bb	audio
Media Type (General type of intermediation, or, device required to view it) – RDA	337 bb	unmediated
Carrier Type (What it is on) – RDA	338 bb	audio disc
Carrier Type (What it is on) – RDA	338 bb	volume
Series	490 1b	Weston Woods ReadAlong CD
Edition and History Note	500 bb	Reading of the book published in 2004 by Atheneum Books for Young Readers (an imprint of Simon and Schuster).
Note	500 bb	Track one has story with page-turn signals ; track two has story with no signals.
Participant or Performer Note	511 0b	Narrated by Randy Travis.
Summary	520 bb	When Duck gets tired of working for Farmer Brown, his political ambition eventually leads to his being elected president.
Library of Congress Subject Heading	650 b0	Ducks $v Juvenile fiction.
Library of Congress Subject Heading	650 b0	Elections $v Juvenile fiction.
CYACP Library of Congress subject heading	650 b1	Ducks $v Fiction.
Genre Subject Heading	655 b7	Children's audiobooks. $2 lcgft
Author	700 1b	Travis, Randy, $e narrator.
Author	700 1b	Lewin, Betsy, $e illustrator.
Author	710 2b	Weston Woods Studios.
Series	830 b0	Weston Woods ReadAlong CD

2. Title (245 Field)

Because this is in RDA, there is no longer a GMD (subfield h) in the 245 field.

3. Publisher (260 Field)

Use the publisher of the CD/book combination in the publisher area, not the publisher of the book itself. It is not unusual for the place of publication on these items (and other AV items for that matter) to be missing. Do not substitute with the place of publication of the book. Instead, if you know the place because perhaps you sent away for the item directly from the publisher or you found it on the Internet, put the name of the place in brackets, which is what was done in this example.

4. Description (300 Field)

Notice that subfield $a contains "1 CD." This designation does not conform to actual RDA terminology, which is "1 audio disc." The Library of Congress recommends "1 CD" as an acceptable option. The value of using that designation is that it gives users a designation that is easily identifiable. They will know this is a "CD," without having to guess what "audio disc" means. Without "CD" in the 300 field, there is no other place in the record that indicates in a user-friendly way just what the format is.

5. Content Type, Media Type, and Carrier Type (336, 337, and 338 Fields)

In this case there are two separate items comprising this title. One is a CD, and the other is a book. The Library of Congress provides two options. Provide these fields for the item you believe is the main item in the set, or provide these fields in duplicate, one of each for each item. The example shows the second option, with the first of each pair of fields representing the CD.

6. Added Corporate Author (710 Field)

Weston Woods is a widely known company famous for transferring picture books to video format with a technique developed by Weston Woods founder Morton Schindel. Called the iconographic technique, it creates the impression that the pictures are moving through the use of panning and zooming a camera over the pages. The record for *Duck for President* is not for one of Weston Woods' films, but for one of its audio books. Weston Woods is usually included as an added entry for its publications because it is well known and teachers may ask for an item made by that company. In 1996 Weston Woods was sold to Scholastic.

For a call number, you could have:

Kit
Cr

(because there are two items, the book and the CD).

CD
Cr

AUDIOBOOK ON CD

Next is an RDA example of a children's book, *The Box-Car Children*, by Gertrude C. Warner, on CD. The physical book is not included. Figure 9.7 shows the CD container, and Table 9.4 is the RDA record.

Table 9.5 is the RDA record for another audiobook, *Alchemy and Meggy Swann*, by Karen Cushman.

1. Publisher (260 Field)

The date of publication is preceded by "p" instead of "c." This is the standard method of indicating copyright for recorded sound.

2. Description (300 Field)

In RDA the specific material designator is "audio disc," but it is acceptable to use "CD" instead (recommended by the Library of Congress).

Special Tidbit: Tracing Narrators

Always trace the narrators of audio books, because many of them are quite famous and readers will know them by name. They should go in the 700 field, which will make them searchable as authors.

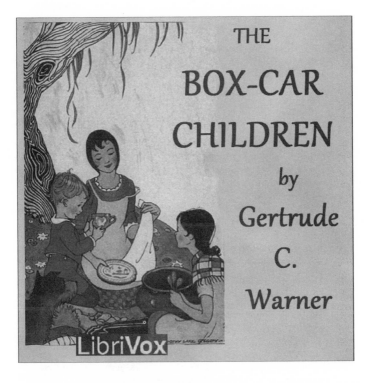

Four children: Henry, Jess Violet and Bennie. They are living alone in a stranded boxcar. They find items they need from the dump and a stray dog whom they name Watch. Henry earns money by working for a man named Dr. McAllister and his wife, Mrs. McAllister. But, while they are living their daily lives, little do they know that the McAllisters are watching their every move. (Summary by francesb)

Read by Librivox volunteers. Total running time: 2:42:33

Gertrude C. Warner

The Box-Car Children

The Box-Car Children

Gertrude C. Warner

This recording is in the public domain and may be reproduced, distributed, or modified without permission. For more information or to volunteer, visit **librivox.org**.
Cover picture from book. Copyright expired in U.S., Canada, EU. and all countries with author's life +70 yrs laws. Cover design by Annise. This design is in the public domain.

Figure 9.7.   Cover and Back of CD Container for *The Box-Car Children*, by Gertrude C. Warner

Table 9.4. RDA Record for *The Box-Car Children*, by Gertrude C. Warner, on CD

Call Number	099 bb	Wa
Author	100 1b	Warner, Gertrude Chandler, $d 1890–1979. $e author
Title	245 10	The box-car children
Publisher	260 bb	[Place of publication not identified] : $b LibriVox, , $c ℗2010.
Physical Description	300 bb	2 CDs (2 hr., 43 min.) ; $b digital ; $c 4 3/4 in.
Content Type (Fundamental form of the communication) – RDA	336 bb	spoken word
Media Type (General type of intermediation, or, device required to view it) – RDA	337 bb	audio
Carrier Type (What it is on) – RDA	338 bb	audio disc
General Note	500 bb	Title from container cover.
Edition and History Note	500 bb	Unabridged reading of the book published in 1924.
Participant or Performer Note	511 0b	Read by LibriVox volunteers.
Summary	520 bb	Four children living alone in an abandoned boxcar find items they need from the dump and earn a little money on their own.
Audience	521 bb	Ages 7-9.
Subject Heading	650 b0	Brothers and sisters $v Juvenile fiction.
Subject Heading	650 b0	Boxcar Children (Fictitious characters) $v Juvenile fiction.
Subject Heading	650 b0	Orphans $v Juvenile fiction.
Subject Heading	650 b1	Brothers and sisters $v Fiction.
Subject Heading	650 b1	Boxcar Children (Fictitious characters) $v Fiction.
CYACP Library of Congress Subject Heading	650 b1	Orphans $v Fiction.
Genre Subject Heading	655 b7	Audiobooks. $2 lcgft
Genre Subject Heading	655 b7	Children's audiobooks. $2 lcgft
Author	710 2b	LibriVox

Table 9.5.   RDA Record for *Alchemy and Meggy Swann*, by Karen Cushman

Field Label	MARC Field Tag and Indicators	Catalog Record Information with MARC Coding and ISBD Punctuation
MARC Code for Organizations/ Cataloging Source Codes	040 bb	DLC $c DLC $d mndueh
International Standard Book Number (ISBN)	020 bb	9780307710246
Publisher Number	028 00	A 1592A $b Listening Library
Call Number	099 bb	Cu
Author	100 1b	Cushman, Karen, $e author.
Title	245 10	Alchemy and Meggy Swann / $c Karen Cushman
Publisher	260 bb	New York : $b Listening Library, $c ℗2010.
Physical Description	300 bb	4 CDs (4 hr., 23 min.) ; $b digital ; $c 4 3/4 in.
Content Type (Fundamental form of the communication) – RDA	336 bb	spoken word
Media Type (General type of intermediation, or, device required to view it) – RDA	337 bb	audio
Carrier Type (What it is on) – RDA	338 bb	audio disc
General Note	500 bb	Title from disc surface
Edition and History Note	500 bb	Unabridged reading of the book published in 2010.
Participant or Performer Note	511 0b	Read by Katherine Kellgren.
Summary	520 bb	In 1573, the crippled, scorned, and destitute Meggy Swann goes to London, where she meets her father, an impoverished alchemist, and eventually discovers although her legs are bent and weak, she has many other strengths.
Audience	521 bb	Ages 9 to 14 (Container)
Subject Heading	650 b0	People with disabilities $v Juvenile fiction.
Subject Heading	650 b0	Alchemy $v Juvenile fiction.
Subject Heading	650 b0	Poverty $v Juvenile fiction.
Subject Heading	650 b0	Fathers and daughters $v Juvenile fiction.
Subject Heading	651 b0	London (England) $x History $y Elizabeth, 1558-1603 $v Juvenile fiction.
CYACP Library of Congress Subject Heading	650 b1	Great Britain $x History $y Elizabeth, 1558-1603 $v Juvenile fiction.
Genre Subject Heading	655 b7	Audiobooks. $2 lcgft
Genre Subject Heading	655 b7	Children's audiobooks. $2 lcgft
Author	700 1b	Kellgren, Katherine, $e narrator.
Author	710 2b	Listening Library.

PICTURE STORYBOOK AND CD

In this situation, the book is cataloged and the CD is an addition in the physical description area. This is different from *Duck for President*, in which the CD was the main item and the book was an addition in the physical description.

Table 9.6 is the RDA record for the book and CD *Puff, the Magic Dragon*.

PLAYAWAYS

"Playaway" refers to a listening device and the audio recording that is housed on it in electronic format. The user needs batteries and some kind of earphone to listen to the recording. It is small, lightweight, and easily carried around by the user. Playways are becoming increasingly popular. Figure 9.8 is an example of this physical format.

Figure 9.8.   A Playaway

Table 9.6. RDA Record for the Book and CD of *Puff, the Magic Dragon*

Field Label	MARC Field Tag and Indicators	Catalog Record Information with MARC Coding and ISBD Punctuation
MARC Code for Organizations/ Cataloging Source Codes	040 bb	DLC $c DLC $d mndueh
Library of Congress Control Number	010	2007002404
International Standard Book Number (ISBN)	020 bb	1402747829 : $c $16.95
Call Number	099	Yar
Author	100 1b	Yarrow, Peter, $d 1938- $e author.
Title	245 10	Puff, the magic dragon / Peter Yarrow, Lenny Lipton ; with paintings by Eric Puybaret
Publisher	260 bb	New York : $b Sterling, $c ©2007.
Physical Description	300 bb	[24] pages : $b color illustrations ; $c 28 x 30 cm. + 1 CD (4 3/4 in.)
Content Type (Fundamental form of the communication) – RDA	336 bb	text
Content Type (Fundamental form of the communication) – RDA	336 bb	performed music
Media Type (General type of intermediation, or, device required to view it) – RDA	337 bb	unmediated
Media Type (General type of intermediation, or, device required to view it) – RDA	337 bb	audio
Carrier Type (What it is on) – RDA	338 bb	volume
Carrier Type (What it is on) – RDA	338 bb	audio disc
General Note	500 bb	"Includes a four-song CD recorded by Peter Yarrow (of Peter, Paul & Mary) with Bethany & Rufus" – Cover. Inserted in envelope at back of book.
Summary Note	520 bb	The adventures of a boy and his dragon friend are recounted in this classic song from the 1960s.
Subject Heading	650 b0	Children's songs, English $z United States $v Texts.
CYACP Library of Congress Subject Heading	650 b1	Dragons $v Songs and music.
Author	700 1b	Lipton, Lenny, $d 1940- $e author.
Author	700 1b	Puybaret, Eric, $e illustrator.

As in DVD cataloging, there is practically no end to what can be included in a Playaway bibliographic record. Table 9.7 is the catalog record for *The Lost Hero*, by Rick Riordan, in RDA.

Table 9.7. RDA Record for the Playaway *The Lost Hero*, by Rick Riordan

Field Label	MARC Field Tag and Indicators	Catalog Record Information with MARC Coding and ISBD Punctuation
MARC Code for Organizations/ Cataloging Source Codes	040 bb	DLC $c DLC $d mndueh
International Standard Book Number (ISBN)	020 bb	9781616572501 : $c $74.99
Call Number	099 bb	Ri
Author	100 1b	Riordan, Rick, $e author
Title	245 10	The lost hero $h / $c Rick Riordan.
Edition	250 bb	Unabridged
Publisher	260 bb	Solon, Ohio : $b Playaway ; $b [Manufactured distributed by] Findaway World, LLC, $c [2010]
Physical Description	300 bb	1 Playaway (16.5 hours) : $b digital ; $c 3 3/8 in. x 2 1/8 in. **Alternatives to 1 Playaway:** 1 audio media player; 1 digital media player **Alternative size:** 8 1/2 x 5 1/2 cm.
Content Type (Fundamental form of the communication) – RDA	336 bb	spoken word
Media Type (General type of intermediation, or, device required to view it) – RDA	337 bb	audio
Carrier Type (What it is on) – RDA	338 bb	other
Series	490 1b	The Kane chronicles ; $v bk. 3
Note	500 bb	Title from Playaway label.
Note	500 bb	Requires headphone and one AAA battery for playback. Not supplied by library. **Alternative:** In container (8 x 5 x 1 in.) with headphone and one AAA battery required for playback.
Performer Note	511 0b	Narrated by Joshua Swanson
Summary Note	520 bb	Jason, Piper, and Leo, three students from a school for "bad kids," find themselves at Camp Half-Blood, where they

Field Label	MARC Field Tag and Indicators	Catalog Record Information with MARC Coding and ISBD Punctuation
		learn they are demigods and begin a quest to free Hera, imprisoned by Mother Earth.
Audience	**521**	Grades 3-6.
Library of Congress Subject Heading	**650 b0**	Mythology, Greek $v Juvenile fiction.
Library of Congress Subject Heading	**650 b0**	Camps $v Juvenile fiction.
Library of Congress Subject Heading	**650 b0**	Hera (Greek deity) $v Juvenile fiction.
Library of Congress Subject Heading	**650 b0**	Gaia (Greek deity) $v Juvenile fiction.
Library of Congress Subject Heading	**650 b1**	Monsters $v Juvenile fiction.
CYACP Library of Congress Subject Heading	**650 b1**	Mythology, Greek $v Fiction.
CYACP Library of Congress Subject Heading	**650 b1**	Camps $v Fiction.
CYACP Library of Congress Subject Heading	**650 b1**	Hera (Greek deity) $v Fiction.
CYACP Library of Congress Subject Heading	**650 b1**	Gaia (Greek deity) $v Fiction.
CYACP Library of Congress Subject Heading	**650 b1**	Monsters $v Fiction.
Genre Subject Heading	**655 b7**	Children's audiobooks. $2 lcgft
Genre Subject Heading	**655 b7**	Audiobooks. $2 lcgft
Author	**700 1b**	Swanson, Joshua, $d 1978- $e narrator.
Author	**710 2b**	Playaway Digital Audio.
Author	**710 2b**	Findaway World, LLC.
Series	**800 1b**	Riordan, Rick. $t . $t Heroes of Olympus ; $v bk. 1

CHILDREN'S MUSIC ON CD

In a children's collection you might have music CDs by the popular children's entertainer Raffi or other similar musicians and groups. Most of the time, the performer is the main entry, and there is a variety of songs on the CD. Sometimes the music might be written by one person and performed by another. In that case, the author is the main entry and the performer an added entry. If no particular performer or composer is apparent, then make it a title main entry. Figures 9.9–9.11 show a typical CD of children's music, this one by Canadian performer Jack Grunsky. Table 9.8 is the RDA record for the CD *Dancing Feet*.

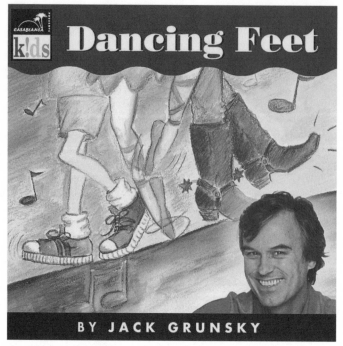

Figure 9.9. Container Cover for CD *Dancing Feet,* by Jack Grunsky

Figure 9.10. Back of Container Cover for CD *Dancing Feet,* by Jack Grunsky

Figure 9.11.   Disc Surface for CD *Dancing Feet,* by Jack Grunsky

1. Author (100 Field)

Grunsky is the performer. Possibly he also wrote the songs.

2. Title (245 Field)

The statement of responsibility comes from the disc surface.

3. Publisher (260 Field)

It is correct to use a "p" in front of the date for sound recordings. It indicates the copyright date of recorded sound.

4. Contents (505 field)

Notice how the record includes the running time of each song. Notice the spaces on either side of the "dash dash."

Table 9.8.   RDA Record for the CD Music Recording *Dancing Feet,* **by Jack Grunsky**

Field Label	MARC Field Tag and Indicators	Catalog Record Information with MARC Coding and ISBD Punctuation
Publisher Number	028 bb	CAS-CD-44009 $b Casablanca Kids
MARC Code for Organizations/ Cataloging Source Codes	040 bb	DLC $c DLC $d mndueh
Author:	100 1b	Grunsky, Jack.
Title	245 10	Dancing feet / $c Jack Grunsky.
Publisher	260 bb	Toronto : $b Casablanca Kids, $c ℗2004.
Description	300 bb	1 CD (36 min.) : $b digital ; $c 4 3/4 in.
Content Type (Fundamental form of the communication) – RDA	336 bb	performed music
Media Type (General type of intermediation, or, device required to view it) – RDA	337 bb	audio
Carrier Type (What it is on) – RDA	338 bb	audio disc
Contents Note	505 0b	Iko Iko (3:25) -- Cumbia cumbia (1:50) -- Carnival parade (3:18) -- Supermarket tango (2:38) -- Alligator stomp (2:34) -- Dance of the seasons (3:15) -- Dancing at the cactus flower (3:37) -- Mexican hat dance (1:37) -- Cha cha cha (2:46) -- Pyjamarama (3:14) -- La bamba (2:16) -- Do the dino rap (2:22) -- Sing & dance (3:48).
Genre Subject Heading	655 b7	Children's songs. $2 lcgft

Table 9.9 is another example of a music CD record in RDA, this time from a musical, *Rock Star*.

1. Title (245 Field)

This is a title main entry, because the item is a collection of songs sung by various musical groups.

2. Added Author (700 Field)

The various musical groups are traced as added corporate author entries.

Table 9.9.   RDA Record for Music CD *Rock Star*

Field Label	MARC Field Tag and Indicators	Catalog Record Information with MARC Coding and ISBD Punctuation
MARC Code for Organizations/ Cataloging Source Codes	040 bb	DLC $c DLC $d mndueh
Title	245 00	Rock star : $b music from the motion picture.
Publisher	260 bb	Los Angeles : $b Posthuman Records/Priority Records, $c ℗2001.
Description	300 bb	1 CD : $b digital ; $c 4 3/4 in.
Content Type (Fundamental form of the communication) – RDA	336 bb	performed music
Media Type (General type of intermediation, or, device required to view it) – RDA	337 bb	audio
Carrier Type (What it is on) – RDA	338 bb	audio disc
Contents	505 0b	Rock star / Everclear -- Into the life / Steel Dragon -- Wild side / Motley Crue -- We all die young / Steel Dragon -- Blood pollution / Steel Dragon -- Livin on a prayer / Bon Jovi -- Stand up / Steel Dragon -- Stranglehold / Ted Nugent -- Wasted generation / Steel Dragon -- Lick it up / Kiss -- Long live rock and roll / Steel Dragon -- Devil inside / INXS -- Colorful / The Verve Pipe -- Gotta have it / Trevor Rabin.
Performer Note	511 0b	Various performers.
Adult Library of Congress subject heading	650 b0	Motion picture music $v Excerpts
Genre Subject Heading	655 b7	Rock music. $2 lcgft
Author	700 1b	Nugent, Ted, $e performer.
Author	700 1b	Rabin, Trevor, $e performer.
Author	710 2b	Everclear (Musical group), $e performer.
Author	710 2b	Steel Dragon (Musical group), $e performer.
Author	710 2b	Mötley Crüe (Musical group), $e performer.
Author	710 2b	Bon Jovi (Musical group), $e performer.
Author	710 2b	Kiss (Musical group), $e performer.
Author	710 2b	INXS (Musical group), $e performer.
Author	710 2b	Verve Pipe (Musical group), $e performer.

Table 9.10 is an example of an RDA record for a music CD with a corporate main entry.

Table 9.10.   RDA Record for a Music CD with a Corporate Main Entry,
Singing Science

Field Label	MARC Field Tag and Indicators	Catalog Record Information with MARC Coding and ISBD Punctuation
MARC Code for Organizations/ Cataloging Source Codes	**040 bb**	DLC $c DLC $d mndueh
Author	**110 2b**	Tickle Tune Typhoon (Musical group), $e performer.
Title	**245 00**	Singing science / $c Tickle Tune Typhoon.
Publisher	**260 bb**	Seattle, WA : $b Tickle Tune Typhoon, $c ℗2000.
Description	**300 bb**	1 CD (48 min.) : $b digital ; $c 4 3/4 in.
Content Type (Fundamental form of the communication) – RDA	**336 bb**	performed music
Media Type (General type of intermediation, or, device required to view it) – RDA	**337 bb**	audio
Carrier Type (What it is on) – RDA	**338 bb**	audio disc
Note	**500 bb**	Children's songs about various scientific subjects with lyrics in container.
Contents	**505 0b**	Science is -- I am an insect -- Arachnids -- Ecology -- Backyard safari -- No backbone backbeat -- Home on the sea -- Ichthyology -- Blue mammal waltz -- Animals down under -- Night creatures -- Form follows function -- Everything grows -- Life in my cells -- That's botany -- Strange food -- Atom matter -- Elements – Weights and measures -- Planet jive -- Constellation cowboy -- Time -- This old bone -- Dirt -- Geography -- Rivers of the world -- Water goes 'round the world -- Ice rap – On into the Amazon -- Adding up the families -- Yes to the world.

Field Label	MARC Field Tag and Indicators	Catalog Record Information with MARC Coding and ISBD Punctuation
Credits Note	**508 bb**	Arranged and orchestrated by Nick Moore.
Performer Note	**511 0b**	Tickle Tune Typhoon is: Dennis Westphall, vocals, guitar ; Lorraine Bayes, vocals, autoharp ; Angie Bolton, vocals, percussion ; Richard Warner, saxophone, flutes ; Eric Chappelle, violin, mandolin ; with assisting musicians.
Genre Subject Heading	**655 b7**	Children's songs. $2 lcgft
CYACP Library of Congress Subject Heading	**650 b1**	Science $v Songs and music.
Author	**700 1b**	Moore, Nick, $e arranger of music.

DOWNLOADABLE AUDIOBOOKS

The downloadable audiobook is a relatively new format. While public libraries are leading the way in offering these to their users, many school libraries are now acquiring them as well. Vendors such as Overdrive and OneClickDigital provide materials for the K–12 audience.

The audiobook is downloadable from a library's website or catalog to the user's iPod, mp3 player, or other listening device. Some libraries do not catalog these items for integration into their OPACs, but rely on a separate listing provided by the vendor of the files.

Table 9.11 is the RDA catalog record for the downloadable audiobook *Splat the Cat Sings Flat*.

1. System Requirements (538 Field)

This field tells you that access to this book is via the Internet, which makes sense because this is a downloadable audiobook. The second 538 field tells the user what device is necessary and the file size.

2. Genre Subject Heading (655 Field)

By using this genre subject heading, you provide the user with a way to find all your downloadable audiobooks.

Table 9.11.   RDA Record for the Downloadable Audiobook *Splat the Cat Sings Flat*

Field Label	MARC Field Tag and Indicators	Catalog Record Information with MARC Coding and ISBD Punctuation
MARC Code for Organizations/ Cataloging Source Codes	040 bb	DLC $c DLC $d mndueh
ISBN	020 bb	97800621247222 (sound recording : OverDrive Audio Book)
Author	100 1b	Strathearn, Chris, $e author.
Title	245 10	Splat the cat sings flat / $c based on the creation of Rob Scotton ; [text by Chris Strathearn]
Edition	250 bb	Unabridged.
Publisher	260 bb	[New York] : $b HarperCollins, $c 2011.
Description	300 bb	1 sound file (7 min.) : $b digital
Series	490 1b	I can read! 1, Beginning reading
Content Type (Fundamental form of the communication) – RDA	336 bb	spoken word
Media Type (General type of intermediation, or, device required to view it) - RDA	337 bb	electronic
Carrier Type (What it is on) – RDA	338 bb	online resource
Note	500	Downloadable audio file.
Note	500	Title from: Overdrive title details screen.
Performer	511 0b	Read by Dan Bittner.
Summary	520 bb	Splat the cat is very nervous when his class prepares to sing on Parents' Night.
System Requirements	538 bb	Mode of access: World Wide Web.
System Requirements	538 bb	Requires OverDrive Media Console (WMA file size: 1548 KB; MP3 file size: 3068 KB)
Library of Congress Subject Heading	650 b0	Cats $v Juvenile fiction.
Library of Congress Subject Heading	650 b0	Schools $v Juvenile fiction.
Library of Congress Subject Heading	650 b0	Stage fright $v Juvenile fiction.
CYACP Library of Congress Subject Heading	650 b1	Cats $v Fiction.
CYACP Library of Congress Subject Heading	650 b1	Schools $v Fiction.
CYACP Library of Congress Subject Heading	650 b1	Stage fright $v Fiction.
Genre	655 b4	Downloadable audiobooks.
Author	700 1b	Scotton, Rob, $e author.
Author	700 1b	Bittner, Dan, $e narrator.
Series	830 b0	I can read book
Link to Resource	856 40	$u http://econtent.hclib.org/ ContentDetails.htm?ID=3D8B18BD- 6277-4764-B466-A485BBAEB3F2

Downloadable Audiobook (1) as Described by Vendor, (2) as It Is Coded in MARC

Figures 9.12 and 9.13 show an example of a downloadable audiobook, the cataloging for which appears in the library's OPAC but also is included in a separate listing from the vendor of all of the library's downloadable audiobooks.

Table 9.12 shows how *The Scorpio Races* would be coded in MARC for display in an OPAC. Notice how much better the subject access is in the MARC record, but how much more technical information is provided in the Overdrive record.

Special Tidbit: 856 Field

The 856 field contains the direct link to the electronic item. Depending on the screen display, this link could be anywhere. A button labeled "Connect Here" might be where this field is used.

DOWNLOADABLE E-BOOKS

Downloadable e-books are fast becoming very popular. These are books the user downloads to a reading device such as a Kindle, Nook, or NetLibrary eReader. Some libraries provide cataloging in the form of vendor-generated information available online to the user, as we have seen for downloadable audiobooks. Depending on the library's cataloging decisions, it may be necessary to search a file separate from the OPAC for any of these titles.

Current cataloging practice dictates that catalog records for e-books be "provider-neutral." This means that each record can be generic, or nonspecific in indicating the producer/distributor of the e-book or the type of reader to use to access it. The basic description is for the print version of the item, and the 300 field (physical description) is to show this: 1 online resource (meaning you retrieve it from the Internet) followed by (x, 278 pages), meaning that is the extent of the item.

Does this work for users, with no mention of the device or provider? This limited information will be puzzling to students looking for an e-book that is playable on a particular device. Some libraries agree with this evaluation of the situation and are providing additional fields relating to the device and publisher of the e-book.

Tables 9.13 and 9.14 are examples of such cataloging in RDA. The first one is for *Looking for Alaska*, by John Green. The second one is for *Colonies and Revolution*, by David C. King.

<u>Sample</u>
The Scorpio Races
by <u>Maggie Stiefvater</u>

<u>Steve West</u>
<u>Fiona Hardingham</u>

With her trademark lyricism, Maggie Stiefvater turns to a new world, where a pair are swept up in a daring, dangerous race across a cliff—with more than just their lives at stake should they...
More...

Available formats-
    OverDrive MP3 Audiobook
    OverDrive WMA Audiobook
Edition- Unabridged
Subjects-
    <u>Science Fiction & Fantasy</u>
    <u>Young Adult Fiction</u>
Copies-
    Available:

                        2

    Library copies:

                        2
Description-
    With her trademark lyricism, Maggie Stiefvater turns to a new world, where a pair are swept up in a daring, dangerous race across a cliff—with more than just their lives at stake should they lose.

Awards-
    <u>Amazing Audiobooks for Young Adults</u>
Young Adult Library Services Association
    <u>Best Fiction for Young Adults</u>
Young Adult Library Services Association
    <u>Michael L. Printz Award Honor Book</u>
American Library Association
    <u>Notable Children's Books</u>
Association for Library Service to Children
    <u>Odyssey Award Honor</u>
American Library Association

Figure 9.12. Overdrive Record (First Part) for *The Scorpio Races*, by Maggie Stief-vater. Display provided by the vendor, Overdrive.

Title Information-
Publisher

Scholastic Audio

OverDrive MP3 Audiobook

File size: 340698 KB
Number of parts: 10
Duration: 12 hours, 6 minutes
ISBN: 9780545357029
Release date:Oct 18, 2011

OverDrive WMA Audiobook

File size: 174050 KB
Number of parts: 10
Duration: 12 hours, 6 minutes
ISBN: 9780545357029
Release date: Oct 18, 2011

Digital Rights Information-
OverDrive MP3 Audiobook

Burn to CD: Permitted
Transfer to device: Permitted
Transfer to Apple® device: Permitted
Public performance: Not permitted
File-sharing: Not permitted
Peer-to-peer usage: Not permitted
All copies of this title, including those transferred to portable devices and other media, must be deleted/destroyed at the end of the lending period.

OverDrive WMA Audiobook

Burn to CD: Permitted
Transfer to device: Permitted
Transfer to Apple® device: Permitted
Public performance: Not permitted
File-sharing: Not permitted
Peer-to-peer usage: Not permitted
All copies of this title, including those transferred to portable devices and other media, must be deleted/destroyed at the end of the lending period.

Figure 9.13. Overdrive Record (Second Part) for *The Scorpio Races*, by Maggie Stiefvater. Display provided by the vendor, Overdrive.

Table 9.12.   MARC Coding of *The Scorpio Races* for Display in an OPAC

Field Label	MARC Field Tag and Indicators	Catalog Record Information with MARC Coding and ISBD Punctuation
MARC Code for Organizations/ Cataloging Source Codes	040 bb	DLC $c DLC $d mndueh
ISBN	020 bb	9780545448550 (electronic audio bk : OverDrive Audio Book)
Author	100 1b	Stiefvater, Maggie, $d 1981- $e author
Title	245 14	The Scorpio Races / $c Maggie Stiefvater.
Edition	250 bb	Unabridged
Publisher	260 bb	New York : $b Scholastic Audio, $c ℗2011.
Description	300 bb	1 sound file (12 hr.) : $b digital
Content Type (Fundamental form of the communication) – RDA	336 bb	spoken word
Media Type (General type of intermediation, or, device required to view it) – RDA	337 bb	electronic
Carrier Type (What it is on) – RDA	338 bb	online resource
Note	500 bb	Downloadable audio file.
Performer	511 0b	Read by Steve West and Fiona Hardingham.
Summary	520 bb	Nineteen-year-old returning champion Sean Kendrick competes against Puck Connolly, the first girl ever to ride in the annual Scorpio Races, both trying to keep hold of their dangerous water horses long enough to make it to the finish line.
System Requirements	538 bb	Mode of access: World Wide Web.
System Requirements	538 bb	Requires OverDrive Media Console (WMA file size: 1548 KB; MP3 file size: 3068 KB)
Library of Congress Subject Heading	650 b0	Racing $v Juvenile fiction.
Library of Congress Subject Heading	650 b0	Orphans $v Juvenile fiction.
Library of Congress Subject Heading	650 b0	Horses $v Juvenile fiction.
CYACP Library of Congress Subject Heading	650 b0	Racing $v Fiction.

Field Label	MARC Field Tag and Indicators	Catalog Record Information with MARC Coding and ISBD Punctuation
CYACP Library of Congress Subject Heading	650 b0	Orphans $v Fiction.
CYACP Library of Congress Subject Heading	650 b0	Horses $v Fiction.
CYACP Library of Congress Subject Heading	650 b0	Teenagers $v Fiction.
CYACP Library of Congress Subject Heading	650 b0	Interpersonal relations $v Fiction.
Genre Subject Heading	655 b7	Love stories. $2 lcgft
Genre Subject Heading	655 b7	Fantasy fiction. $2 lcgft
Genre Subject Heading	655 b4	Downloadable audiobooks.
Genre Subject Heading	655 b4	Audiobooks.
Genre Subject Heading	655 b4	Children's audiobooks.
Author	700 1b	West, Steve, $e narrator
Author	700 1b	Hardingham, Fiona, $e narrator
Author	710 2b	Scholastic Audiobooks.
Author	710 2b	OverDrive, Inc.
Link to Resource	856 40	$u http://econtent.hclib.org/ContentDetails.htm?ID=696CB506-57CC-4BCB-8171-D5FAE8E171C0

Table 9.13.   RDA Coding for Downloadable E-book *Looking for Alaska*, by John Green

Field Label	MARC Field Tag and Indicators	Catalog Record Information with MARC Coding and ISBD Punctuation
MARC Code for Organizations/ Cataloging Source Codes	040 bb	DLC $c DLC $d mndueh
ISBN	020 bb	9781429526999 (electronic)
Author	100 1b	Green, John $d 1977-
Title	245 10	Looking for Alaska : $b a novel / $c by John Green.
Edition	250 bb	Kindle edition
Publisher	260 bb	New York : $b Dutton, $c ©2005.
Description	300 bb	1 online resource (221 pages)
Content Type (Fundamental form of the communication) – RDA	336 bb	text
Media Type (General type of intermediation, or, device required to view it) – RDA	337 bb	electronic
Carrier Type (What it is on) – RDA	338 bb	online resource

(continued)

Table 9.13. *(continued)*

Field Label	MARC Field Tag and Indicators	Catalog Record Information with MARC Coding and ISBD Punctuation
Note	500 bb	Kindle eBook.
Summary	520 bb	Sixteen-year-old Miles' first year at Culver Creek Preparatory School in Alabama includes good friends and great pranks, but is defined by the search for answers about life and death after a fatal car crash.
System Requirements	538 bb	Requires Adobe digital editions software.
Awards Note	586 bb	Michael L. Printz Award for Excellence in Young Adult Literature, 2006.
Library of Congress Subject Heading	650 b0	Interpersonal relations $v Juvenile fiction.
Library of Congress Subject Heading	650 b0	Boarding schools $v Juvenile fiction.
Library of Congress Subject Heading	650 b0	Schools $v Juvenile fiction.
Library of Congress Subject Heading	650 b0	Death $v Juvenile fiction.
CYACP Library of Congress Subject Heading	650 b1	Interpersonal relations $v Fiction.
CYACP Library of Congress Subject Heading	650 b1	Boarding schools $v Fiction.
CYACP Library of Congress Subject Heading	650 b1	Schools $v Fiction.
CYACP Library of Congress Subject Heading	650 b1	Death $v Fiction.
Genre	655 b4	Downloadable books.
Genre	655 b4	Electronic books.
Genre	655 b4	Kindle ebooks.
Additional Physical Form	776 08	Print version: $t Looking for Alaska .$d New York : Dutton, 2005 $z 9780525475064

Table 9.14. RDA Coding for Downloadable E-book *Colonies and Revolution*, by David C. King

Field Label	MARC Field Tag and Indicators	Catalog Record Information with MARC Coding and ISBD Punctuation
MARC Code for Organizations/ Cataloging Source Codes	040 bb	DLC $c DLC $d mndueh
ISBN	020 bb	9780471443919 (electronic)
Author	100 1b	King, David C.
Title	245 10	Colonies and revolution / $c David King
Edition	250 bb	Netlibrary edition
Publisher	260 bb	Hoboken, N.J. : $c Wiley, $c 2003
Description	300 bb	1 online resource (ix, 134 pages : $b illustrations, map)
Series	490 1b	American heritage, American voices
Content Type (Fundamental form of the communication) – RDA	336 bb	text
Media Type (General type of intermediation, or, device required to view it) – RDA	337 bb	electronic
Carrier Type (What it is on) – RDA	338 bb	online resource
Bibliographical references note	504 bb	Includes bibliographical references (p. 129-131) and index.
Contents	505 0b	Colonizing a new world -- Daily life in colonial America -- Many people, many voices -- Prelude to revolution -- The American Revolution -- Creating a national government.
Summary	520 bb	Presents a picture of life in America prior to and during the American Revolution using excerpts from diaries, advertisements, court proceedings, speeches, and political documents of the day.
Reproduction note	533 bb	Electronic reproduction. Boulder, Colo. : $b NetLibrary, $d 2003. Available via World Wide Web to Netlibrary subscribers.
Library of Congress Subject Heading	651 b0	United States $x History $y Colonial period, ca. 1600-1775 $v Sources $v Juvenile literature.
CYACP Library of Congress Subject Heading	651 b1	United States $x History $y Colonial period, ca. 1600-1775 $v Sources.
Genre	655 b4	Electronic books.
Author	710 2b	Netlibrary, Inc.
Series	800 1b	King, David C. $t American heritage, American voices
Electronic access link	856 4b	$u http://www.netLibrary.com/urlapi.asp ?action=summary&v=1&book id=82046

OVERVIEW OF SOME MARC FIELDS RELATING TO ELECTRONIC FORMATS

Table 9.15 shows MARC fields applicable to electronic formats. For sample RDA records from OCLC, see Appendix B.

Table 9.15.   MARC Fields for Electronic Formats

Field and Indicators	Name	Function
250 bb	Edition statement	This field's content is varied. Sometimes it is used in the traditional sense, for example, "Unabridged edition," or "Second edition." Sometimes it is used to name the type of e-book reader, for example, "Netlibrary edition.
538 bb	System Details Note (Called Technical Details in MnPALS)	Kindle, Adobe Digital Editions, DVD, CD, World Wide Web. Any number of designations can go here.
776 08	Additional Physical Form	Use this to indicate bibliographic information for the original print version of the e-book being cataloged. This alerts your users to the fact that the item exists in both print and electronic formats. The indicators mean: • 1 = Display a note • 8 = No display constant. In other words, you must provide your own, such as "Print version:"
856 4b	Electronic Location	Contains the hotlink to the actual item. The first indicator "4" indicates the item is accessible via http.

SUMMARY

Only the most common nonprint materials being used in schools today were included in this chapter. AACR2 and RDA provide rules for cataloging many others, such as games, manipulatives, puppets, globes, pictures and photographs, toys, and microforms. The process of cataloging these materials can seem overwhelming, but deciding first which fields are the most important for your users and making a special effort to include these fields in your records will make the process and products relevant and, in the long run, affect resource discovery. Through both description and multiple access points, all stakeholders can be inspired to use these materials, which are powerful catalysts for student learning.

TEST YOUR BASIC KNOWLEDGE

Answer the questions below to solve the quotation puzzle. When you determine the answer (word) for the blank line in each statement, write it on the line. Then find that word in Table 9.16 (for Puzzle 1) and Table 9.17 (for Puzzle 2). Each word is paired with a word for the quotation. Place the paired words in the quotation puzzle on the corresponding numbered lines (e.g., the paired word for the answer to question 1 goes on line 1. in the quotation puzzle). In this way you can answer the questions and fill in the quotation simultaneously.

Puzzle 1

1. Another word for audiovisual is multi-media or _____.
2. With RDA, the _____ is gone.
3. If you include names of individuals in the statement of responsibility in DVD cataloging, they should be people with _____ _____ for the content.
4. The specific material designator for a DVD is _____, but LC prefers CD.
5. _____ _____ is extremely important in nonprint cataloging, because teachers are on a classroom schedule.
6. Recording the size of a DVD in _____ is not recommended by RDA, but is acceptable to the Library of Congress.
7. Credits, if not in the statement of responsibility, go in MARC field _____.
8. In the field 511, a first indicator of "1" generates this display constant: _____
9. Nonprint material catalog records should have a summary note (520), because you cannot _____ these materials like you can books.
10. The 538 field is used for the _____ of the video, be it cassette or DVD.
11. In the NTSC standard, 30 _____ are transmitted each second.
12. The fact that the DVD has closed captioning or subtitles for a foreign-language film goes in the _____ field.
13. A movie about organized crime could have Organized crime--_____ as a subject heading.
14. A subject heading for what something *is* instead of what it is *about* is called a _____ subject heading.
15. An item *about* the history of horror films could be given the _____ subject heading Horror films.
16. _____ in subfield "e" of a 655 field means the genre subject heading is from a new authority file at the Library of Congress.
17. Actors, directors, narrators, etc., in your cataloged movies can all be traced in the _____ field, or the added author field(s).
18. Weston Woods and Films for the Humanities are _____ companies that should be traced in the 710 field.

19. The 336 field in RDA is for _____ _____, which is *two-dimensional moving image* for DVDs.

20. Cherokee Legacy is a _____ title, or, in this case, a portion of the title.

21. The cataloging for a DVD in RDA will show the _____ in the 538 instead of the type of media (DVD).

22. RDA allows the cataloger to use the _____ _____ as the preferred source of information for the title field.

23. RDA terminology in the physical description area is "1 video disc," but the Library of Congress recommends "__ _____" as an acceptable option.

24. RDA records may have a new field for the publication, distribution, and manufacture area, field _____, rather than the earlier 260.

25. The publisher area in the RDA record for *Little Women* shows the _____ date of the film after the date of the DVD release.

26. In the notes field of a film adaptation of a novel, there should be a reference to the novel and its author. The author should also be _____ in a 700 field.

27. In the CD recording/book example *Duck for President*, the author and title information in the catalog record came from the disc label, not the _____ _____ of the book.

28. Regarding the place of publication of a CD/book combination, it is not _____ to not be able to find this information on the item.

29. The second 337 field in the RDA record for *Duck for President* is the media type for the _____.

30. *Puff, the Magic Dragon* shows the _____ as the main item, not the CD.

31. *Puff, the Magic Dragon* in RDA assigns the second of two 338 fields to the _____.

32. One type of listening device with an audio recording housed on it is the _____.

33. *The Lost Hero* is book number 3 in the _____ _____ series.

34. An _____ size for a playaway is 8 1/2 x 5 1/2 cm.

35. "Grades 3-6" is an _____ note.

36. "Not supplied by library" refers to _____.

37. Musical groups get a relationship designator of _____.

38. A downloadable audiobook is called a _____ file in RDA.

39. For most children's music collections on CD, the _____ is the main entry.

Quotation 1

1. _____ 2. _____ 3. _____ 4. _____
5. _____ 6. _____ 7. _____ 8. _____
9. _____ 10. _____ 11. _____
12. _____ 13. _____ 14. _____

15. _____   16. _____   17. _____
18. _____   19. _____   20. _____
21. _____   22. _____. 23. _____
24. _____   25. _____   26. _____
27. _____   28. _____   29. _____
30. _____   31. _____   32. _____
33. _____   34. _____   35. _____
36. _____   37. _____   38. _____
39. _____.—ACRL Visual Literacy Competency Standards for Higher Education

Table 9.16.

copyright = is	performer = forms	book = imagery	alternative = supplemental
variant = the	inches = visual	format = culture	disc = is
unusual = and	videodisc = images	Region = 21st	GMD = importance
508 = media	frames = is	production = literate	singer = information
700 = be	nonprint = The	content type = in	browse = contemporary
traced = highly	Drama = what	batteries = other	book = visual
major responsibility = of	title page = visual	546 = changing	Running time = and
topical = means	genre = it	Playaway = no	lcgft = to
264 = society	disc label = century	1 DVD = Today's	cast = in
Kane chronicles = longer	audience = to	sound = of	

Puzzle 2

1. Most of the time for collections of performed children's music, the _____ is the main entry.
2. The contents note for Jack Grunsky's *Dancing Feet* shows the _____ time of each song.
3. A copyright date for _____ _____ is preceded by ℗.
4. The dimension of the CD is given in _____ .
5. There is a _____ on either side of "- -" in the 505 field.
6. The music CD titled *Rock Star* has a title ____ _____ because many musical groups contributed to compilation.
7. The subfield "v" in Motion picture music -- Excerpts is a _____ subdivision.
8. There are many corporate added entries in this catalog record for the numerous _____ _____.
9. In the record for *Rock Star*, the "Fundamental form of communication" is _____ _____.

10. The record for *Singing Science* is an example of a collection of songs being assigned a _____ _____ _____.

11. Nick Moore is traced in this record because he arranged and _____ the music.

12. One vendor for the new downloadable audiobooks is _____.

13. Some libraries do not _____ records for audiobooks into their OPACs.

14. In the record for *Splat the Cat,* the field telling the user what kind of listening device is necessary and the file size is the _____.

15. The 856 field connects the user to the _____ audiobook.

16. The Overdrive record for *The Scorpio Races* shows that it is _____ to burn the text to a CD.

17. The Selco record for *The Scorpio Races* in the downloadable audio format shows no _____ _____, or physical description, such as paging.

18. In the MARC record the 856 field is at the end of the record, but could display _____ or take any form in the OPAC screen display.

19. Concerning cataloging practice for downloadable e-books, it is best not to adhere to the _____-_____ practice and include the type of reader the book will display on.

20. A catalog record for a downloadable e-book will display the _____ in the 300 field, which is different from a record for a downloadable audiobook, which has no 300 field.

21. The 250 field for *Looking for Alaska* and *Colonies and Revolution* gives information on what type of _____ the user will need to read these e-books.

22. The 776 field is used to alert the user that the e-book exists in an additional _____ form, most likely print.

Quotation 2

1. _____ 2. _____ 3. _____ 4. _____
5. _____ 6. _____ 7. _____ 8. _____
9. _____ 10. _____ 11. _____
12. _____ 13. _____ 14. _____
15. _____ 16. _____ 17. _____
18. _____ 19. _____ 20. _____
21. _____ 22. _____.—Author Unknown

Table 9.17.

main entry = way	Overdrive = theoretical	recorded sound = be	reader = the
provider-neutral = world	paging = outside	permissible = concepts	corporate main entry = connect
anywhere = a	performer = Film	space = interesting	physical = classroom

integrate = or	downloadable = course	orchestrated = sometimes	running = can
inches = an	form = for	300 field = to	musical groups = teachers
538 = abstract	performed music = to		

TEST YOUR CRITICAL THINKING

1. What are the advantages and disadvantages of having MARC records in your OPAC for downloadable audiobooks and e-books rather than relying on vendor-supplied non-MARC records?
2. Think about all the elements in a catalog record for a DVD. Which elements would you consider absolutely necessary for both the access and description needs of your users? Are there any you believe could be left out?

RESOURCES

Adamich, A. (2006). CE-MARC: The library educator's "receipt." *Knowledge Quest, 35*(1), 64–68.

Culbertson, B., Mandelstam, Y., & Prager, G. (2011, September). *Provider-neutral e-monograph MARC record guide.* Washington, DC: Program for Cooperative Cataloging.

DVD region code. (2012, September 20). Retrieved from: http://en.wikipedia.org/wiki/DVD_region_code.

International Historic Films. (2012). *What is NTSC and PAL standard?* Retrieved from: http://ihffilm.com/videostandard.html.

LC training for RDA: Resource description and access. (2012). *Module 2: Describing carriers and identifying works.* Retrieved from: http://www.loc.gov/catworkshop/RDA%20training%20materials/LC%20RDA%20Training/LC%20RDA%20course%20table.html.

Olson, N. B. (2008). *Cataloging of audiovisual materials and other special materials: A manual based on AACR2 and MARC 21* (5th ed.). Westport, CT: Libraries Unlimited.

10

Cataloging Books in Series

This chapter addresses the sometimes confusing arena of publications that are not complete in one physical item. They could be seen as the "gift that keeps on giving," but in reality they also present special problems and considerations for catalogers.

THE SERIAL

A serial is a publication that comes out at regular or irregular intervals. It retains the same title with each item, is issued in successive parts, and is intended to be continued indefinitely. Several types of publications fit this definition. Magazines, journals, yearbooks, and newspapers fall under the broad category of serial. A *semi-annual* serial is one that comes out twice a year. *Biannual* means the same thing. A *biennial* serial is one that comes out every two years.

The current trend in school libraries is for students to access journal and magazine articles via online subscription databases for class assignments, but magazines for leisure reading are often made available in print format. Typical print magazines in schools include a whole range of items for the K–12 schools, including *Cricket* and many others from the same publisher, *Sports Illustrated for Kids*, *Teen People*, *Teen Vogue*, *Seventeen*, and many others. High schools will have at least a few subscriptions to titles appropriate for all populations. You will seldom, if ever, have to catalog any of these items.

Serials cataloging, particularly for magazines, journals, and newspapers, is best left to the specialists in public, academic, and special libraries. Here we will look at typical monographs (books) that are published in series. One way of doing this is to consider them as two broad types.

SERIES TYPE 1: NONFICTION SERIES

A series is a group of separate titles related to one another through a common series title for every item in the group. The item in hand might be titled *Nine-Eleven: Attack on the World Trade Center*, but it could belong to a series titled Terrorists in the 20th Century. Each title receives a separate bibliographic record. Individual titles within series are often numbered, but they do not have to be. Their title and number, if there is one, should go in the 490 and 830 fields.

Table 10.1 is an RDA record for the individual title *Methamphetamine: The Dangers of Crystal Meth*, which is in the series Drug Abuse and Society.

SERIES TYPE 2: FICTION SERIES

Series Meant to be Read in a Particular Order

This refers to the popular fiction that follows a single character or group of characters and has a single story arc from book to book. The following cogent definition comes from Jen Robinson on PBS's *Booklights* blog (2009): "While there are, of course, multiple plot streams within each of these series, the books are meant to be read together, to tell a single, epic, story. Clues are planted in one book that are not explained until the end. There are sometimes major cliffhangers between books." Examples of this type are the Twilight series by Stephenie Meyer, the Inkhearts *s*eries by Cornelia Funke, and The Shadow Children series by Margaret Haddix.

Series Meant to Be Read as Episodic Tales

An episodic series could have many volumes, each meant to be read as a separate story. The same characters populate the stories, and each book presents a complete story. The books may be read out of order without confusing the reader (Robinson, 2009). Popular episodic series include Encyclopedia Brown and Junie B. Jones.

Formula vs. Literary Series

Looking at series another way, Van Orden and Strong (2007) define formula series and literary series as having the same character in several separate volumes, but in the formula series this character never grows or develops (Nancy Drew, Encyclopedia Brown, The Magic Tree House, Sweet Valley High, and some manga series are examples). Literary series, on the other hand, have three-dimensional characters who grow and possibly grow up. Such series include the Harry Potter books by J. K. Rowling, *The Hunger Games* by Suzanne Collins and its sequels, the Ramona books by Beverly Cleary, and the Diary of a Wimpy Kid series by Jeff Kinney.

Table 10.1. RDA Record for *Methamphetamine: The Dangers of Crystal Meth* in series Drug Abuse and Society

Field Label	MARC Field Tag and Indicators	Catalog Record Information with MARC Coding and ISBD Punctuation
ISBN	020 bb	9781404209121
Location	092 bb	362.29 Sp
Author	100 1b	Spalding, Frank, $e author
	245 10	Methamphetamine : $b the dangers of crystal meth / $c Frank Spalding.
Edition	250 bb	First edition
Publisher	260 bb	New York : $b Rosen, $c ©2007.
Description	300 bb	64 pages : $b illustrations (some color) ; $c 24 cm
Series	490 1b	Drug abuse and society
Content Type (Fundamental form of the communication)	336 bb	text
Media Type (General type of intermediation, or, device required to view it)	337 bb	unmediated
Carrier Type (What it is on)	338 bb	volume
Bibliography	504 bb	Includes bibliographical references (pages 57-62) and index.
Contents	505 0b	Meth : an addictive stimulant -- Users and pushers -- Human behavior and drug addiction -- Meth and the legal system -- Meth and society -- Meth and the media.
Summary	520 bb	Summary: Discussion of methamphetamine abuse and its social costs.
Adult Library of Congress subject heading	650 b0	Methamphetamine abuse $x Social aspects.
Adult Library of Congress subject heading	650 b0	Methamphetamine $x Social aspects.
CYACP Library of Congress Subject Heading	650 b1	Methamphetamine.
CYACP Library of Congress Subject Heading	650 b1	Drug abuse.
Series	830 b0	Drug abuse and society

HOW WILL YOUR USERS FIND THE
SERIES TITLES THEY WANT?

Bibliographic control of all these types of series can be problematic. Students may have a favorite series and ask for it by series name and number rather than the individual title. They may want to see the "next one" in the series and are not sure how to identify it. Think about those needs and requests as you catalog the individual items. Also understand your online catalog and its capabilities for dealing with the series fields. You may have to experiment a bit.

Once users get to the shelves, it would be helpful for them to see the volume numbers on the spines of each book. Position the volume number on a sticker or write it on the spine.

Table 10.2 is an RDA record for the series title Avalon High Coronation, with both the individual item title and series title together in the 245 field.

Meg Cabot has written a series of young adult fiction under the series title Avalon High Coronation. There are currently three volumes: *The Merlin Prophecy*, *Homecoming*, and *Hunter's Moon*. In the bibliographic record in Table 10.2 the title of the series was entered first in the 245 field, along with a subfield code "n" (number) of the item, in this case Volume 1. This is followed by subfield "p" (part) for the individual volume title, *The Merlin Prophecy*. There is no series statement (490), because it is the title proper in the bibliographic record.

Table 10.3 is an RDA record with the series title Avalon High Coronation in the 245 field and individual item titles in the contents note (505) and added title entries (740).

In this example, the series title is in the title proper field (245), and the individual titles are in the contents note. The individual titles are also traced in analytical added titles (740). The description field (300) shows an "open entry." The space in front of the lower case "v." is meant to be filled in with a number when the series is complete. If it is complete in five volumes, enter "5 v." Any time a new title comes into the collection, it must be added to the contents note and traced in a 740 field.

Notice the date in the Publisher field (260); it is 2007- . The hyphen means that the date of closure is still open. When the final volume in a series is acquired, the span of dates for the entire set is recorded in this manner: 2007-2013.

Table 10.4 is an RDA record with the individual item title *The Merlin Prophecy* in the 245 field and the series title in the 490 field.

In this example the title proper (245) is the individual volume title, *The Merlin Prophecy*. The series title is in the series statement (490) and traced in the 830 field. In this case it is an author/title series added entry. The subfield "t" ought to be searchable in a title search rather than exclusively in a keyword search.

Table 10.2.   RDA Record for the Series Avalon High Coronation (Book and Series Both in 245 Field)

Field Label	MARC Field Tag and Indicators	Catalog Record Information with MARC Coding and ISBD Punctuation
ISBN	020 bb	9780061177071
Location	099 bb	Fiction $a Cabot
Author	100 1b	Cabot, Meg, $e author
Title	245 10	Avalon High coronation. $n Volume 1, $p The Merlin prophecy / $c created and written by Meg Cabot ; illustrated by Jinky Coronado.
Alternate Title	246 30	Merlin prophecy
Publisher	260 bb	Los Angeles, CA : $b Tokyopop ; $a New York : $b HarperCollins, $c 2007.
Description	300 bb	107 pages ; $b chiefly illustrations ; $c 19 cm
Content Type (Fundamental form of the communication)	336 bb	text
Media Type (General type of intermediation, or, device required to view it)	337 bb	unmediated
Carrier Type (What it is on)	338 bb	volume
Audience Note	521 bb	Rated T for Teen, age 13+
Summary	520 bb	Ellie, the new student at Avalon High School, and her boyfriend, Will, wonder if their teacher Mr. Morton could be right that Will is the reincarnation of King Arthur--especially when Ellie begins having nightmares about Will's murderous brother, Marco.
LC Subject Heading	600 00	Arthur, $c King $v Comic books, strips, etc.
LC Subject Heading	650 0b	Reincarnation $v Comic books, strips, etc.
LC Subject Heading	650 0b	Prophecies $v Comic books, strips, etc.
Genre Heading	655 b7	Fantasy comic books, strips, etc. $2 lcgft
Genre Heading	655 b7	Graphic novels. $2 lcgft
Added Author	700 1b	Coronado, Jinky, $e illustrator

Table 10.3. RDA Record for the Series Avalon High Coronation (Only Series in 245 Field)

Field Label	MARC Field Tag and Indicators	Catalog Record Information with MARC Coding and ISBD Punctuation
ISBN	020 bb	9780061177075 (pbk. ; v. 1)
ISBN	020 bb	9780061177071 (pbk. : v. 1)
ISBN	020 bb	9780061177095 (pbk. ; v. 2)
Location	099 bb	Cabot
Author	100 1b	Cabot, Meg, $e author
Title	245 10	Avalon High coronation.
Publisher	260 bb	Los Angeles, CA : $b Tokyopop, $c 2007-
Description	300 bb	v. ; $b chiefly illustrations ; $c 19 cm
Content Type (Fundamental form of the communication)	336 bb	text
Media Type (General type of intermediation, or, device required to view it)	337 bb	unmediated
Carrier Type (What it is on)	338 bb	volume
General Note	500 bb	Illustrated by Jinky Coronado.
Audience Note	521 bb	Rated T for Teen, age 13+
Contents	505 0b	v. 1. Merlin prophecy -- v. 2. Homecoming.
LC Subject Heading	600 00	Arthur, $c King $v Comic books, strips, etc.
LC Subject Heading	650 0b	Reincarnation $v Comic books, strips, etc.
LC Subject Heading	650 0b	Prophecies $v Comic books, strips, etc.
Genre Heading	655 b7	Fantasy comic books, strips, etc. $2 lcgft
Genre Heading	655 b7	Graphic novels. $2 lcgft
Added Author	700 1b	Coronado, Jinky, $e illustrator
Added Title	740 42	The Merlin prophecy.
Added Title	740 02	Homecoming.

Table 10.4. RDA Record for Individual Item *The Merlin Prophecy* (Individual Item in 245 Field)

ISBN	020 bb	9781427801067 (pbk.)
Location	099 bb	Fiction $c Cabot
Author	100 1b	Cabot, Meg, $e author.
Title	245 14	The Merlin prophecy / $c created and written by Meg Cabot ; illustrated by Jinky Coronado & Larry Tuazon.
Publisher	260 bb	Los Angeles, CA : $b Tokyopop, $c 2007.
Description	300 bb	105 pages : $b chiefly illustrations ; $c 19 cm.
Series	490 1b	Avalon High coronation ; $v 1
Content Type (Fundamental form of the communication)	336 bb	text
Media Type (General type of intermediation, or, device required to view it)	337 bb	unmediated
Carrier Type (What it is on)	338 bb	volume
Summary	520 bb	Ellie, the new student at Avalon High School, and her boyfriend, Will, wonder if their teacher Mr. Morton could be right that Will is the reincarnation of King Arthur--especially when Ellie begins having nightmares about Will's murderous brother, Marco.
Audience Note	521 bb	Rated T for Teen, age 13+
Study Program	526 0b	Accelerated Reader $c 3.1
LC Subject Heading	600 00	Arthur, $c King $v Comic books, strips, etc.
LC Subject Heading	650 0b	Reincarnation $v Comic books, strips, etc.
LC Subject Heading	650 0b	Prophecies $v Comic books, strips, etc.
Genre Heading	655 b7	Fantasy comic books, strips, etc. $2 lcgft
Genre Heading	655 b7	Graphic novels. $2 lcgft
Added Author	700 1b	Coronado, Jinky, $e illustrator
Added Author	700 1b	Tuazon, Larry, $e illustrator
Series	830 b0	Cabot, Meg. $t Avalon High coronation ; $v 1

SUMMARY

There are several ways to handle series titles in your OPAC. It is especially important to make these popular titles accessible to students, because they love to read them and will seek them out. Consider the users' needs for access and the amount of time each of these bibliographic records would cost and make a decision based on a careful balance between the two.

TEST YOUR BASIC KNOWLEDGE

Answer the questions below to solve the quotation puzzle. When you determine the answer (word) for the blank line in each statement, write it on the line. Then find that word in Table 10.5. Each word is paired with a word for the quotation. Place the paired words in the quotation puzzle on the corresponding numbered lines (e.g., the paired word for the answer to question 1 goes on line 1. in the quotation puzzle). In this way you can answer the questions and fill in the quotation simultaneously.

Puzzle

1. A serial is a publication that comes out at regular or _____ intervals.
2. A serial that comes out once every two years is a _____.
3. A typical serial is a _____.
4. In media centers you will often find nonfiction series consisting of _____ titles all linked to one another through a common series title.
5. A literary series differs from a formula series in that its characters are more _____-_____ and exhibit growth.
6. Sweet Valley High is a _____ series.
7. It would be helpful to put a _____ on the spine of a series book with the volume number on it.
8. The first record for the Avalon High series traces *The Merlin Prophecy*, or the individual title in the series, as an _____ title.
9. The second record for the Avalon High series placed all the individual titles in a contents note and is an example of an _____ entry.
10. The title added entry for *The Merlin Prophecy* (740) has a first indicator "4," which designates the _____ characters in the title.
11. If the series is complete at five volumes, the subfield "a" in the 300 field will look like this: ___.
12. In the third record for the Avalon High series, the ____ field has an author/title added entry for accessing the series title.
13. There is no period after ___ because it precedes a series statement.
14. _____ and your students' needs must be balanced when considering how to handle series books.

Quotation

1. _____ 2. _____ 3. _____ 4. _____
5. _____ 6. _____ 7. _____ 8. _____
9. _____ 10. _____ 11. _____
12. _____ 13._____ 14. _____.

—Jane Smiley

Table 10.5.

nonfiling = mere	sticker = better	separate = among	open = the
three-dimensional = them	830 = of	formula = feel	biennial = people
cm = a	irregular = Many	alternate = at	5 v. = sight
newspaper = myself	Time = book		

TEST YOUR CRITICAL THINKING

Identify several series that are popular with students, determine how you would catalog them, and explain why you chose a particular approach for each.

RESOURCES

Robinson, J. (2009, September 7). Two types of series books. In *Booklights* [blog]. PBS. http://www.pbs.org/parents/booklights/archives/2009/09/two-types-of-series-books.html.
Van Orden, P., & Strong, S. (2007). *Children's books: A practical guide to selection.* New York: Neal-Schuman.

III

SUBJECT CATALOGING
AND CLASSIFICATION

11

Using *Sears List of Subject Headings*

Besides main and added entry access, it is necessary to assign one or more subject headings to an item so users can locate material according to its content in addition to its authors. This chapter covers *Sears List of Subject Headings*, the subject authority commonly used in school and small public libraries. It operates by a few easily understood principles explained in one volume, which is not nearly as overwhelming as the 2012 six-volume set of the *Library of Congress Subject Headings* or its latest incarnation as a pdf document available online. Both LCSH and Sears subject headings are "controlled languages," or systematically compiled lists of terms that, when applied, provide consistency and comprehensiveness in retrieval.

There are a number of differences between Sears and LCSH:

- Sears is not intended to be a comprehensive list, but rather a list of those topics most commonly seen in small public and school libraries.
- Sears is updated every three years, whereas LCSH comes out annually.
- Sears uses simpler, broader, less technical, and less specialist-oriented language than does LCSH.
- Sears uses fewer subdivisions with its subject headings than does LCSH.

The first edition of Sears (originally called *List of Subject Headings for Small Libraries: Compiled From Lists Used in Nine Representative Small Libraries*) was published in 1923 (*Bulletin of Bibliography*, 1923). Minnie Earl Sears was the leading force in this endeavor, and beginning with the 1950 edition (sixth), these subject headings bear her name. Today Sears is available to users online through Ebsco, a commercial database provider, and in print format. For a detailed and highly readable history of Sears, see Satija and Haynes (2008).

CONTROLLED LANGUAGE VS.
NATURAL LANGUAGE (KEYWORD SEARCHING)

Although there are journal article databases that do not have controlled language subject headings applied to them, you will never find an online catalog that does not use a controlled language. Databases without a controlled language are often said to use "natural language." In other words, the user plugs in whatever word comes to mind, and the system looks through the database for records with that word. Using this kind of unreliable system, users would never know if they had found everything on their chosen topic residing in the database, because there is no consistent gathering point (controlled subject heading) for all the records on that particular topic.

WHY IS IT NECESSARY TO USE A
SUBJECT HEADINGS AUTHORITY FILE?

The reason to use a subject headings "authority file" such as Sears is to maintain uniformity in subject access. Inconsistencies caused by using one term at one time and a different term to describe the same thing at a later time result in a poor discovery tool. For example, a book on the war in Vietnam is given the subject heading Vietnam War, 1961-1975 not Vietnamese War or Vietnamese Conflict. The same principle works here as with name authority work. Pick a form and stick to it.

MARC CODING

Subject heading fields in MARC records are 600s (600, 650, 651). How can you tell which 6XXs are for adults, which are for children from the CYACP, and which are from Sears? Look at the second indicator. The first indicator on each of these is "blank." The second indicator tells you what kind of subject heading it is:

- An adult LC subject heading will have a "0." CYACP subject headings will have a "1." Sears subject headings will have a "7," and there will be a subfield $2 that will have the name of the subject heading authority in it, in this case: Sears.
- The Library of Congress does not assign Sears subject headings, but other cataloging agencies will. Your vendor may supply Sears subject headings in your catalog records and should assign a second indicator of "7" and specify the source (Sears). A second indicator of "4" might be used instead, meaning the source is not specified.

MARC Tags, Indicators, and Subfield Codes for Subject Headings

1. **600 10 Library of Congress Personal Name Subject Heading,** such as

   600 10 $a Shakespeare, William, $d 1564-1616.

   The first indicator in the 600 field is not blank, as it is in the 650. A first indicator of "1" means that this is a personal surname. The second indicator is "0," which means Library of Congress subject heading.

2. **600 11 CYACP Personal Name Subject Heading.** If the Shakespeare heading were assigned in the CYACP, it would be 600 11. The first "1" means this is a personal surname; the second "1," which is the second indicator, means this personal name subject heading is from the CYACP and is suitable for children's catalogs. For example:

   600 11 Shakespeare, William, $d 1564-1616.

3. **650 b0 Library of Congress Topical Subject Heading.** These are such things as Dogs, Folklore, and Teenagers. The first indicator is blank; the second indicator is "0," which means Library of Congress topical subject heading (for adults). For example:

   650 b0 Dogs

4. **650 b1 CYACP Topical Subject Heading.** Notice the difference in the indicators. The second indicator "1" means this is a subject heading from the CYACP. For example:

   650 b1 Extreme sports

5. **651 b0 Library of Congress Geographic Subject Headings.** These are such things as Duluth (Minn.) or United States -- History -- Civil War, 1861-1865 -- Fiction. These are adult geographic subject headings. The second indicator is "0." For example:

   651 b0 United States $x History $y Civil War, 1861-1865 $v Fiction

   Subfield $v is for form subdivisions.
   Subfield $x is for general subdivisions.
   Subfield $y is for chronological subdivisions.
   Subfield $z is for geographical subdivisions.

6. **651 b1 CYACP Geographic Subject Headings.** If the subject heading were 651 b1, that would mean it is a CYACP subject heading. For example:

   651 b1 Duluth (Minn.)

ASSIGNING SEARS SUBJECT HEADINGS

Sears consists of two parts, an introduction that explains the principles of assigning subject headings, and the alphabetical listing of the subject headings. The section on the principles is invaluable. At first glance it may look like a lot to wade through, but this clearly written guide is well worth your time. Giving practical advice on all aspects of assigning subject headings, it makes a seemingly complex endeavor crystal clear. Table 11.1 is intended to set forth this same information in a visually accessible format, but the information can easily be comprehended by reading the Sears introduction carefully. It is inadvisable to attempt to apply Sears without first thoroughly understanding the principles set forth in the introduction. It is not necessary to memorize all the subject headings and their permutations. There are prompts everywhere in Sears about what to do in every case. Learn to read the fine print at each entry in Sears.

Sears subject headings tend to be expressed in simple language. Many are single nouns such as **Health** or **Plants**. A large number are two-word phrases such as **Human rights** or **Hazardous wastes**. There are also multiword phrases such as **Violence in mass media**. If a word or phrase has more than one meaning, parenthetical qualifiers are added to distinguish between them. **Depression (Psychology)** is used to distinguish it from **Depressions**, which is used for economic depression. Over the years revisions have been undertaken to neutralize racial and gender bias in the terminology (e.g., Negro changed to African Americans, Indians of North America changed to Native Americans, and Firemen to Fire fighters), and a Christian bias has been reduced.

Catalogers cannot rely solely on the title of the book when determining what the book (or other media) is about. The title may, on the surface, seem to indicate what the book is about, but it could be misleading. A book titled *Indians of the Plains* may not be as general as it sounds, because the book may specifically focus on the Ojibwa. It is necessary to open the book and look at it to determine precisely what it is about. The foreword, the table of contents, and the body of the work will all give clues as to its "aboutness" and how broad or narrow its scope is. Subject analysis with Sears and classification with Dewey Decimal numbers are closely related. Both indicate what the item is "about." But while there can be several subject headings for any one item, it is impossible for the item to shelve in more than one place. Consequently, it can have only one classification number attached to it as long as the classification has to serve as a shelving device.

Sears does not specifically name all possible headings that can be used. Given the vastness of human knowledge, that would be impossible. What it does instead is apply patterns and examples that allow the cataloger to add needed new headings that are not specifically in Sears. Furthermore, Sears is constantly revising and updating its subject headings to conform to the latest trends in many areas, most particularly in the areas of computers, personal relations, politics, and popular culture. Subject headings are removed if they represent topics of little interest to the current public. In each new edition of Sears there is a list of canceled headings and new terms taking the place of old terms.

After determining what the item is about, fit that "aboutness" to the vocabulary and principles of Sears. In order to do a consistent and professional job, it is necessary to know the big picture of how Sears works. Knowing that you can assign a specific subject heading, such as "Apples," when all you can find in Sears is "Fruit," and that you can assign a subdivision such as -- History, or -- Economic conditions to any named city, is enormously useful and will make your job much easier. Again, the introductory section in Sears clearly explains such principles.

Another principle is specificity. A subject heading should be as specific as possible. A book on cats should receive Cats as a subject heading, not Mammals or Zoology. What if all your books on cats as pets gathered under Mammals along with all the other books on various kinds of mammals? Finding everything the library has specifically on cats would be quite a chore. While Sears recommends that you not assign both a specific and a general subject heading, in school libraries assigning both can actually be helpful for the child catalog user. The Children's and Young Adults' Cataloging Program has a policy called Standard Second Headings for CYAC Records. After assigning the most specific subject heading possible, when appropriate the cataloger also assigns a broader subject heading to accommodate children's searching habits. This now applies only to fiction, which can have nonfiction-type subject headings followed by -- Fiction, since the CYAC is not assigning subject headings to nonfiction.

Choosing the number of subject headings to assign and determining whether they should be general or specific or a combination of both are professional decisions the school librarian will have to make (or the vendor will make those decisions). Standard practice guidelines suggest that no more than three subject headings be assigned, but in today's OPAC environment, assigning more does not entail a lot of extra work, nor do additional headings consume too much storage space. Above all else, know your collection, know your users, and do not hesitate to assign a subject heading you know will help them discover a useful resource even if it does not seem to follow Sears principles precisely.

Note also that every subject heading is accompanied by one or more Dewey Decimal Classification numbers from Abridged Dewey. These are meant to be used as a guide only and are not to be relied upon for all classification needs. While it may be a good starting point, consult the schedules and tables of Dewey itself before making the final decision about a classification number.

Figure 11.1 is a typical page from Sears. Notice that some items are in boldface print and others in regular print, and there are abbreviations in various positions on the page (BT, NT, and UF). There are also dashes embedded in some subject headings (Women -- Health and hygiene). These features and Sears principles are explained in the table of information following the figure.

Hazardous substances—*Continued*
    Inflammable substances
    Toxic substances
  BT Materials
  NT Hazardous wastes
    Poisons and poisoning
Hazardous substances—Transportation
    363.17; 604.7
  BT Transportation
Hazardous waste disposal
  USE Hazardous wastes
Hazardous waste sites (May subdiv.
    geog.) 363.72; 628.4
  UF Chemical landfills
    Dumps, Toxic
    Toxic dumps
  BT Landfills
  NT Love Canal Chemical Waste
    Landfill (Niagara Falls,
    N.Y.)
Hazardous wastes 363.72
  UF Hazardous waste disposal
    Toxic wastes
    Wastes, Hazardous
  BT Hazardous substances
    Industrial waste
    Refuse and refuse disposal
  RT Medical wastes
    Pollution
HDTV (Television)
  USE High definition television
Head 611; 612
  BT Anatomy
  NT Brain
    Ear
    Eye
    Face
    Hair
    Mouth
    Nose
    Phrenology
    Teeth
Head pain
  USE Headache
Headache 616.8
  UF Head pain
  BT Pain
  NT Migraine
Heads of state (May subdiv. geog.)
    352.23; 920
  UF Rulers
    State, Heads of

  SA names of individual heads of
    state [to be added as needed]
  BT Executive power
    Statesmen
  NT Dictators
    Kings and rulers
    Presidents
Healing 615.5
  BT Therapeutics
Healing, Mental
  USE Mental healing
Healing, Spiritual
  USE Spiritual healing
Health 613
  Use for materials on physical, mental, and
  social well-being. Materials on personal body
  care are entered under Hygiene.
  UF Personal health
  SA parts of the body with the sub-
    division *Care*, e.g. Foot—
    Care; classes of persons and
    ethnic groups with the subdi-
    vision *Health and hygiene*,
    e.g. Women—Health and
    hygiene; and subjects and
    names of wars with the sub-
    division *Health aspects*, e.g.
    World War, 1939-1945—
    Health aspects [to be added
    as needed]
  BT Medicine
    Physiology
    Preventive medicine
  NT Children—Health and hygiene
    Diet
    Elderly—Health and hygiene
    Exercise
    Health education
    Health self-care
    Infants—Health and hygiene
    Mental health
    Nutrition
    Physical fitness
    Public health
    Rest
    Sleep
    Stress management
    Women—Health and hygiene
  RT Diseases
    Holistic medicine
    Hygiene

Figure 11.1.   Sample Page From *Sears List of Subject Headings*

GUIDE TO BASIC CONCEPTS OF SEARS

Table 11.1 lists the basic concepts of Sears.

Table 11.1. Basic Concepts of Sears

Scope notes	These are explanatory notes that delineate the meaning of the subject heading. One type starts with the words "Use for" followed by a definition of the subject. (**Inner cities**. Use for materials on the densely populated, economically depressed, central areas of large cities) The second type is a definition of the subject coverage of one heading, followed by a distinction between it and another closely related heading (**Protestant churches**. Use for materials on Protestant denominations treated collectively. Works on Protestant church buildings are entered under **Church buildings**).
Boldface vs. light (regular) text	Any word or group of words in **boldface print** is an authorized subject heading. The other items in lighter print are not authorized.
Subdivisions within subject headings	Subject headings frequently consist of a main word or word followed by a subdivision that consists of another word or words. Between the main word(s) and subdivision(s) are two dashes that look like this -- (dash, dash, OR hyphen, hyphen); for example, **American poetry -- Collections**. There is an alphabetical list of all subdivisions in the preliminary material of Sears. Also, within the main body of Sears you can look up the subdivision and find instructions on how to apply it.
Parenthetical qualifiers are used to distinguish between synonyms.	**Stress (Psychology)** is one subject heading, and **Stress (Physiology)** is another.
Some concepts are conveyed in a phrase heading.	Examples of these are: **"Arts and crafts movement," "Urban sociology,"** and **"Life on other planets."**

(continued)

Table 11.1. *(continued)*

Capitalization in the Sears subject headings is based on capitalization rules in AACR2.	The first word and proper nouns are capitalized in the main heading and any subdivisions. In a parenthetical subject heading, the first word of the subject heading and the first word of the parenthetical words are capitalized.
Sears and the Dewey Decimal System	Sears displays suggest Abridged Dewey classification numbers for all subjects. Look for these classification numbers in boldface print. This is not meant to be a substitute for the actual Dewey volume, but as a pointer to classification numbers in Dewey. The intent is that the cataloger will check the number in the Dewey before assigning it.
Sears says to use the most specific word possible to describe your subject. If the book is on Penguins, use that word, not Birds or Water birds.	In children's libraries, it is helpful to use both a general and a specific heading, and this is often done. For example, if a book is about **Monarch butterflies**, Sears would authorize that specific name as a subject heading. It would be a good idea to also use the subject heading **Butterflies**. The subject tracings in a MARC record would look like this: 650 b7 Monarch butterflies. 650 b7 Butterflies. If the book is about the Ojibwa Indians, first assign a subject heading for that specific tribe. It would be a good idea to add a second subject heading for Native Americans. (This used to be "Indians of North America," and that is what you will find in older editions of Sears.) These would be the subject headings: 650 b7 Ojibwa Indians. 650 b7 Native Americans. It is not necessary to do this in all cases, but think about the collection and your users and apply this if it would be helpful.

Materials about literature	These are assigned subject heading such as Poetry, Drama, and Fiction. A book about the history of poetry would be under **Poetry -- History and criticism**. A book about writing plays would be under **Drama -- Technique**.
Literature from a particular country	If the literature is focused on one nationality, that nationality is the entry point for the subject heading. For example, a book about the art and technique of Russian fiction would have **Russian fiction** as the subject heading. A history of Italian poetry would have **Italian poetry -- History and criticism** as its subject heading. Nationality trumps anything else.
Literary form headings	Literary form headings for *some* literary forms, such as Fiction, Poetry, Drama, and Essays, are used for collections of items in those formats, but not for works in those formats by individual authors. A collection of poetry by one American poet *does not* have Poetry as a subject heading: for example, a collection of poems by Jack Kerouac *does not* get Poetry or Poetry -- Collections as a subject heading. It does not get any subject heading at all. A collection of plays by one playwright does not get any subject heading at all. A collection of poems by many poets from around the world gets **Poetry -- Collections** as a subject heading. A collection of poems by many American poets gets **American poetry -- Collections** as a subject heading. A collection of plays by many American playwrights gets the subject heading **American drama -- Collections**. Again, nationality is the most important element.
Short stories	Short stories. Do not use the subdivision -- Collections. Use only **Short stories**. Even if the book is a collection by only one author, you may assign the subject heading "Short stories."

(continued)

Table 11.1. (*continued*)

Fiction as subdivision	Many works of fiction deal with real events or physical items. The subdivision **Fiction** following the topical subject heading is authorized. For example, it would be fine to give the following subject heading to *Gone With the Wind*:
	United States -- History -- 1861-1865, Civil War -- Fiction
	The first part of that subject heading is the authorized subject heading for the American Civil War. The last part, or Fiction, tells you that this is a work of fiction about that event in American history.
	Another example: The work of fiction titled *Watership Down* could receive a subject heading **Rabbits -- Fiction**.
Geographic subdivisions	A common subdivision of subject headings is a geographic location. For example, if the book is on Agriculture in Texas, the subject heading is **Agriculture -- Texas**. You are tipped off to that situation right at the subject heading of Agriculture in Sears. It says Agriculture (may subdiv. geog.). The instruction, "may subdiv. geog." is used throughout Sears. It means "may subdivide geographically," if the situation calls for it.
Geographic place subdivided by subject	Some situations call for the name of the place (the geographic area) to be subdivided by the subject. This is the exact opposite of subject subdivided by place.
	If your book is on the climate in Alaska, first look up Climate. Here you will find a reference that says **SA** (this stands for SEE ALSO) **names of countries, cities, etc. with the subdivision Climate [to be added as needed]**.
	So your subject heading will be **Alaska -- Climate**, not **Climate -- Alaska**.
Biography	If the book is about a famous person (is either a biography or autobiography), use that person's name as the subject heading. Determine the form of the name by using the Library of Congress name authority file. Do not add -- Biography.

Nonbook materials	Nonbook materials (audiovisual items) follow the same principles as above and should not include form subdivisions. For example, *do not* enter a DVD on birds like this: **Birds -- DVDs**. Just **Birds** will do.
Form subdivisions	Standard terms known as "form subdivisions" may be added to any subject heading where the use of such a subdivision is appropriate. Five frequently used form subdivisions are

Dictionaries
Pictorial works
Fiction
Biography
Bibliography

For example, a subject heading for a book on Jazz music would look like this: **Jazz music**. If it were a dictionary of terms relating to Jazz music, it would look like this: **Jazz music -- Dictionaries**. The introduction to Sears has a list of the form subdivisions.

History of countries

The subject heading for the history of any country starts with the name of the country. Following that name is -- History. Then, *depending on the amount of detailed breakdown* in that country's history that the authors of *Sears* felt was needed, there may be other subdivisions. For example, the history of the colonial period of American history is this:

United States -- History -- 1600-1775, Colonial period.

NOTE: "American History" will be found under "United States" in Sears.

Here is another example, this one from the history of France. *Sears* authorizes:

France -- History -- 1589-1789, Bourbons.

Sears was constructed based on the idea that it would be used in small public libraries and schools. Therefore, it *does not provide detailed breakdown* for the history of some countries. LCSH, on the other hand, has a very detailed breakdown for many countries, because that level of differentiation would be needed in libraries with large, diverse collections.

(*continued*)

Table 11.1. (*continued*)

If the country for which you need a subject heading is not listed in Sears, you are authorized to create a subject heading for it yourself, but with no breakdown. So, for example, the colonial history of Brazil (which is not listed in Sears) would just be **Brazil -- History.

Follow this procedure: Once you determine that you have a book on some aspect of the history of a country,

- Start in Sears by looking up the name of the country.
- If you don't find it, you're authorized to use Name of Country -- History, and that's all. (Brazil -- History)
- If you do find the country name in Sears, check for the detailed breakdown of the history of the country and choose the one that *most closely matches* the item you have.

Extremely Important:** Students learning cataloging want to match the wording of the title of a book to the wording of the subject heading subdivision. For example, if a book is called *Colonial America Between the Years 1640 and 1690*, students want to substitute those dates for the dates in the authorized subject heading subdivision. That is incorrect. It is correct to use the subject heading and the historical subdivision just as you find it in Sears, no matter what the precise title of the book is. Use a subdivision that most closely matches (not perfectly matches) the historical content of the book.

Headings to be added by the cataloger

Find the section in the front material titled "Headings to Be Added by the Cataloger." This is a list of categories that will evoke specific names. You are being authorized here to use specific names for items that fall into any of those categories. These are specific names that are not listed in the body of the Sears book because they would take up too much space. Examples of these are:

Names of persons
Names of places

Names of wars and battles
Names of Indian peoples
Names of hotels, shops, ships, etc.
Names from categories such as animals, birds, fish, games, fruit, trees, vegetables
Names of diseases
Names of minerals

For example, if you need a subject heading for a disease not listed in Sears, you are authorized to establish the subject heading yourself. For example, **Lupus**.

As another example, if you need a subject heading for sunfish, but do not find sunfish listed in Sears, you are authorized to establish the subject heading yourself, because "fish" is one of the categories. **Sunfish**

As another example, if you need a subject heading for any individual person, you are authorized to establish a heading for that person's name (keeping in mind the rules for constructing a form of entry). So, if you have a DVD about Thomas Jefferson, you are authorized to make a subject heading for his name: **Jefferson, Thomas, 1743-1826**.

Key headings; Key headings for the president

Now find the section in the introductory material titled "'Key' Headings."

This is a difficult concept for students, but it is very useful and important. The **subdivisions** following these subject headings in the main body of Sears apply to specific cases of these general categories.

1. **Presidents -- United States.** Use this to find the correct subdivisions for materials about any individual president.
2. **Shakespeare, William, 1564-1616.** Use this to find the correct subdivisions for materials about any famous author.
3. **Native Americans.** Use this to find the correct subdivisions for materials about any individual Indian tribe.
4. **United States.** Use this for subdivisions for other countries *except* for the historical subdivisions that obviously must be country specific.

(*continued*)

Table 11.1. *(continued)*

5. **Ohio.** Use this to find the correct subdivisions for materials about any U.S. state.
6. **Chicago (Ill.).** Use this to find the correct subdivisions for materials about any U.S. city.
7. **English language.** Use this to find the correct subdivisions for materials about any language.
8. **English literature.** Use this to find the correct subdivisions for materials about any world literature.
9. **World War, 1939-1945.** Use this to find the correct subdivisions for materials about any war.

Examples:

A. Presidents -- United States. Look this up in Sears. Notice that there is a rather lengthy list at Presidents -- United States, all with different subdivisions.

Here's how this works: If you have a book or video about an aspect of all the presidents (as found in the subdivisions, such as Assassination or Children), your subject heading would be: **Presidents -- United States -- Assassination** or **Presidents -- United States -- Children**.

Now note that every subdivision (such as -- Assassination and -- Children) can be used when needed with individual presidents' names. So if the book is on the assassination of John F. Kennedy, you are authorized to use Assassination as a subdivision after his name, like this:

Kennedy, John F. (John Fitzgerald), 1917-1963 -- Assassination

Note that this subject heading starts with the president's last name. So it is not Presidents -- United States -- Kennedy, John F. (John Fitzgerald), 1917-1963, it is Kennedy, John F. (John Fitzgerald), 1917-1963 -- Assassination.

For a book about Kennedy's children, the subdivision Children is authorized, like this:

Kennedy, John F. (John Fitzgerald), 1917-1963 -- Children

NOTE: Students find this concept extremely difficult to grasp. They want to tack Presidents -- United States onto every president's name. It does not work that way. Select the subdivision needed (such as Assassination, or Children, or Religion, etc.) and append just that subdivision to the names of individual presidents as needed.

Key heading for Native Americans

B. Native Americans. Look it up in Sears and note that all subdivisions listed after that subject heading may be used with any individual tribe name. So a book on Christian missions with the Ojibwa Indians could have the following subject heading:

Ojibwa Indians -- Christian missions

Key heading for states

C. Ohio. Look up that state name in Sears and note that all subdivisions listed in Sears after that state may be used with any state. So for a book about the population of California, you are authorized to use the subdivision -- Population after the state name, like this:

California -- Population

Key heading for cities

D. Chicago (Ill.). Look up that city name in Sears and note that all subdivisions listed in Sears after that city may be used with any city. So for a book on the climate in Minneapolis, you are authorized to use the subdivision -- Climate after the city name, like this:

Minneapolis (Minn.) -- Climate

Key heading for languages

E. English language. Look up that subject heading in Sears. There are at least two pages with English language as the main heading, followed by many different subdivisions. One of those subdivisions is -- Idioms. By analogy, you are authorized to use -- Idioms after any language. You must include the word "language." So it is **French language -- Idioms**, not French -- Idioms.

(continued)

Table 11.1. (*continued*)

Key heading for literature	**F. English literature.** Look up that subject heading in Sears. There are only a few subdivisions. They are authorized to be used with any literature, for example: **German literature -- Study and teaching.**
Key heading for wars	**G. World War, 1939-1945.** Look up that subject heading in Sears. There are several pages for that heading and its subdivisions. Any subdivision may be used with any war, as applicable, for example: **Vietnam War, 1961-1975 -- Aerial operations.**

SEARS IN MARC RECORDS

If you want to apply Sears subject headings in your MARC records, ask your vendor. Follett in particular will provide this service. See the Follett vendor form online at their website, which includes a check-off for Sears vs. Library of Congress.

CROSS-REFERENCES

Cross-references are used in catalogs to help ensure readers will find what they are looking for. In a controlled vocabulary, they are "helps" to lead readers from the term not used to the term that is used. They also direct readers from broader and related topics to a "better" term. The cross-reference structure in Sears is indicated through the use of the following abbreviations:

BT = Broader Term
NT = Narrower Term
RT = Related Term
UF = Used for

This cross-reference structure was perhaps more understandable in the days of card catalogs. Cross-reference cards were typed and filed in the catalog. They would guide users around in the subject catalog. Today, a similar cross-reference structure is found in online catalogs, at least in the catalogs that are well-designed. Here we cover the basics of the cross-reference structure.

As an example, here is the entry for **Extinct cities** in Sears:

Extinct cities (may subdiv. geog.)
    UF Abandoned towns

Buried cities
Ruins
Sunken cities
SA names of extinct cities and towns, e.g.
Delphi (Extinct city) [to be added
As needed]
BT Archeology
Cities and towns
NT Ghost towns
RT Excavations (Archeology)

The first abbreviation right under the boldface printed **Extinct cities** is **UF**. It stands for **Used for**. Any subject heading following **UF** represents terminology deemed "not preferred." These are often words that are synonymous or nearly synonymous with the main word. In other words, you would not use Abandoned towns as a subject heading. You would use **Extinct cities**. You would not use Buried cities; you would use **Extinct cities**. Think of it this way: Extinct cities is **USED FOR** Abandoned towns. Extinct cities is **USED FOR** Buried cities, and so forth. Or, in terms of a **SEE** reference, it would be: Abandoned towns **SEE** Extinct cities. Buried cities **SEE** Extinct cities.

USE

In contrast to the situation described in the preceding paragraph, nonpreferred subject headings are printed in regular, not boldface, print at their alphabetical point in Sears, meaning that they are not authorized to be used. Following the heading is the word **USE**. After that comes the preferred heading (in this case, **Extinct cities**). There are **USE** references throughout Sears. Any time that word appears, it means the subject heading right above it is not to be used. The subject heading right after it is the one to be used instead. For example, look up Extraterrestrial life. It says Extraterrestrial life **USE Life on other planets**. Extraterrestrial life is not authorized. **Life on other planets** is authorized.

SA, or SEE ALSO

SA stands for **SEE ALSO**. This provides the authorization to use specific terms that cannot all be listed in Sears because of space constraints. For example, Sears has **SA** names of extinct cities and towns; e.g., **Delphi (Extinct city); to be added as needed**. This SA is not the same thing as "See also" (discussed below), which is used to take users from one authorized subject heading to another.

For a book titled *A Ruined City of the North*, about Fairbanks, Alaska, as it existed thousands of years ago but has since been destroyed, the librarian is authorized to use the name of that city in a subject heading, like this:

Fairbanks (Extinct city)

Another example may be found at **Fabrics**. Here Sears has *SA Types of fabrics to be added as needed*. This means if the book is on polyester fabric, the cataloger is authorized to establish the subject heading **Polyester**. The instructions say: specific names to be added as needed. If you need it, add it.

USING BOTH SPECIFIC AND GENERAL TERMS TOGETHER IN ONE CATALOG RECORD

It is fine to add the general subject heading Extinct cities, so there could be two subject headings for one book that look like this:

1. Delphi (Extinct city)   2. Extinct cities.

For the Polyester subject heading, this would be appropriate:

1. Polyester. 2. Fabrics.

Broader Terms, Narrower Terms, and Related Terms

Returning to **Extinct cities**, note the abbreviation **BT**. It stands for **Broader Term**. This is telling the user that **Archeology** is a broader term (in concept) than **Extinct cities** and that **Cities and towns** is a broader term than **Extinct cities**. You can use the list of Broader Terms as suggestions for subject headings that could be helpful in addition to the narrower, more specific term. "See also" cross-references may be made from the broader term to the narrower one, like this:

Archeology See also Extinct cities
Cities and towns See also Extinct cities

However, the librarian must be cautious not to make blind cross-references. If there are no items in the catalog for the subject heading **Extinct cities**, do not supply a cross-reference to that heading.

Next is **NT**, which stands for **Narrower Term** and authorizes a subject heading narrower in concept than **Extinct cities**.

Next is **RT**, which stands for **Related Term**. **Excavations (Archeology)** is a concept essentially equivalent hierarchically to **Extinct cities**. Related terms are somewhat difficult for catalogers to create, as there are no particular standards or rules to follow. It helps to imagine what catalog users might be looking for and generate RTs based on that. "See also" cross-references may be made among the RTs.

Main Points to Be Aware Of

- There is a linking structure among all the subject headings. It is called the **syndetic structure**. BTs, NTs, RTs, USE, and "See also" are the indicators of this linking structure.

- Any subject heading in light (regular) typeface is not authorized to be used.
- Any subject heading in boldface typeface is an authorized subject heading.
- If you have a book about a specific something, you are often given authorization at the subject heading for the general thing to use the specific name as needed. For example, at **Cooking** there is an **SA** note that allows you to use specific types of cooking, for example, **Microwave cooking**.
- Use the **NT** items to get ideas for a subject heading that is more specific to your topic than a general subject heading. For example, **Extrasensory perception** is an authorized subject heading. If the book happens to specifically be on **Telepathy**, you are authorized to use that. It is listed under **Extrasensory perception** as an **NT**. You would, of course, also find **Telepathy** at its own spot alphabetically in the Ts.
- If you have already selected a very narrow term, note the **BTs** at that term in Sears. Those are the broader terms, any one of which may be assigned also if you choose to offer your users access by both the most specific term possible and the broader concept of which it is a part.

SUMMARY

Subject headings in the OPAC should be based on a controlled vocabulary so that consistency and comprehensiveness in retrieval are achieved. For school libraries, the most often used controlled vocabulary is *Sears List of Subject Headings*. While it is only one volume, through the use of various principles and practices it provides a wide range of specific subject headings on nearly any topic appropriate to the K–12 audience. Learning the relatively few principles and practices thoroughly will make it easy to provide precise and consistent retrieval terms. Book and MARC record vendors will add Sears subject headings to catalog records if requested. MARC records from the Library of Congress do not include them.

Sears List of Subject Headings is more than a list of authorized terms. Those terms taken together form a syndetic, or linking, structure through the use of designators that define the type of link. Sears identifies Broader Terms, Narrower Terms, and Related Terms in addition to using See and SA, Use, and Used For. By understanding the meaning of the terms and the overall concept of the syndetic structure, the cataloger will be able to provide users with a rich subject network. If purchasing a new system, librarians should be certain to ask the vendors about the linking structure among subject headings in their OPAC.

TEST YOUR KNOWLEDGE

Determine the correct subject heading(s) for each of the following:

1. A book on Robins. Assign two subject headings.
2. The health of children

3. Race relations in Los Angeles
4. A collection of plays by five American playwrights
5. A history of China covering roughly the first half of the twentieth century
6. A bibliography of materials on pesticides
7. A book about the many homes lived in by President Ulysses S. Grant
8. Medical care for Ojibwa Indians. Assign two subject headings.
9. A Swahili language grammar
10. A work of fiction set during the French and Indian War (U.S. history)
11. A biography of Bill Gates
12. A collection of poems by one American poet
13. Home care for the aged
14. A DVD on mountain climbing
15. A book on the disease smallpox
16. A collection of short stories all written by one author
17. Conscientious objectors during the Vietnam War
18. Economic conditions in Arizona

19. Library of Congress and Sears subject headings are examples of a:

   A. structured language
   B. natural language
   C. controlled language

20. Sears is updated every:

   A. year
   B. three years
   C. time the editors believe there have been a significant number of changes since the previous edition

21. If a subject heading is authorized for use it is printed in:

   A. boldface
   B. italics
   C. 14 pt. type

22. In MARC, subject headings are in which fields?

   A. 6XX
   B. 7XX
   C. 8XX

23. To indicate a Sears subject heading in MARC, the second indicator should be:

   A. 0
   B. 1
   C. 7

24. The designator _____ in Sears means if you look below it you will find the correct term, and above it, the incorrect term.

   A. SA
   B. See
   C. NT

What is the MARC coding for the following Library of Congress subject headings?

25. Predatory animals
26. Great Britain -- History -- Henry, VIII, 1509-1547 -- Fiction
27. Individual Mark Zuckerberg, born in 1984
28. Penguins -- Juvenile films
29. African Americans -- Civil rights -- Alabama -- Montgomery -- History -- 20th century
30. Poisonous snakes (as a CYACP subject heading)

TEST YOUR CRITICAL THINKING

1. Look at the subject heading **Health** on the sample page from Sears in this chapter. Explain in your own words the meaning of **SA** on this page and how it economizes on the total number of pages in an edition of Sears.
2. You have decided to have your book vendor add *Sears* subject headings to your MARC records for a small extra fee per record. Defend that decision to your budget-minded principal.
3. Define "syndetic" and explain how it applies in Sears.

RESOURCES

Bulletin of Bibliography. (1923). *11*(10), 180.
Miller, Joseph. (2011). Sears list of subject headings In S. S. Intner, J. F. Fountain, & J. Weihs (Eds.), *Cataloging correctly for kids* (5th ed.) (pp. 129–34). Chicago: American Library Association.
Satija, M. P., & Haynes, E. (2008). *User's guide to Sears list of subject headings*. Lanham, MD: Scarecrow.
Sears, M. E. (2010). *Sears list of subject headings* (20th ed.). New York: Wilson.

12

Using *Abridged Dewey Decimal Classification*

CONCEPTUAL BACKGROUND:
FIXED LOCATION VS. RELATIVE LOCATION

Classification in libraries may be said to have two purposes. One is to group items by subject so users can find like items together and browse through them. Although any intellectual item can be classified in more than one area, it is necessary to choose only one, because the second purpose of classification is to give the item a physical place to reside in the collection. Both purposes were quite problematic in the early days of libraries before Dewey's scheme of relative location was developed. Until the end of the nineteenth century, fixed location was the common way of physically placing a book on the shelves. This meant a book had the same location on the shelf all the time, usually in order of accession. Some kind of mark was put on the book, signifying the book's physical location on the shelf. The book would always be in that one spot, having nothing to do with subject arrangement.

With the introduction of subject arrangements, librarians had the freedom to *interpolate*, meaning it became possible to add a new item among the items already there. Items could be lined up according to subject, always with room for one more item to be moved into the mainstream of items. Each item was shelved *relative* to other items in the collection and relative to its subject. A good classification scheme is *infinitely hospitable*, or amenable to new subject areas being added as knowledge grows in multiple directions.

MELVIL DEWEY, THE MAN WHO INVENTED A
RELATIVE LOCATION CLASSIFICATION SCHEME

As a young man, Melvil Dewey was the individual who conceived a solution to the difficulties inherent in a fixed location scheme. His decimal system made it possible to flexibly shelve materials according to intellectual content with whole numbers representing broad categories of knowledge and decimal number extensions permitting refinement of the broad categories. These numbers could be written on the spines of the books and serve as a relative order shelving device. Dewey's story is quite interesting.

He was born in 1851 in Adams, New York, into a poor family. His given name was Melville Louis Kossuth Dewey. The area of New York in which he was born was known as the "Burned-Over District," because of the many religious reform movements that swept through it. The believers stressed hard work, social responsibility, and education. Dewey's parents were among the stalwart and instilled the same values in their son. Early in Melvil's life he cataloged his mother's pantry, later taught himself shoemaking, and learned bookkeeping so he could help keep the accounts for his father's store. By age thirteen he had saved enough money to purchase an unabridged dictionary.

As a passionate proponent of spelling reform (he helped found The Spelling Reform Association), he changed his name to Melvil Dui, but the Dui part did not stick. Dewey also devised a simplified system of spelling words that he used throughout his life, sometimes bringing him scorn, which he ignored. This simplified spelling was used in Unabridged Dewey until the 14th edition in 1942 (and in the introductions until the 18th edition).

While a student and library assistant at Amherst College in Massachusetts, he began studying the operations of the library and various proposed classification schemes from around the country. At the time, the library was shelving according to a fixed location system, something that greatly disturbed Dewey. For several months, he pondered the problem until one Sunday, while sitting in church, half listening to a long sermon, the idea for his decimal system crystallized in his mind. He later described this event in exuberant prose. ". . . the solution flasht over me so that I jumpt in my seat and came very near to shouting, 'Eureka!'" In 1874, after he graduated, Amherst hired him as an assistant librarian and allowed him the freedom to carry out his reformist ideas, including classifying the entire collection. In 1876 he obtained the copyright for his classification scheme, titled *A Classification and Subject Index for Cataloguing and Arranging the Books and Pamphlets of a Library*. Eventually he established Forest Press, his own publishing company, to disseminate his classification. In 1988, OCLC Online Computer Center, Inc., took over Forest Press and now sells the DDC.

Dewey's system ordered human knowledge into hierarchical concepts and linked hierarchical decimal classification numbers to these concepts. The result was that books could now be shelved relative to their subject, and new books and subjects could be easily interpolated into the existing collection. this was a highly creative solution to the constraints of inflexible fixed location. Now in its 21ˢᵗ edition, the DDC is still the world's most widely used classification system despite being quite ethnocentric and not used much by academic and research libraries, which tend to use the Library of Congress classification.

We can thank Melvil Dewey for making librarianship a female-dominated profession. He was hired at Columbia University as the head librarian and decided to open the country's first library school (after all, his decimal system could not be used by libraries unless it was taught) in 1887. Columbia was a males-only college, but this did not deter Dewey. He opened the school anyway (much to the wrath of the college), filling his first class with seventeen female and three male students.

It was an experience none of them would forget. As one student said, "For his lectures, Dewey would rush in at the last moment. . . . He would begin almost immediately to pace back and forth and talk at the rate of 180 words per minute (some students actually counted), while students took notes furiously. Occasionally he would stop pacing, turn full square towards the class, draw his six foot frame erect before them, and while tipping his head back, address them by looking down his nose" (Wiegand, p. 205). Some students could not endure these intense classroom encounters and quit within a short time. Most, however, were inspired and stayed with the program.

Dewey also contributed to the founding of the American Library Association in 1876 and *Library Journal*. In addition, he started a company, The Library Bureau (library supplies vendor), which still exists. He and his first wife, Annie Dewey, developed the Lake Placid Club, a resort that was intended for members' "social, cultural, and spiritual enrichment in the Adirondack Mountains," but it excluded certain individuals from membership. Dewey and his only child, Godfrey, played a prominent role in bringing the Olympic Games to Lake Placid in 1932 (Lake Placid Club Demolition, 1993).

Despite his considerable accomplishments, Dewey was known to bestow inappropriate attention on many women, was accused of racism and anti-Semitism, and was a champion of the so-called Anglo-Saxon race. He was driven, intense, obsessed with rules and details, arrogant, and egotistic. All of these traits contributed to his passionate reformist ideas and the energy with which he carried them out. He died in 1931 at age eighty. For better or worse, his mark on the library world is immutable.

Special Tidbit: Call Numbers

No doubt you have heard the Dewey Decimal Classification number referred to as the "call number." What does that terminology mean? It goes back to the days when books were kept on closed shelves to which the public had no access. If you wanted a book, you had to "call for it." You did this by filling out a slip with the title and classification (call) number. Someone would then go to the shelves and return with the book. (Ferro & Lushington, 1998)

VERSIONS OF DEWEY

Unabridged Dewey is four volumes and is used in larger libraries. A shorter, abridged version in one volume is also available. K–12 schools and small public libraries use Abridged Dewey. The Dewey Decimal System is also available in electronic format on the Internet from OCLC. In this format, called *WebDewey*, both Unabridged and Abridged Dewey are kept up to date, and it has numerous searching and browsing features. A site license for one user is currently $260 a year, an expense probably not necessary for the school librarian. A book vendor can classify school items, and if the need arises for a copy of Dewey in the school library, it is less costly to purchase an Abridged Dewey.

THE DEWEY DECIMAL CLASSIFICATION SYSTEM: NOT A PERFECT SCHEME

Time is not on the side of any classification system, and the DDC is not immune to the problems that arise as new areas of knowledge evolve while previously established areas become less prominent or fade away entirely. Terminology and concepts both are subject to change and revision. History, of course, is constantly advancing, and the DDC must accommodate new events. While the editors try to incorporate new knowledge into the DDC, a complete revamping of the classification scheme is not economically feasible, and no library could afford to reclassify its existing collection to conform to a radically changed classification scheme.

To make matters more problematic, libraries in more than 135 countries use the DDC to organize their collections for their users. The DDC, however, was constructed in North America over a hundred years ago and as such reflects a nineteenth-century Western bias. It is often criticized for its detailed breakdown of subtopics within Christianity while gathering numerous other religions into single classification numbers. Similarly, European languages span numbers 420–489, while other world languages are squeezed into numbers 490–499. For a detailed discussion of the biases in the DDC, see Kua (2004).

The first DDC was published in 1876 by Dewey as a pamphlet. Today the DDC is owned and published by OCLC. All references to Dewey in this book are to the one-volume, 15th abridged edition (2012).

Preliminaries

All Dewey numbers are a minimum of three digits. If further notation is needed, a decimal point is placed at the end of the first three digits and more numbers are added. These are, of course, all decimal numbers. That must be taken into account when shelving. For example, 221.451 shelves before 221.46.

There are empty spaces in some of the longer numbers, for example, 947.540 8. The empty space between the 0 and the 8 is there only to make long numbers easier to read. The theory is that the space helps your eyes and brain work together better. The space is not part of the completed number as affixed to your item.

Sometimes there is a segment symbol in the midst of the digits following the decimal point that looks like this: / or this: ' This is called a "prime" mark. It identifies a conceptual segment of the number that may be dropped if you do not wish to have such a finely defined subject represented by the number. This works well in converting full numbers to something more like Abridged Dewey. For example, Unabridged Dewey has 973.758 to classify armored vessels in the Civil War. Expressed as 973.7 / 58, this means "58" may be dropped. That will leave just "Civil War" (973.7) and eliminate the refinement of "armored vessels," "58."

The Library of Congress assigns classification numbers from Unabridged Dewey. In a MARC record, it is in the 082 field, which has coding at the end of it indicating the edition of Unabridged Dewey it was assigned from. It is possible to classify school library materials in these Dewey numbers, but it might be better to truncate (cut off) the number the segment symbol.

The DDC classifies knowledge starting with the "general" and narrowing down to the "specific," making it a hierarchical arrangement. The broader the topic, the shorter the number. Each refinement in the meaning represented is indicated symbolically through extensions of the number. For example, 793 is used for Indoor games and amusements, but to indicate the narrower topic of "Word games, including Scrabble," the number is 793.734.

Assigning Classification Numbers

Typically, the school librarian fills out a profile with the MARC record vendor in which its catalogers are authorized to assign DDC numbers. They will probably use the numbers they find in the 082 field, but convert them to Abridged Dewey numbers. Or they may devise the number themselves using Abridged Dewey.

As you might think, it is most common to assign a classification number that represents the entire subject of the book. That works fine if the book is about one concept, but what about a book about more than one concept? If one subject occupies more space in the item than a second subject does, assign the classification number to that one. If they seem to be covered equally, even if there are two or three subjects in the book, assign the classification number that comes first in the Dewey classification. If there are more than three subjects in one item, presumably they are related to one another, and you can assign a broader number that would encompass all the concepts (Weihs & Intner, 2009).

Using Subject Headings to Compensate for Limitations of Classification Numbers

Remember, an item can be shelved in only one place, but this disadvantage can be compensated for through subject headings in the OPAC. In the OPAC you can make an item accessible by several subject headings and other access points. It is not advisable to expect patrons browsing the shelves to find everything they need, and you cannot always rely on users finding everything through the OPAC, either. There has to be a balance between browsing and specific searching. So think about that when you are in a quandary about where to place a particular item. Physically, where is this item the most likely to be found by users? If there is an 80 percent chance they will find it in the biographies section (920 or 921) of the library, but it is a book about a rock star, should it go in 784.092 for rock musicians instead? It probably is better to put it with biographies and compensate by having a subject heading not just for the particular rock artist, but for rock music as well.

Classifying Graphic Novels and Graphic Nonfiction

Another example of a classification dilemma is where to put graphic novels and nonfiction. Some libraries put graphic novels in the Dewey Decimal number for cartooning (741.5). If they are very simple graphic novels, such as the Owly series, which is wordless, they could go in the Easy or Everybody collection (E). There is a series titled Graphic Modern History—World War II that has individual, independent volumes about various fronts in the war. Each of those could be placed in the Dewey Decimal history number for its particular aspect of the war. Similarly, there is a science series titled Graphic Library, Graphic Science that covers many aspects of science. One title in this series is *The Whirlwind World of Hurricanes*, which the Library of Congress has placed in a science classification number. Again, use the subject headings to compensate for the single classification number. If you want your students to be able to find all your "graphic novels" no matter where they are shelved in the library, use a genre subject heading (655 Graphic novels). There is some discussion in the library community about what to call nonfiction in the graphic format. One suggestion is simply Graphic nonfiction.

Doing It Yourself

The school librarian should not agonize over the local assignment of a classification number. Dewey seems so rule-bound, as does all of cataloging, that we too often think there is only one right way to do something. But the library, the users, and the curriculum are your first concern. Put any item in a location that will ensure it gets the most use possible given your particular audience.

ORGANIZATION OF THE
ABRIDGED 15TH EDITION OF DEWEY

The *Abridged 15th Edition of Dewey* (2012) has seven main preliminary sections:

1. New Features (pp. xix–xxvii)
2. Introduction (pp. xxix–liv)

3. Glossary (pp. lv–lxiv)
4. Index to the Introduction and Glossary (pp. lxv–lxvii)
5. Notes on Table Numbers (pp. 5–19)
6. Notes on Schedule Numbers (pp. 23–118)
7. Relocations and Discontinuations (pp. 119–123)

Following those are the four major sections of the book, A–D.

A. Tables

Table 1. Standard Subdivisions (pp. 127–138)
Table 2. Subdivisions for Geographic Areas (pp.139–189)
Table 3. Subdivisions for Individual Literatures, for Specific Literary Forms (pp. 190–196)
Table 4. Subdivisions of Individual Languages and Language Families (pp. 197–202)

B. Summaries (pp. 203–214)

1. First Summary: 10 main classes (the 000s, 100s, 200s, 300s, 400s, 500s, 600s, 700s, 800s, and 900s)
2. Second Summary: 100 divisions, or 10 per class (110, 220, 440, 650, 940, etc.)
3. Third Summary: 1,000 sections, or up to 10 per class (for further refinement of the subject and its accompanying classification)

Look at the First Summary (p. 203). Dewey originally divided all of knowledge into ten main classes. Today, with modifications, they are:

000 Computer science, information, & general works
100 Philosophy & psychology
200 Religion
300 Social sciences
400 Language
500 Science
600 Technology
700 Arts & recreation
800 Literature
900 History & geography

It is in the Summaries that the conceptual and numerical hierarchical order of human knowledge becomes apparent. Each of the ten main classes (000, 100, etc.) is further divided into ten divisions per class. Each division represents a concept that is a part of, but narrower than, the class to which it is assigned. For example, Class 100 is Philosophy & Psychology. That is a vast subject area, so it must be subdivided by divisions such as Metaphysics (110), Psychology (150), and Ethics (170). The hierarchical arrangement in the 500s shows the "Sciences" as the broad category, with specific divisional breakdowns by "10s" or subtopics in science, such as Mathematics (510) and Plants (580).

Look at the Third Summary (pp. 205–214). Now things become very detailed. Under each division there are ten "sections." For example, under the Class of Philosophy & Psychology, or 100, there is the Division of Parapsychology & occultism, or 130. Under the Division of Parapsychology & occultism is the Section of Dreams & mysteries, or 135.

C. The Schedules (pp. 217–961)

This is the full array of classification numbers in order first by the ten main classes, and within each class in order by the divisions and within each division, in order by sections. There is much fine print here. The accomplished user of Dewey learns to read and heed it.

D. Relative Index (pp. 964–1228)

Start here when trying to decide on a classification number. It is more efficient to start alphabetically in this index than to try to find a classification number by just looking around in the Schedule. After identifying a potential classification number, go to the classification schedules section itself to the potential number.

HOW TO APPLY NUMBERS FROM THE TABLES

Look at Table 1, Standard Subdivisions. *These are never used alone.* They are always used in conjunction with a three-digit (or more) Dewey Decimal number. The most important for school libraries are the following:

--03 Dictionaries, encyclopedias, concordances
--07 Study and teaching
--09 Historical and geographical treatment

Look at Table 2, Geographic Areas. *These are never used alone.* They are always used in conjunction with a three-digit (or more) Dewey Decimal number.

Look at Table 3, Subdivisions of Individual Literatures. *These are never used alone.* They are always used in conjunction with a three-digit (or more) Dewey Decimal number. We are especially concerned with

--08

and

--1-8   Specific forms of Literature

Within specific forms we are most concerned with

--1 Poetry
--2 Drama

Look at Table 4, Subdivisions of Individual Languages. *These are never used alone.* They are always used in conjunction with a three-digit (or more) Dewey Decimal number. We are especially concerned with

--03 Dictionaries
--3 Dictionaries

Yes, there are two ways of using the subdivision "3" in Individual Languages (03, or 3). Either way, a 3 means a dictionary.

Standard Subdivisions

Standard subdivisions can be used where needed to delineate certain aspects of the item being classified. If the book is a dictionary, its classification number gets a standard subdivision meaning "dictionary." For a book on child psychology, here is how to find a classification number:

- Start at the Relative Index at the back of Dewey (starts on p. 965). Look up child psychology. It leads you to 155.4. Turn to the page in the Schedules with 155.4 on it. There is the classification number, along with a definition of "child psychology."
- If the book is a general one on child psychology, use that call number (155.4). If it is a dictionary of child psychology, use a standard subdivision from Table 1: -03 (find -03 in Table 1, p. 132). Drop the hyphen and tack the "03" onto the end of 155.4, making it 155.403. Unfortunately, standard subdivisions *do not all work this easily.*

If only the rest of Dewey were this straightforward! In general, remember this: *If you are not told otherwise, if you are not given any special instructions, just use the standard subdivisions by tacking them on at the end of your chosen call number. That includes the zero, for example: -03. Do not use the hyphen.*

Merging Zeros in Standard Subdivisions

Dewey gets murkier now. Turn to the classification number 370 for education. Notice that 370 has a zero at the end of it. That zero is a warning, of sorts. Return to Table 1, Standard Subdivisions. Notice that standard subdivisions start with a 0. If a standard subdivision is needed and the main number ends in a zero, the 0 in 370 merges with the 0 at the beginning of the standard subdivision. In other words, an encyclopedia (remember -03 means dictionaries or encyclopedias) of education has a call number of 370.3, not 370.03. The two zeros merge.

If you are not told otherwise at the point of the call number that has a 0 at the end of it, this is how you build the number using the standard subdivision. The zeros merge. *But they do not always merge.* Sometimes you are told otherwise under the word Summary, followed by an example of how to apply the standard subdivisions.

- Here is an example of a situation in which the zeros do not merge. Turn to classification number 230 for Christianity. Find the word Summary. Under that it shows 230.002-.007 Standard subdivisions of Christianity. By that example you are being told not to merge the zeros. A dictionary of Christianity would go in 230.003.

- Turn to the classification number for Engineering and allied operations (620) and look at the first line of the Summary, where it shows 620.001-.009 Standard subdivisions. You are told by example here that a dictionary or encyclopedia in this subject area should have two zeros placed before the "3" with no merging of zeros. So the dictionary of Engineering goes in 620.003.

Standard Subdivisions for Classification Numbers with No Ending Zero

Here is an example of the application of .001-.009, but without a zero at the end of the main number:

- See Animal Husbandry 636. Then find 636.7, Dogs. Notice that it shows .700 1-.700 9 Standard subdivisions right below. That means two zeros are used with any of the standard subdivisions. The space between the second zero and the last digit is there only to help the eyes and mind perceive the number clearly and transcribe it correctly when writing out the full number for the item. A dictionary of dogs would have the following for a classification number: 636.7003.

Standard Subdivision for Historical or Geographical Treatment: "9" or "09"

The standard subdivision for historical or geographical treatment is -09. Any region or country number found in Table 2, Areas may be added to -09. Once they become practiced at this, librarians are attuned to -09. Any time 9 or 09 appears in a call number, it will immediately call to mind either geography or history.

For a book on castles in Spain, look up castles in the Relative Index. It says 728.8. Turn to that classification in Dewey. Here there aren't any special instructions. Therefore the authorized DDC number is 728.80946. Break that number down:

728.8 is castles.
09 means geographical designation to follow.
46 means Spain. To verify this, look up Spain in the Relative Index. First it says Spain 946, but under that it says T2--46. T2 stands for Table 2, or the Geographic Areas table. Go there and find -46. It says Spain, Andorra, Gibraltar, Portugal.

What if this book were on castles in Monaco? Then it would be 728.80944. 728.8 = castles, 09 = geographical treatment, and 449 = Monaco (T2).

Special Tidbit: Finding Geographic Locations in Dewey

Using the Relative Index to find a geographic location is far more efficient than trying to browse through the Area tables.

Special Instructions for Geographic Treatment

Another way to apply geographic treatment requires following special instructions in Dewey at the number being used as the main classification number. This is a rather difficult concept to grasp, so take your time and read and follow the instructions carefully.

How to Figure Out "Geographic Treatment": Force Your Eyes to Wander Down the Page

For geographic treatment of political parties today, start at 324.2 and look below that, where it states ".209 4-.209 9 Specific continents, countries, localities in modern world." The "09" in that number is the Dewey standard subdivision for geographic treatment, and the "4" and the "9" represent the range of country numbers in Table 2, Geographic Areas.

Next is "Do not use for parties in specific countries and localities in modern world; class in 324.24-324.29." Look a little further down to find ".24-.29. Parties in specific countries and localities in modern world." This is the stopping point.

So for geographic treatment of political parties in the modern world, it is necessary to scan down the page and read everything under 324.2 Political parties, then arrive at the final instruction, which directs you to "add to **base number** 324.2 notation 4-9 from Table 2 for the specific country."

The meaning of the final instruction is that "09" is not used to designate geographic treatment. Go straight to the country number and affix it to the classification number directly. Thus, 324.273 is the number for Political parties in the United States. The notation "73" is the geographic area number for the United States. Unfortunately, this kind of verbiage is used throughout Dewey. Use it as a reminder that "it is wrong if you are using -09 with an area number after it."

Base number is the important concept to remember. *You add an area number to a base number without the intervening "09."*

Review of Base Number

• The base number for political parties is 324.2. What if the book is about political parties in a country? Expand the Dewey number by adding the area number to it.

• Therefore, "political parties in Ireland" would start with the *base number* 324.2. Next, look up Ireland in the Relative Index or find Ireland in the Area tables. Ireland's number is "415."

• So the classification number for political parties in Ireland would be 323.2415. Always add a decimal point three spaces to the right of the first digit in the call number.

Here is another example.

To classify a book on public policy issues in education in Algeria, start in the Relative Index under Public education, Policy issues. It says 379.

Turn to that number in the Schedules. Then look for the reference to [.094-099]. Notice that it is in brackets. Brackets here mean that this standard subdivision concept is represented in *another location* within Dewey. Indeed, that is the case. It states "Specific continents, countries, localities in modern world. Do not use; class in 379.4-379.9."

Let your eyes wander further to .4-.9 on the next page, where it states "Public policy issues in specific continents, countries, localities in modern world. Add to base number 379 notation 4-9 from Table 2."

Write down 379 and then find "Algeria" in the Relative Index. Its number is 65, the number for policy issues in Algerian public education is 379.65.

Statistics is another areas in which this number building with a base number and an area number is used all the time.

Statistics

Find the classification numbers 314-319. Here it states that the *base number* for statistics is 31. To build a number for a book on statistics in a specific continent, country, or locality in the modern world, such as Spain, write down "31" and add the number for Spain to it, which is 46, making the number for a book of statistics of Spain 314.6. Statistics of Michigan works the same way. Write down 31, meaning statistics. Go to the Relative Index. Find Michigan. Its number is 774, making the classification number 317.74.

Standard Subdivision for Bibliographies

A bibliography is a compiled list of citations to materials, usually on a specific topic. If the book is a bibliography on a stated topic, it may be classified with its subject or topic (such as flowers or psychology) or in the number that is set aside for bibliographies. Here is how this works:

- 016 is the standard subdivision for bibliography, and it is the actual classification number for bibliographies. Look in the standard subdivision table. Find where it shows "-(016)." It also states: Optional number; prefer 016. That sounds as if it makes no sense, right? What this is saying is that -(016) in parentheses means that it is possible to use -016 as a tacked-on standard subdivision to any subject area classification number, but Dewey suggests that you not do this. Instead, classify bibliographies in 016 with an extension that stands for the subject area.
- So a book on electricity (537) in the form of a bibliography would be classified in bibliographies (016) with the *extension* of 537 for electricity. 016.537.
- If you prefer, the book may go in electricity, 537, with 016 added to it (537.016), meaning bibliography.

Special Tidbit: Bibliography vs. Biography

People often confuse the words *bibliography* and *biography*. A bibliography is a list of resources. A biography is a document about someone. For example: "I need a bibliography of materials about Barack Obama because I need several sources in my research project." vs. "I want to know more about Barack Obama's life, so I want to read his biography."

Rules for Standard Subdivisions Review

1. Add them anywhere, using the zero as in -03 or -07 or -09, unless you are told you can't.
2. If the number onto which you are adding a standard subdivision has a zero at the end (such as 570 for life sciences) the zeros "overtake" each other. The number for a dictionary of Life Sciences would be 570.3, not 570.03, unless you're told differently by example at the classification number in question. Watch for the word Summary and look right below that for the example.
3. Always look for instructions relating to building on base numbers and follow them. Let your eyes wander down the page until you find the exact point of the number building instructions.
4. Once in a great while you will be instructed to use two zeros (-003, for example) instead of one zero (-03).

Single Biographies

An item about one individual can go in a general classification number for "biography," alphabetically subarranged by the last name of the person (the biographee) in the biography (or autobiography). This is the way these biographies are most often handled in schools and public libraries. Biographies are shelved together because school and public library users love to browse in the biography section, or the 921s. The "one" in 921 is something that should help you remember that it represents one individual. The number 921 for Abraham Lincoln would look like this:

921
Lin

The "Lin" makes the biographies in 921 subarrange by biographee, in this case, Lincoln.

Alternatively, these biographies can go with the subject area of the famous person. That is done with a standard subdivision of -092. After you become practiced at this, any time you see 092 in a classification number, it will jump right out at you as identifying a biography. Here is how it works:

* A book about a famous teacher would go in 370.92. Why is it not 370.092? 370 is for education. -092 is the standard subdivision meaning "biography." The zeros merge in the middle of this number.
* These books would then subarrange by the person the book is about. So if it were about Marva Collins (famous teacher of inner-city youth in Chicago), it would go in 370.92 Col (first three letters of the subject's last name).

Collective Biographies

A book that is a collection of biographies (such as a book containing a chapter on each president) goes in 920. These would be subarranged by the author of the book. So the number for a book by Smith on all the presidents would look like this:

920
Smi

Folklore and Fairy Tales

A very important area in the elementary school library is the section for folklore and fairy tales. Any aspiring school librarian should memorize the fact that 398.2 is the general number used for folklore and fairy tales. In Dewey it is broken down into further subcategories, but for our purposes, 398.2 is sufficient. Mother Goose nursery rhymes and other kinds of rhymes go in 398.8.

SUMMARY

The *Abridged Dewey Decimal Classification* is a single volume designed for schools and small public libraries. In a departure from having fixed locations for books on shelves, the Dewey Decimal System facilitates the shelving of books relative to each other and in a subject arrangement. This classification scheme is built on a hierarchical arrangement of concepts symbolized by a scheme of three-digit whole numbers (such as 100, 530, 640, etc.), often (but not always) followed by decimal numbers of varying length. Only one classification number is assigned to each book or other item in the collection. This limited subject access on the shelves may be compensated for by assigning more than one subject heading. The Dewey Decimal System has a number of conventions that expand its capacity for defining subjects. There are directions throughout the scheme on how to apply these conventions. As when using *Sears List of Subject Headings*, ask the MARC record provider if including Abridged Dewey classification numbers is an option.

TEST YOUR KNOWLEDGE

1. What is an acceptable classification number for an autobiography of Bill Gates, including the second line? _____
2. What is an acceptable classification number for a dictionary of cats? _____
3. What is an acceptable classification number for a book on the architecture of farmhouses in France? _____
4. What is an acceptable classification number for a book on secondary education in California? _____
5. What does 613.8016 stand for? _____
6. True or False: 799.202 is the DDC number for bow and arrow hunting. _____
7. Find the DDC number for taxidermy. What is it? Going up the hierarchy that includes taxidermy, what are the two broader areas of which taxidermy is a part? _____
8. What does 016.6138 stand for? _____
9. What is an acceptable classification number for a book on the geography of Colorado? _____
10. What is an acceptable classification number for a book on hunting in Wisconsin? _____

TEST YOUR CRITICAL THINKING

You are hired as the new librarian, and you learn that your predecessor has been classifying materials according to Abridged Dewey. You had a difficult time learning the various aspects of the Dewey Decimal System in your library education and have decided to simply use the DDC number assigned by the Library of Congress (field 082). Why is this not a good idea? What could you do instead with the numbers you find in the 082 field that would compensate for your perceived weaknesses in assigning Abridged DDC numbers?

RESOURCES

Bealle, J. (2011). Dewey decimal classification. In S. S. Intner, J. F. Fountain, & J.Weihs (Eds.), *Cataloging correctly for kids* (5th ed.) (pp. 135–147). Chicago: American Library Association.

Bowman, J. H. (2005). *Essential Dewey.* New York: Neal-Schuman.

Dewey, M. (2004). *Abridged Dewey decimal classification and relative index* (14th ed.). Albany, NY: Forest Press.

Ferro, F., & Lushington, N. (1998). *How to use the library: A reference and assignment guide for students.* Westport, CT: Greenwood.

How one pioneer profoundly influenced modern librarianship. (n.d.). Retrieved from: http://www.oclc.org/dewey/resources/biography/.

Kua, E. (2004). Non-western languages and literature in the Dewey Decimal Classification scheme. *Libri, 54,* 256–265.

Lake Placid Club demolition undertaken at Mirror Lake facility. (1993, February 16). *Watertown Daily Times* (Online in Newsbank).

Prescott, S. (2001). If you knew Dewey . . . Melvil Dewey. *School Library Journal, 47*(8), 50–53.

Weihs, J., & Intner, S. S. (2009). *Beginning cataloging.* Santa Barbara, CA: Libraries Unlimited.

Wiegand, W. (1996). *Irrepressible reformer: A biography of Melvil Dewey.* Chicago: American Library Association.

13

Building Dewey Numbers in Three Major Areas

This chapter looks at Abridged Dewey numbers in languages, literature, and history to complete our coverage of the DDC. The 400s are used for anything having to do with the various languages of the world. Dictionaries of all languages go in the 400s. The lower 400s are reserved for items *about* all languages in general, from Philosophy and Theory (401) to Linguistics (410). After Linguistics, other aspects of language are classified in Dewey numbers from 411 to 419. Sign language is classified in 419. In a school library, you will not have many items between 401 and 419. The rest of the 400s apply to languages of specific countries and are more important in school libraries. Once again, the complete number is formed by building on base numbers.

THE BASE NUMBER AS USED IN THE
LANGUAGES CLASSIFICATION (400s)

The classification number range for materials about various languages is 420 to 490. In a school situation, what you will find is mostly dictionaries or grammar books in various languages, such as 423 for an English-language dictionary. Read the fine print under 420-490 Specific Languages. Note especially the instruction that reads like this:

add to **base number** for each language identified by * notation 01-8 from Table 4.

Look at Table 4 at the place where it shows -3 and -5. Those are the numbers to be added to a base number in languages to define certain aspects of languages. There are other numbers there as well, but our needs here are limited, just -3 (dictionary) and -5 (grammar).

To classify a French dictionary or French grammar, first locate the base number for the French language. This may be done by browsing through the 400s or by looking up French language in the Relative Index. The base number for French language is only two digits: 44. Watch for where it states 441-448 Subdivisions of French language, "add to base number 44 notation 01-8 from Table 4, e.g., grammar of French language 445." If the book is a French grammar, add "5" to 44, making it 445. If it is a French dictionary, add "3" to 44, making it 443.

Following are the essential steps for assigning these numbers:

1. Determine the language of your item.
2. Look up the language in the Relative Index or scan through the 400s starting at 420, looking for selected language. Find the small print that says "add to base number."
3. Write down your base number.
4. Determine the aspect of the language. Is it a grammar, a dictionary, or something else? In a school situation, you will have mostly grammars and dictionaries, but you may also have items about word origins or the history of a particular language (etymology) or other aspects.
5. Add the standard subdivision meaning either dictionary (-3) or grammar (-5) to your base number. This is *not* -03. It's just "3" or "5."

NUMBERS OF DIGITS IN THE BASE NUMBERS FOR LANGUAGES

*   Often a base number consists of two digits (i.e., "42" for English, "44" for French, etc.). Major European languages will have just two digits for their base numbers.
*   Some languages have three digits. For those, use the three digits and then place the appropriate -3 or -5 onto the number like this: 469.3 (for a Portuguese dictionary), 469.5 (for a Portuguese grammar). There must be a decimal point three spaces from the left.
*   Some language numbers have four digits in their base numbers. The Japanese language goes in 495.6. A dictionary of the Japanese language is 495.63.

Catalogers working with a large collection of language materials need to know more about the various other aspects of classifying in the 400s, but this is not all within the scope of this book.

Special Tidbit: Finding the Language Number

If you can't find the language that you want in the 400s, look it up in the Relative Index first, which will give you the language number. Then go to the 400s and find it there.

In the following sections the 800s, or literature, is covered. The literature area can be a complicated one to comprehend, but again, here we concentrate on just a few concepts, those most often encountered in a school library. The first type of literature to consider is fiction.

CLASSIFYING FICTION IN THE SCHOOL LIBRARY

Fiction in school libraries is almost always shelved in a Fiction area separate from nonfiction. These books should be in order by author's last name and usually with something like this on the spine:

F
Wi

or

Fic
Har

In the first option, the "F" tells your users the book is shelved in a special "Fiction" area of the library, separate from the nonfiction shelved in Dewey classification order. "Wi" is the first two letters of the author's last name. For a book by Laura Ingalls Wilder, "Wi" could be placed beneath "F." "Fic" in the second option also means "Fiction." This label could be affixed to a work of fiction by children's author Bob Hartman.

Think of fiction as living in its own world, apart from its cousins such as poetry and drama. It is possible to classify fiction using a Dewey classification number based on the nationality of the author, but few, if any, libraries do that. A separate fiction collection in order by author's last name, particularly for American authors, is the usual arrangement in school and public libraries.

Shelving by Popular Genres

Related to shelving fiction separately from other types of literature is the practice of segmenting it into certain genres, such as Fantasy, Science fiction, Historical fiction, or Graphic novels. A literary genre is characterized by a particular style, form, or content. Having popular genres shelved separately means that students can browse in their favorite areas. In the catalog, it is necessary to have a way of indicating that these items are shelved separately from the larger group of general fiction. This is best done in the circulation record. While it is possible to assign a genre *subject heading* to each item, that is not enough to clearly and unambiguously indicate the shelving of the item in a genre area, for these reasons:

- Viewing of subject headings in a screen display might take an additional click, slowing down the process of identifying the book as being shelved in a particular genre.
- Any one particular record could have numerous subject headings listed, making it difficult to quickly identify a genre heading.
- Even if there is a genre subject heading, that is not a guarantee to the OPAC user that the library classified the item in that particular genre for shelving purposes.
- The item being viewed on the screen might actually be a work of nonfiction about a particular genre and be shelved in the nonfiction area of the library.

Also, besides having the designator in the circulation record, have either genre stickers or letters on the spine of the item indicating the genre, to help both your users and shelvers (figure 13.1). Science fiction, Fantasy, Historical fiction, and Mystery are just a few of the popular genres.

Doing this takes advance planning and a clear idea of how far one wants to take the practice of shelving by genre. Some school libraries use genre stickers on the spines of books, but rather than being used for shelving, these designators serve as an alert to students browsing in the general fiction section. While this works to alert browsers to "Animal stories," or "Humor," it is at odds with using the stickers to indicate shelving areas and should be considered before using genre stickers or shelving by genres.

Figure 13.1.   Genre Stickers on Spines of Books

VARIETIES OF POETRY AND DRAMA

- A book of poems or plays by one author. For example, a book of poetry by Robert Frost.
- A collection of poems or plays by many authors, all from the same country. For example, a book of poems by five American poets, or a collection of plays by British playwrights.
- A collection of poems or plays by many authors, from many countries. For example, a book of plays in this category might be titled: *European Drama of the 20th Century* (many countries, all on the continent of Europe).
- A collection of literature consisting of a variety of types of literature. For example, a book with poetry, plays, short stories, etc., all in one volume.

Follow these steps in determining the classification number for the literary work:

- Consider the country of origin of the literature first, followed by its type (or genre).
- Then consider if the book is by a single author or is a collection of literary works by more than one author.

ADDING TO BASE NUMBERS IN LITERATURE

Since countries are the first consideration, locate 810, American literature in English. Look down to the 811-818 subdivisions for specific forms of American literature in English. Here the instructions state: "add to base number 81 as instructed at the beginning of Table 3, e.g., American poetry in English 811." Table 3 shows Subdivisions for Individual Literatures for Specific Literary Forms. Here you can see that -1 means poetry and -2 means drama.

Looking again at the base number for American literature in English, we see that it is 81. For a book of poetry all by one individual, use 81, meaning American literature, and add a -1 to it for poetry.

The countries of the world having two-digit base numbers are the United States (base number 81), England (82), Germany (83), France (84), Italy (85), and Spain and Portugal (86). For the countries, drop the "0" and add a "1" if you are classifying a book of poetry. If you are classifying a book of plays (drama), drop the "0" and add a "2." Essentially that is what is done in the list of classification numbers starting at 811, American poetry (p. 887). The "0" is dropped, and the Specific Forms number is added, with poetry always being "1" and drama always being "2." American fiction could be classified in 813 rather than Fiction, but again, that is seldom done in any library.

Next you will see 814 for American essays, 815 for American speeches, 816 for American letters, and 817 for American humor. The digits 1, 2, 3, 4, 5, 6, and 7 may be added to any country number and will mean the same thing that they do here for American literature.

A few base numbers are three or even four digits. For example, take a look at Portuguese (869). Add the appropriate single digit to this number for the genre, such as poetry or drama. Portuguese poetry would go in 869.1. Portuguese drama would go in 869.2. Each of these items would have to be by one person. Collections by more than one person are designated with a standard subdivision for Collections.

COLLECTIONS, SINGLE COUNTRY

In number building in literature, -008 means a collection. This used to be -08 rather than -008, so you will find many materials in Dewey collections that have -08 rather than the newer -008. This *does not* mean a collection of anything by one individual person. It means a collection of literary forms by many people. It is a standard subdivision under -1-8 in Table 3. The -1-8 means the range of specific forms (poetry, drama, fiction, essays, etc.). One standard subdivision for all these forms is -008, "collections." The collection must be of authors all from the same country. If they are from *different* countries, see further instructions in this chapter in the section "Collections, Many Countries, One Type of Literature (Poetry or Drama)."

POETRY

Again, the country of the author is the most important thing to think about first. For a book of poetry by Robert Frost, American poet, use 811 for its classification number, followed by the first two letters of Frost's last name.

811 = American poetry
Fr = Author's last name

A book of poetry by five different American poets, for example *Journeys in American Poetry*, is an occasion to use the designator for "collection." First you need the number for American poetry:

811

Then add -008 onto it.

811.008
Jo

The last line is the first two letters of the main entry, which should be the first word of the title (a title main entry) of the book, because editors of collections are not main entries in a catalog record.

DRAMA

For a book consisting of only one play by Tennessee Williams, the American playwright, use the base number 81 and add -2 onto it, meaning this is a work of drama.

812
Wi

The letters are the first two letters of the author's last name.

A book of five plays by Tennessee Williams sounds like a "collection," but in terms of assigning a classification number, it is not. It would be incorrect to place this in 812.008. The plays are all by one author, so the book, whether it consists of one play or several by the same author, gets this:

812
Wi

Plays often are not published conveniently as collections by one playwright. Most often the collection of plays will be of many plays, perhaps American plays by several playwrights. This is when you use the -008. The number would look like this for a book titled *Modern American Drama*:

812.008
Mo

Special Tidbit: Cutter Numbers

The second lines of the call numbers are often called "Cutter numbers," named for Charles Ammi Cutter, who invented this system. In school libraries there are usually no actual numbers associated with that line. Rather, just a letter or two (sometimes called Cutter letters) are sufficient for the first word in the main entry. In large public libraries, numbers are associated with the Cutter designation as a device for alphabetically arranging by main entry (usually the author's last name) multiple books on the same topic. A school situation will never be that complicated. If you had five books on American birds, they would all go in the same Dewey classification number and would be subarranged by the main entries, usually the author's last name designated by one or two letters, for example: 598 Zi or 598 ZIM for *Birds: A Guide to Familiar Birds of North America*, by Herbert Spencer Zim.

In this case "81" is the base number for American literature, "2" means drama, and -008 means it is a collection of plays by more than one author. "Mo" underneath the classification number stands for the first word of the title. This item is given a title main entry because the plays would have been collected under an editor's direction.

As with languages, literature base numbers may be more than two digits long. For example, the Portuguese base number is 869. A book of poetry by one Portuguese poet goes in 869.1 (the -1 is for poetry). A book of poetry by more than one Portuguese poet goes in 869.1008.

COLLECTIONS, MANY COUNTRIES, ONE TYPE OF LITERATURE (POETRY OR DRAMA)

If the book is a collection of poetry from many countries, dispense with the 810s–890s, because those go only on items specific to a country. Instead, start with 808, Rhetoric and collections of literary texts from more than two literatures.

Locate ".8," Collections of literary texts from more than two literatures. This means 808.8 is assigned to a collection of several genres (plays, poetry, short stories, etc.) from more than one country.

Next, locate 808.81-808.88 Collections in Specific Forms. Here are the major ones to remember:

* 808.81 is assigned to a collection of poetry by poets from more than one country (808.8 = collections, 1 = poetry).
* 808.82 is assigned to a collection of drama by playwrights from more than one country (808.8 = collections, 2 = drama).

COLLECTIONS, ONE COUNTRY, SEVERAL TYPES OF LITERATURE (POETRY, DRAMA, SHORT STORIES, IN AN ANTHOLOGY)

Since this is a collection from one country, start with the base number for that country. For example, Spanish literature's base number is 86. Add the standard subdivision for collections from Table 3. Individual Literatures is -08. That would give you 860.8. Alternatively, think of the base number as being 860. When the standard subdivision for "Collections [of various types of literature]" is added, -08, the zeroes merge, making the number 860.8, not 860.08.

An example with a four-digit base number is Norwegian literature, 839.8. There is no zero as the third digit. A collection of various types of Norwegian literature goes in 839.808. The "08" portion of the classification number means "Collections of literary texts in more than one form."

For the same reason, a collection of Japanese literature goes in 895.608. 895.6 is for Japanese and -08 is for collections of various types, or "Collections of literary texts in more than one form."

Special Tidbit: Standard Subdivision for Collections

When should you use the -08 standard subdivision, and when should you use -008? Use -08 when a designation of form is not used. Collections of many types of literature in one volume, from one country, get -08. Collections of the form of poetry or the form of drama get -008, preceded by the designator for the form, either "1" for poetry or "2" for drama. For example: 891.81008.

HISTORY AND GEOGRAPHY

Base Number for History

Turn to 940-990, History of specific continents, countries, localities in modern world; extraterrestrial worlds. History's base number is "9." Add the country number to the base number from Table 2. The other way is to look them up by country name in the Relative Index. If you start at the Relative Index, do not stop there:

- After finding what appears to be the appropriate number in the Relative Index, double check it in the Schedules.
- Once you find your country number in the 900s history area, scan the historical breakdown given for the country.
- For those countries that schools and small public libraries are likely to have a wide range of materials on, Dewey provides detailed breakdowns in the call numbers.
- For example, if you have a book about the Norman period of British history, it would go in 942.02.

Dewey provides call numbers for the history of individual states as well:

- You can look up any state in the Relative Index.
- The state number gets tacked onto a "9," because "9" is your base number in history. So if you find the number for Massachusetts (744) in the Relative Index, you tack that onto "9" and add the decimal point three spaces to the right of the first number. Hence, Massachusetts is 974.4

Another way to build a number for the history of a state is to start in United States history, 973. Look further to 974-979. This is for history of specific states.

- The instruction states "Add to base number 97 the numbers following –7 notation 74-79." You are to build your number by using the state number in Table 2.
- Look at the Area tables, Specific States of United States. All the numbers for the states begin with "7." When number building in states' history, drop the initial "7" from the state number. This missing "7" is picked up in the base number for states, or "97." This is for history, not geography, which starts with the base number 91.
- That is what the fine print under 974-979 is saying. Whatever number is left over gets tacked onto 97. So a history of Maine would be 974.1. 97 = History of the States, and 41 = Maine (minus the initial "7," or 741, which is in the Area table designating Maine, the "7" meaning "United States," so actually the "7s" merge. The 7 in 974-979 merges with the "7" or the first digit in the state number).

Remember that you are working with Abridged Dewey. It is only one volume. If you were working with Unabridged Dewey (four volumes), you would find much more detailed classification numbers for the 900s and for other areas as well, because a larger library is likely to have many more materials on any one state and so will need a more refined classification scheme to delineate those items. It would not want to collect all its books on New York City into a general New York classification number, but rather would want something more refined that would isolate the New York City books from the general New York books, and other such finer delineations.

Geography or Travel

Locate 913-919 Geography of and travel in specific continents, countries, localities; extraterrestrial worlds. See the explanation of the base number 91 in the small print right beneath the 913-919 heading.

- For geography books, write down the base number for these two types of materials, 91, then add the number for the geographic area to it. Insert the decimal point.
- For example, for British geography: Add "42" from the Area table to the base number of 91. 914.2 is for atlases and geographies about Great Britain: 91 = Geography; 42 = British.

For travel guides (like Fodor's, Frommer's, or Michelin), do the same as above, but add the subdivision 04. You will see that in the list under 913-919. A travel guide to Costa Rica would go in 917.28604.

The Presidents

Look at 973.921. This is a number specifically for the Eisenhower administration. Notice the breakdown that follows under that number. The presidential administrations of the United States in the twentieth century are specifically each given an Abridged Dewey classification number.

Dewey's Mnemonic Feature

You should start to see a pattern to geographic treatment. Area table numbers are affixed to subject numbers. They do not change. Therefore, any time you see, for example, a "44" in the last position in a call number, it is very likely that book has something to do with France. It might be about political parties in France (324.244), or statistics of France (314.4), or geography of France (914.4), and "42" is the Area number for Britain. Taking "42" to history, if we affix "42" to the base number "9," we get the number for history of England and Wales (942). By the same token, "44" is the base number for the French language, while "44" is the Area number for France. This numbering system within Dewey is known as a *mnemonic* device, which means it functions as an aid to one's memory.

CONFUSED, DON'T FEEL YOU KNOW QUITE WHAT YOU ARE DOING?

Go to an OPAC on the Internet for a library that classifies using the DDC and test your classification number by doing a call number browse command. See if the resulting titles are similar to the title you are classifying. If a MARC display is available, click on that. The tag for a DDC number assigned by the Library of Congress is 082. The tag for a DDC number assigned by the specific library whose catalog you are searching is 092. There is no substitute for practice when learning Dewey.

BISAC SUBJECT HEADINGS LIST: THE MOST RECENT EXPERIMENT IN BOOK CLASSIFICATION AND SHELVING

Some librarians have been questioning whether the Dewey Decimal System, with all its complexity, is really necessary. If the goal is to find a book on a shelf and there is a less labor-intensive (hence less costly) way of doing it, should librarians try it?

Some libraries have done this. They are arranging their books by subject categories used in bookstores. Some users love it. They find what they want and also run across other books that look appealing. Others say its drives them crazy because they can't find books that do not fit neatly into a category.

This is not a free-for-all, haphazard arrangement. Like Dewey, it is a codified classification scheme called the BISAC Subject Headings List, also known as the BISAC Subject Codes List. BISAC stands for Book Industry Standards and Communications and is a standard used by bookstores to categorize and shelve books based on topical content. The major subject categories and subcategories are available on the

Internet at no cost. The Library of Congress began including BISAC subject codes in its cataloging in 2011 (*Ask Ms. MARC*, n.d.). Some public libraries are experimenting with shelving arrangements and signage meant to entice readers as bookstores do, while not completely abandoning the DDC, but rather using a "mashup style" incorporating both (Ambrosius, 2012).

This concludes the discussion of the DDC. You are now familiar with the main concepts of library materials classification using this system and should be able to proceed and practice from a well-informed knowledge base.

TEST YOUR KNOWLEDGE

What are the classification numbers in the 400s for the following?

1. Spanish-language dictionary
2. Latin grammar
3. Swahili dictionary
4. Korean dictionary
5. Russian grammar
6. Hebrew dictionary

What are the classification numbers in the 800s for the following?

1. A book of plays by the British playwright Tom Stoppard. Include the "Cutter" line (the second line of the classification number) as well.
2. A collection of American plays by several playwrights.
3. A book of poetry by Carl Sandburg, an American. Include the Cutter line as well.
4. A collection of poems by one Japanese poet.
5. A book of plays by several Swedish playwrights.
6. An anthology of several types of literature (poetry, short stories, plays) from more than one country.
7. A collection of plays by several Slovanic authors.
8. A book titled *Anthology of Best Portuguese Short Stories, Plays and Poetry of the 20th Century*.

What are the classification numbers in the 900s for the following? (Hint: Do not forget to the use Relative Index when the Schedules do not tell you enough.)

1. British history during the era of Queen Elizabeth II.
2. The African country of Botswana after it achieved independence from Great Britain in 1966.
3. The American Civil War.

4. World War II as it relates to all of Europe.
5. The 1974–1975 period of the Vietnamese War in U.S. history.
6. The history of Texas.
7. A geography of the western United States.
8. A travel guide to Tibet.
9. The rule of Saddam Hussein.
10. An atlas of Ireland. (This is not covered in the chapter specifically, but check the Relative Index and use your number building skills.)

TEST YOUR CRITICAL THINKING

1. A teacher wants each student to memorize a short poem and needs a selection from various poets. You find him browsing in the 800s for poetry collections. Where do you steer him in the collection, and what do you tell him about the placement of poetry in your library?
2. Think about using bookstore arrangement in your school library. What are the strengths and weaknesses of such an arrangement?

RESOURCES

Ambrosius, A. (2012, January 13). *Libraries rethinking the Dewey Decimal System*. Retrieved from: http://sussex.patch.com/groups/editors-picks/p/libraries-ditching-or-doctoring-the -dewey-decimal-system.
Ask Ms. MARC. (n.d.). Retrieved from: http://www.follettsoftware.com/askmsmarc.cfm.
Dewey, M. (2012). *Abridged Dewey decimal classification and relative index* (15th ed.). Dublin, OH: OCLC.
McCoppin, R. (2011, February 19). Dewey's days numbered? Some suburban libraries shelve old classification system, which still has its defenders. *Chicago Tribune*. News Section, 1.1.

IV

CONCLUSION

14

From Resource Discovery to Information Fluency

The theme throughout this book has been a catchphrase taken from the stated principal goal of RDA: to facilitate *resource discovery* through library catalogs in a more consistent and powerful way than is currently possible with AACR2. In the information age, resource discovery has become an exciting concept, albeit more complex than it was in the predigital era. When seeking information, everyone is faced with a vast landscape of choices, with some resources easily uncovered, while others take longer and require deeper digging to discover. To be successful at deeper discovery, students need to achieve skills in information fluency, a concept without a universally agreed upon definition. In terms of the OPAC, only one research tool among many others in the digital age, students can be considered information fluent if they can mine the OPAC for deep retrieval, understand what records they have retrieved and why their search retrieved them, and make a preliminary judgment about the usefulness of the resources identified.

It would be most beneficial if OPAC skills were in some way part of the Common Core State Standards Initiative, but unfortunately the language used very briefly in the Standards more closely relates to Internet searching. For example, Standard RI-5 (Reading Informational Text) at grade level 3 reads as follows:

- Use text features and tools (e.g., keywords, sidebars, hyperlinks) to locate information relevant to a given topic efficiently.

Although every librarian knows the shortsightedness of this reliance on search engines like Google, it is well to keep in mind that teachers and students will first think of the Internet rather than the online catalog when contemplating research. This is like relying on a poor index in a multivolume encyclopedia to yield precise information on the myriad subjects within its covers. The user needs accurate information on a chosen main topic, in addition to related, broader and narrower aspects of it. Without a controlled vocabulary, precision of retrieval on the Internet is not guaranteed. The catalog, on the other hand, has consistency as its foundation, making search results more precise and reliable. Also, resources identified through the OPAC have passed editorial tests before being published, unlike information on the Internet, where there are no such restrictions.

Resource discovery for K–12 students presents another challenge for teachers and librarians. Students are at various stages of development, which affects their ability to use keyboards, formulate searches, spell search words correctly, and interpret OPAC displays. Unfortunately, most of the research in this area has been focused on Web searching rather than OPACs, at least in recent years. Child-friendly search interfaces are available from some vendors, who have developed icon-based functions to supplement text-based commands.

Aside from such icons, OPACs do not appear to be designed with the child in mind. Indeed, given the variety of displays now available from OPAC software designers, it is a wonder that anyone, child or adult, can mine all the information embedded in a catalog record. While the new digital technology and screen designs can exploit bibliographic information in ways not possible in the days of static card display, OPACs can also leave the user confused by the nonstandardized displays, making it difficult to navigate through them and discover all they have to offer. Making the transition from one OPAC to another and interpreting what appears on the screen is not as easy as using card catalogs in different libraries was. All bibliographic records based on cards were alike in structure and display. For this reason, it is important to teach K–12 students not only how to search in their own school's OPAC, but also something about the basic structure of an OPAC record and how to identify its various elements in a way that is not tied directly to screen display.

The library profession as a whole must become highly attuned to the current information landscape, realizing, accepting, and adapting to the reality that digitization has created competition. While catalog-based information retrieval was once almost the librarian's exclusive domain, today everyone is in the game. The Internet-at-large, LibraryThing, library discovery systems, Novelist, GoodReads, Shelfari, and Bibliocommons are across-the-board competitors. Bibliocommons, a newly developed library discovery system, in particular is aiming at redefining the OPAC with the goal of creating a search interface that "combines the ease of use that users find on Google and Amazon with the power and precision library professionals require" (BiblioCommons, 2013). The days of the traditional OPAC may be numbered.

The catalog as social space is supported by LibraryThing, GoodReads, and Shelfari, sites where books are "cataloged" by users and given subject tags, reviews, ratings, and commentaries, some even accompanied by user-input short videos reflecting their feelings and reactions to the book. While this is not a substitute for a professionally constructed catalog, it does seem to offer something the inventory structure of the catalog does not: the chance for users to exchange their thoughts about what they are reading. This could easily be seen as a function akin to the stated purpose of RDA, resource discovery, in this case directed by students themselves rather than by teachers or librarians.

With the implementation of RDA and the potential of FRBR to create an OPAC display based on relationships between and among entities, the OPAC should be able to contribute more meaningfully to information fluency among students and information discovery for all users. The OPAC is only one player in the information game today, but a very important one, because this finding tool, above all others, has a long tradition behind it. It was built on experience and codification and discussion and interaction among the national and international communities, and was the first large-scale resource discovery system to harness the wonders of digitization. It still has a role to play in student learning and achievement, and school librarians must be ever mindful of creating and maintaining a catalog that lives up to its potential in this role.

RESOURCES

BiblioCommons. (2013). *Search that is as intuitive as it is intelligent*. Retrieved from: http://www.bibliocommons.com/products/bibliocore/for-users/search.

Gross, M. (2006). *Studying children's questions: Imposted and self-generated information seeking at school*. Lanham, MD: Scarecrow Press.

Heine, C., & O'Connor, D. (2014). *Teaching information fluency: How to teach students to be efficient, ethical, and critical information consumers*. Lanham, MD: Scarecrow Press.

Intner, S. S., Fountain, J. F., & Weihs, J. (2011). *Cataloging correctly for kids: An introduction to the tools* (5th ed.). Chicago: American Library Association.

Tarulli, L. (2012). *The library catalogue as social space*. Santa Barbara, CA: Libraries Unlimited.

A

Differences Between AACR2 and RDA to Aid Quick Recognition of an RDA Record

AACR2	RDA
Has a GMD in brackets following the title in bibliographic records for nonprint items.	There is no GMD. It is replaced by Content Type, Media Type, and Carrier Type, three new fields. These fields are in bibliographic records for both print and nonprint items.
Many abbreviations used. For example, 45 p., ill., ed.	Fewer abbreviations used. "45 pages," "illustrations," "edition" are spelled out.
Uses [et al.] in the Statement of Responsibility to indicate there were more than three individuals contributing to the publication.	No use of [et al.] permitted. Indicate any or all of the named individuals. One option is "by Arthur Levine [and five others]."
If the place of publication is not known, it is indicated as S.l. (Latin for *sine loco*).	S.l. is no longer used. Use this instead: [Place of publication not identified].
If the publisher is not known, it is indicated as s.n. (Latin for *sine nomine*).	s.n. is no longer used. Use this instead: [publisher not identified].
Copyright dates are indicated as c2007.	Copyright symbol is required. ©
No more than three individuals having the same function are traced.	Rule of three is out. Trace one or all individuals, or use the "and others" option.
Inaccuracies in spelling in the title are indicated by [sic], with the correction being traced in the 246 field.	Inaccuracies in the title are not indicated by [sic], but the corrected form is traced in the 246 field.

B

RDA Sample Records in MARC From OCLC

1. RDA RECORD FOR A BOOK, WITH A PERSONAL MAIN ENTRY

I Am Malala, the Girl Who Stood up for Education and Was Shot by the Taliban, by Malala Yousafzai

050 b4 LC2330 ‡b .Y69 2013b
020 bb 9780297870913 (hbk.)
082 04 954.91053092 ‡2 23
100 1b Yousafzai, Malala, ‡d 1997- ‡e author.
245 10 I am Malala : ‡b the girl who stood up for education and was shot by the Taliban / ‡c Malala Yousafzai ; with Christina Lamb.
264 b1 London : ‡b Weidenfeld & Nicolson, ‡c 2013.
300 bb viii, 327 pages, 16 unnumbered pages of plates : ‡b color illustrations, maps ; ‡c 25 cm
336 bb text ‡2 rdacontent
337 bb unmediated ‡2 rdamedia
338 bb volume ‡2 rdacarrier
505 b0 Before the Taliban -- A daughter is born -- My father the falcon -- Growing up in a school -- The village -- Why I don't wear earrings and Pashtuns don't say thank you -- Children of the rubbish mountain -- The mufti who tried to close our school -- The autumn of the earthquake -- The Valley of Death -- Radio Mullah -- Toffees, tennis balls, and the Buddhas of Swat -- The clever class -- The bloody square -- The diary of Gul Makai -- A funny kind of peace -- Leaving the valley -- Three bullets, three girls -- The Valley of Sorrows -- Praying to be tall -- The woman and the sea -- A private Talibanization -- Who is Malala? -- Between life and death -- 'God, I entrust her to you' -- Journey into the unknown -- A second life -- 'The girl shot in the head, Birmingham' -- 'They have snatched her smile' -- Epilogue: One child,

one teacher, one book, one pen -- Glossary -- Acknowledgements -- Important events in Pakistan and Swat.
600 10 Yousafzai, Malala, ‡d 1997-
650 b0 Young women ‡x Education ‡z Pakistan ‡z Swāt District ‡v Biography.
650 b0 Young women ‡x Crimes against ‡z Pakistan ‡z Swāt District ‡v Biography.
650 b0 Children's rights ‡z Pakistan.
700 1b Lamb, Christina, ‡e author.

2. RDA RECORD FOR A BOOK, WITH A TITLE MAIN ENTRY

Sharkopedia, the Complete Guide to Everything Shark

020 bb 1603209646
020 bb 9781603209649
050 14 QL638.9 ‡b .S45395 2013
082 04 597.3 ‡2 23
245 00 Sharkopedia : ‡b the complete guide to everything shark / ‡c with an introduction by Andy Dehart, marine biologist and "Shark Week" expert.
246 1b ‡i Title appears on item as: ‡a Discovery sharkopedia
264 b1 Des Moines, Iowa : ‡b Time Home Entertainment, ‡c [2013]
300 bb 192 pages : ‡b color illustrations ; ‡c 26 cm
336 bb text ‡2 rdacontent
337 bb unmediated ‡2 rdamedia
338 bb volume ‡2 rdacarrier
500 bb "Shark week" -- Title page.
520 bb Presents facts, trivia, photographs, and anecdotes about over four hundred known species of sharks in the world.
650 b0 Sharks ‡v Juvenile literature.
650 b1 Sharks.
710 2b Time Inc. Home Entertainment, ‡e publisher.
710 2b Discovery Channel (Firm), ‡e sponsoring body.

3. RDA RECORD FOR AN E-BOOK

Other Worlds, edited and with an introduction by Jon Scieszka.

020 bb 9780062239129 (electronic bk.)
020 bb 0062239120 (electronic bk.)
020 bb ‡z 9780061963803
020 bb ‡z 0061963801
020 bb ‡z 9780061963797
020 bb ‡z 0061963798
050 b4 PZ5 ‡b .O85 2013eb
082 04 [Fic] ‡2 23

245 00 Other worlds / ‡c edited and with an introduction by Jon Scieszka ; stories by Tom Angleberger [and 9 others] ; with illustrations by Greg Ruth.
264 b1 New York, NY : ‡b Walden Pond Press, an imprint of HarperCollinsPublishers ‡c 2013.
300 bb 1 online resource (ix, 331 pages) : ‡b illustrations.
336 bb text ‡b txt ‡2 rdacontent
337 bb computer ‡b c ‡2 rdamedia
338 bb online resource ‡b cr ‡2 rdacarrier
490 1b Guys read ; ‡v #4
520 bb An anthology of original science fiction and fantasy stories.
505 00 ‡t Before we begin / ‡r by Jon Scieszka -- ‡t Percy Jackson and the singer of Apollo / ‡r by Rick Riordan -- ‡t Bouncing the grinning goat / ‡r by Shannon Hale -- ‡g The ‡t Scout / ‡r by D.J. MacHale -- ‡t Rise of the RoboShoes / ‡r by Tom Angleberger -- ‡g The ‡t dirt on our shoes / ‡r by Neal Shusterman -- ‡t Plan B / ‡r by Rebecca Stead -- ‡g A ‡t day in the life / ‡r by Shaun Tan -- ‡g The ‡t Klack Bros. Museum / ‡r by Kenneth Oppel -- ‡g The ‡t warlords of recess / ‡r by Eric Nylund -- ‡t Frost and fire / ‡r by Ray Bradbury.
588 bb Description based on print version record.
650 b0 Children's stories, American.
650 b0 Science fiction, American.
650 b0 Fantasy fiction, American.
650 b1 Science fiction.
650 b1 Fantasy.
650 b1 Short stories.
655 b4 Electronic books.
700 1b Scieszka, Jon, ‡e editor of compilation.
700 1b Ruth, Greg, ‡e illustrator.
700 1b Angleberger, Tom. ‡t Rise of the Robo Shoes.
700 1b Riordan, Rick. ‡t Percy Jackson and the singer of Apollo.
700 1b Hale, Shannon. ‡t Bouncing the grinning goat.
700 1b MacHale, D. J. ‡t Scout.
700 1b Shusterman, Neal. ‡t Dirt on our shoes.
700 1b Stead, Rebecca. ‡t Plan B.
700 1b Tan, Shaun. ‡t Day in the life.
700 1b Oppel, Kenneth, ‡d 1967- ‡t Klack Bros. Museum.
700 1b Nylund, Eric S. ‡t Warlords of recess.
700 1b Bradbury, Ray, ‡d 1920-2012. ‡t Frost and fire
776 08 ‡i Print version: ‡t Other worlds ‡z 9780061963803 ‡w (DLC) 2013021863 ‡w (OCoLC)827259355
830 b0 Guys read ; ‡v 4.
856 40 ‡3 OverDrive (EPUB) ‡u http://www.contentreserve.com/TitleInfo .asp?ID={DE032844-FD19-4C5D-9E4B-FD78504C80C2}&Format=410
856 40 ‡3 OverDrive (Kindle) ‡u http://www.contentreserve.com/TitleInfo .asp?ID={DE032844-FD19-4C5D-9E4B-FD78504C80C2}&Format=420
856 40 ‡3 OverDrive (READ) ‡u http://www.contentreserve.com/TitleInfo .asp?ID={DE032844-FD19-4C5D-9E4B-FD78504C80C2}&Format=610
856 4b ‡3 Image ‡u http://images.contentreserve.com/ImageType-100/0293-1/ {DE032844-FD19-4C5D-9E4B-FD78504C80C2}Img100.jpg

4. RDA RECORD FOR A BOOK, WITH A
TITLE MAIN ENTRY AND VARIANT TITLES

Official 2013 National Football League Record & Fact Book

020 bb 9781603209809 (paperback)
020 bb 1603209808 (paperback)
050 14 GV955 ‡b .N334 2013
082 04 796.33202/02 ‡2 23
245 00 Official 2013 National Football League record & fact book / ‡c compiled by
   the NFL Communications Department. and Seymour Siwoff, Elias Sports Bureau
   ; statistics by Elias Sports Bureau ; edited by Jon Zimmer, NFL Communications
   Department and Matt Marini.
246 3b Record and fact book
246 3b 2013 National Football League record & fact book
246 3b National Football League official 2013 record and fact book
246 14 2013 official NFL record and fact book : 94th season
264 b1 New York, N.Y. : ‡b Time Home Entertainment Inc., ‡c 2013.
300 bb 688 pages : ‡b illustrations ; ‡c 23 cm
336 bb text ‡2 rdacontent
337 bb unmediated ‡2 rdamedia
338 bb volume ‡2 rdacarrier
500 bb "94th season"-- Cover and spine.
520 bb A resource of complete statistics includes all-time records, team rosters,
   schedules, past standings, and Super Bowl results, and also features a digest of NFL
   rules, team directories, and active and career coaching records.
610 20 National Football League ‡v Handbooks, manuals, etc.
610 20 National Football League ‡v Statistics.
650 b0 Football ‡v Handbooks, manuals, etc.
650 b0 Football ‡x Records ‡z United States.
700 1b Siwoff, Seymour, ‡e compiler.
700 1b Zimmer, Jon, ‡e editor.
700 1b Marini, Matt, ‡e editor.
710 2b National Football League. ‡b Public Relations Department, ‡e compiler, ‡e
   editor.
710 2b Elias Sports Bureau, ‡e researcher.

5. RDA RECORD FOR A BOOK, WITH
TWO EXTERNAL LINKS (856 FIELDS)

Cooking for Your Gluten-Free Teen: Everyday Foods the Whole Family Will Love, by
Carlyn Berghoff and Sarah Berghoff McClure.

020 bb 9781449427603
020 bb 144942760X

050 00 RM237.86 ‡b .B468 2013
082 00 641.3 ‡2 23
100 1b Berghoff, Carlyn.
245 10 Cooking for your gluten-free teen : ‡b everyday foods the whole family will love / ‡c by Carlyn Berghoff and Sarah Berghoff McClure ; with Suzanne P. Nelson and Nancy Ross Ryan.
260 bb Kansas City, Mo. : ‡b Andrews McMeel, ‡c c2013.
300 bb 181 p. : ‡b col. ill. ; ‡c 23 cm.
500 bb Includes index.
505 0b Pt. I The new lifestyle: -- Why I wrote this book / Carlyn Berghoff -- Eating with the enemy / Carlyn Berghoff -- Nothing helped -- and then finally something did / Sarah Berghoff McClure -- The inside track on celiac / Suzanne P. Nelson -- The survey: top thirty foods kids miss most -- Guide to gluten-free eating and cooking / Carlyn Berghoff -- Eating out: school, restaurants, and away from home / Sarah Berghoff McClure -- Sharing tips / Suzanne P. Nelson -- Helpful links -- Pt. II The cookbook: -- The best place to start -- Recipe guidelines for gluten-free cooking -- Lactose intolerance, dairy allergies, and a gluten-free diet -- Resources for gluten-free products -- ch. 1 Breakfast and bread -- ch. 2 Starters and snacks -- ch. 3 Soups, salads, and sandwiches -- ch. 4 Main dishes -- ch. 5 Side dishes -- ch. 6 Desserts.
650 b0 Gluten-free diet ‡v Recipes.
650 b0 Gluten-free foods.
655 b7 Cookbooks. ‡2 lcgft
700 1b McClure, Sarah Berghoff.
700 1b Nelson, Suzanne P.
700 1b Ryan, Nancy Ross.
856 42 ‡3 Contributor biographical information ‡u http://catdir.loc.gov/catdir/ enhancements/fy1317/2012955066-b.html
856 42 ‡3 Publisher description ‡u http://catdir.loc.gov/catdir/enhancements/ fy1317/2012955066-d.html

6. RDA RECORD FOR A BLU-RAY DVD

Oz the Great and Powerful

028 42 111592 ‡b Buena Vista Home Entertainment
028 42 8028407 (Blu-ray) ‡b Buena Vista Home Entertainment
028 42 8028409 (DVD) ‡b Buena Vista Home Entertainment
090 bb PN1997.2 ‡b .O9 2013
245 00 Oz the great and powerful / ‡c Disney presents a Roth Films Production in association with Curtis-Donen Productions ; screen story by Mitchell Kapner ; screenplay by Mitchell Kapner and David Lindsay-Abaire ; produced by Joe Roth ; directed by Sam Raimi.
246 1b ‡i At head of title: ‡a Disney.
250 bb [Blu-ray/DVD combo edition]
257 bb United States. ‡2 naf
260 bb Burbank, Calif. : ‡b Distributed by Buena Vista Home Entertainment, ‡c c2013.

300 bb 1 Blu-ray disc (ca. 130 min.) : ‡b sd., col. ; ‡c 4 3/4 in. + ‡e 1 DVD-video + 1 digital copy
336 bb two-dimensional moving image ‡b tdi ‡2 rdacontent
337 bb video ‡b v ‡2 rdamedia
338 bb videodisc ‡b vd ‡2 rdacarrier
344 bb digital ‡b optical ‡g surround
347 bb video file ‡b DVD video ‡e Region 1 ‡2 rda
380 bb Motion picture
538 bb Blu-ray ; 1080p high definition ; Widescreen (beginning of features plays in 1.33:1) ; Surround sound
538 bb DVD; NTSC; Region 1; widescreen (2.40:1) presentation (beginning of features plays in 1.33:1); 5.1 Dolby digital (English, French, Spanish), 2.0 Dolby digital (English, DVS).
546 bb English, Spanish or French dialogue; Spanish or French subtitles; subtitled for the deaf and hard of hearing; English described video.
511 1b Rachel Weisz, James Franco, Michelle Williams, Mila Kunis, Zach Braff.
500 bb Originally released as a motion picture in 2013.
521 8b MPAA rating: PG; for sequences of action and scary images, and brief mild language ‡a CHV rating: PG.
508 bb Based on the works of L. Frank Baum ; music by Danny Elfman ; film editor, Bob Murawski ; director of photography, Peter Deming.
520 bb Disney's fantastical adventure Oz The Great And Powerful, from the director of the Spider-Man trilogy, follows Oscar Diggs, a small-time circus magician with dubious ethics. When Diggs is hurled away to the vibrant Land of Oz, he thinks he's hit the jackpot -- until he meets three witches who aren't convinced he's the great wizard everyone's expecting. Reluctantly drawn into epic problems facing Oz and its inhabitants, Oscar must find out who is good and who is evil before it's too late. Putting his magical arts to use through illusion, ingenuity -- and even some wizardry -- Oscar transforms himself into the great wizard and a better man as well.
500 bb Special features: bloopers; featurette "Walt Disney and the road to Oz", Walt's fascination with Oz.
650 b0 Wizard of Oz (Fictitious character) ‡v Drama.
650 b0 Oz (Imaginary place) ‡v Drama.
650 b0 Witches ‡v Drama.
650 b7 Wizard of Oz (Personaje literario) ‡v Teatro. ‡2 bidex
655 b7 Action and adventure films. ‡2 lcgft
655 b7 Fiction films. ‡2 lcgft
655 b7 Feature films. ‡2 lcgft
655 b7 Fantasy films. ‡2 lcgft
655 b7 Video recordings for the hearing impaired. ‡2 lcgft
655 b7 Video recordings for people with visual disabilities. ‡2 lcgft
700 1b Weisz, Rachel, ‡d 1971- ‡e actor
700 1b Franco, James, ‡d 1978- ‡e actor
700 1b Williams, Michelle, ‡d 1980- ‡e actor
700 1b Kunis, Mila, ‡d 1983- ‡e actor
700 1b Braff, Zach, ‡d 1975- ‡e actor
700 1b Kapner, Mitchell. ‡e screenwriter
700 1b Lindsay-Abaire, David. ‡e screenwriter

700 1b Roth, Joe, ‡d 1948- ‡e producer
700 1b Raimi, Sam. ‡e director
710 2b Curtis-Donen Productions.
710 2b Walt Disney Pictures.
710 2b Buena Vista Home Entertainment (Firm)
710 2b Roth Films.

7. RDA RECORD FOR A PLAYAWAY

The Book Thief, by Markus Zusak

020 bb 9781615875825 (Playaway)
020 bb 1615875824 (Playaway)
028 bb 0180123 ‡b Findaway World
028 bb 0116682 ‡b Findaway World
050 14 PZ7.Z837 ‡b Boo 2013e
100 1b Zusak, Markus, ‡e author.
245 14 The book thief / ‡c Markus Zusak.
250 bb Unabridged.
264 1b Solon, Ohio : ‡b Findaway World, LLC, ‡c [2013]
300 bb 1 audio media player (approximately 14 hr.) : ‡b digital, HD audio ; ‡c 3 3/8 x
   2 1/8 in. + ‡e 1 book.
336 bb spoken word ‡b spw ‡2 rdacontent
336 bb text ‡b txt ‡2 rdacontent
337 bb audio ‡b s ‡2 rdamedia
337 bb unmediated ‡b n ‡2 rdamedia
338 bb other ‡b sz ‡2 rdacarrier
338 bb other ‡b nz ‡2 rdacarrier
338 bb volume ‡b nc ‡2 rdacarrier
500 bb Title from Playaway label.
500 bb "HDAUDIO."
500 bb "Listening Library"-- Container.
500 bb In hanging bag (13 x 10 cm).
511 0b Read by Allan Corduner.
500 bb Previously released by Random House, Inc., ℗2005.
500 bb Issued on Playaway, a dedicated audio media player.
500 bb One set of earphones and one AAA battery required for listening.
520 bb Trying to make sense of the horrors of World War II, Death relates the story
   of Liesel -- a young German girl whose book-stealing and story-telling talents help
   sustain her family and the Jewish man they are hiding, as well as their neighbors.
651 b0 Germany ‡x History ‡y 1933-1945 ‡v Juvenile fiction.
650 b1 Books and reading ‡v Fiction.
650 b1 Storytelling ‡v Fiction.
650 b1 Death ‡v Fiction.
650 b1 Jews ‡z Germany ‡x History ‡y 1933-1945 ‡v Fiction.
650 b1 World War, 1939-1945 ‡x Jews ‡x Rescue ‡v Fiction.

651 b1 Germany ‡x History ‡y 1933-1945 ‡v Fiction.
655 b7 Children's audiobooks. ‡2 lcgft
655 b7 Audiobooks. ‡2 lcgft
700 1b Corduner, Allan, ‡e narrator.
710 2b Random House (Firm)
710 2b Listening Library.
710 2b Playaway Digital Audio.
710 2b Findaway World, LLC.

8. RDA RECORD FOR BOOK ON COMPACT DISC

Sycamore Row, by John Grisham

020 bb 9780385366472
020 bb 0385366477
028 bb 01Z8585 ‡b Blackstone Audio
043 bb n-us-ms
050 14 PS3557.R5355 ‡b S93 2013d
082 bb 04813/.54 ‡2 23
100 1b Grisham, John, ‡e author.
245 10 Sycamore Row / ‡c by John Grisham.
250 bb Unabridged, [library edition].
264 1b [Ashland, Oregon] : ‡b Blackstone Audio, Inc., ‡c [2013]
264 4b ‡c ℗2013
300 bb 16 audio discs (20 hours) : ‡b digital ; ‡c 4 3/4 in.
336 bb spoken word ‡b spw ‡2 rdacontent
337 bb audio ‡b s ‡2 rdamedia
338 bb audio disc ‡b sd ‡2 rdacarrier
344 bb digital ‡b optical ‡g stereo ‡2 rda
347 bb audio file ‡b CD audio ‡2 rda
500 bb Compact discs.
500 bb Tracks every 3 minutes for easy bookmarking.
520 bb When wealthy Seth Hubbard hangs himself from a sycamore tree and leaves
    his fortune to his black maid, Jake Brigance once again finds himself embroiled in
    a controversial trial that will expose old racial tensions and force Ford County to
    confront its tortured history.
650 b0 Criminal defense lawyers ‡z Mississippi ‡v Fiction.
650 b0 Trials (Murder) ‡v Fiction.
650 b0 Race relations ‡v Fiction.
650 b0 African American women ‡v Fiction.
651 b0 Mississippi ‡v Fiction.
655 7b Legal stories. ‡2 gsafd
655 7b Suspense fiction. ‡2 gsafd
655 7b Mystery fiction. ‡2 gsafd
655 7b Audiobooks. ‡2 lcgft
700 1b ‡i Sequel to (Work): ‡a Grisham, John. ‡t Time to kill.
710 2b Blackstone Audio, Inc., ‡e publisher.

9. RDA RECORD FOR CHILDREN'S MUSIC ON COMPACT DISC, CORPORATE MAIN ENTRY

Japanese Children's Songs, by Dino Lingo

045635824645
02800EX316e7 ‡b Dino Lingo
110 2b Dino Lingo.
245 00 Japanese children's songs / Dino Lingo.
264 1b [Place of publication not identified] : ‡b Dino Lingo, ‡c [2013]
300 bb 1 audio disc : ‡b digital, optical, 1.4 m/s, stereo ; ‡c 4 3/4 in.
336 bb performed music ‡b prm ‡2 rdacontent
337 bb audio ‡b s ‡2 rdamedia
338 bb audio disc ‡b sd ‡2 rdacarrier
546 bb In Japanese.
588 bb Title from disc.
505 00 ‡t Bunbunbun -- ‡t Donguri -- ‡t Hato -- ‡t Kagome -- ‡t Kirakiraboshi -- ‡t Koinoburi -- ‡t Kurinoki -- ‡t Nekofunjyatta -- ‡t Sakur a-- ‡t Shabondama -- ‡t Tewoutte -- ‡t Yuki.
650 b0 Children's songs, Japanese ‡v Juvenile sound recordings.

10. RDA RECORD FOR CHILDREN'S MUSIC ON COMPACT DISC, PERSONAL MAIN ENTRY

The Best in Me, by Dave Kinnoin

020 bb 9781881304166
024 1b 744757910822
028 02 SW108-2 ‡b Song Wizard Records
037 bb ‡b Midwest Tape ‡n http://www.midwesttapes.com
050 4b M1997.K56 ‡b B47 2013
082 04 782.42083 ‡2 23
100 1b Kinnoin, Dave, ‡e composer, ‡e performer.
245 14 The best in me / ‡c Dave Kinnoin.
264 1b South Pasadena, CA : ‡b Song Wizard Records, ‡c [2013]
264 b4 ‡c ℗2013
300 bb 1 audio disc : ‡b CD audio, digital ; ‡c 4 3/4 in.
336 bb performed music ‡b prm ‡2 rdacontent
337 bb audio ‡b s ‡2 rdamedia
338 bb audio disc ‡b sd ‡2 rdacarrier
344 bb digital ‡2 rda
347 bb audio file ‡b CD audio ‡2 rda
500 bb Title from container.
511 0b Performed by Dave Kinnoin ; with assisting musicians.
508 bb Produced by Randy Sharp, Jimmy Hammer, and Dave Kinnoin.
500 bb Compact disc.

505 00 ‡t A lot of good in there ‡g (3:06) -- ‡t Enormously inconvenient ‡g (3:24) -- ‡t Happy for myself ‡g (3:45) -- ‡t Things kids figure out ‡g (2:50) -- ‡t It's good to love somebody ‡g (3:51) -- ‡t Person of character ‡g (3:28) -- ‡t I'll be me ‡g (3:52) -- ‡t Lemonade stand ‡g (3:33) -- ‡t Place of character ‡g (3:06) -- ‡t What you do ‡g (4:12) -- ‡t High achiever ‡g (3:28) -- ‡t Give us a chance ‡g (3:31) -- ‡t Greater than our fears ‡g (3:28) -- ‡t It could've been me ‡g (2:51) -- ‡t Everywhere all the time ‡g (3:22) -- ‡t I don't want an easy life ‡g (3:21) -- ‡t My dog brings out the best in me ‡g (2:59) -- ‡t A lot of good in there (music track only) ‡g (3:14) -- ‡t Enormously inconvenient (music track only) ‡g (3:30) -- ‡t Lemonade stand (music track only) ‡g (3:40) -- ‡t Place of character (music track only) ‡g (3:09) -- ‡t I don't want an easy life (music track only) ‡g (3:26) -- ‡t My dog brings out the best in me (music track only) ‡g (3:06).
650 b0 Children's songs ‡v Juvenile sound recordings.
650 b0 Character ‡x Songs and music ‡v Juvenile sound recordings.
650 b0 Fairness ‡x Songs and music ‡v Juvenile sound recordings.
650 b1 Songs.
650 b1 Character ‡v Songs.
650 b1 Fairness ‡v Songs.

Key to the Quizzes

CHAPTER 4, UNDERSTANDING CATALOGING IN PUBLICATION (CIP)

Test Your Knowledge

1. This book is nonfiction, and therefore its summary note should have something about its source, such as -- Provided by publisher. Also, there should be no children's subject headings, or the subject headings in brackets.

CHAPTER 5, CREATING ACCESS POINTS

Test Your Knowledge

Title Page 1. Best Shot in the West: The Adventures of Nat Love
By Patricia and Fredrick McKissack, Jr.
Illustrated by Randy DuBurke

ME: 100 1b McKissack, Pat, $d 1944- (You will not necessarily know this form of her name. If you answered by using McKissack, Patricia, for purposes here that would be correct.)
AE: 245 10 Best shot in the West
AE: 700 1b McKissack, Fredrick, $c Jr.
AE: 700 1b DuBurke, Randy, $e illustrator

Reason: AACR2 Rule 21.6C1. Works of Shared Responsibility: If responsibility is shared between two or three persons or bodies and principal responsibility is not attributed to any of them by wording or layout, enter under the heading for the one named first. Make added entries under the headings for the others. Optional: Make an added entry for the illustrator; this is almost always done for children's literature.

Title Page 2. Summer Reading for Teens: How to Close the Achievement Gap
Edited by Richard L Allington, Anne McGill, & Lynn Bigelman

M.E.: 245 00 Summer reading for teens
A.E.: 700 1b Allington, Richard L., $e editor
A.E.: 700 1b McGill, Anne, $e editor
A.E.: 700 1b Bigelman, Lynn, $e editor

Reason: AACR2 Rule 21.7B1: Collections of works by different persons . . . enter it under its *title* . . . make added entries under the headings for the compilers or editors if there are not more than three. RDA: The same, but if there are more than three editors, you *may* trace all of them.

Title Page 3. Encyclopedia of World War II
By Dwight D. Eisenhower, George Patton, Omar Bradley, and Douglas MacArthur

M.E.: 100 1b Eisenhower, Dwight D. $q (Dwight David), $d 1890-1969
A.E.: 245 10 Encyclopedia of World War II
A.E.: 700 1b Patton, George S. $q (George Smith), $d 1885-1945
A.E.: 700 1b Bradley, Omar Nelson, $d 1893-1981
A.E.: 700 1b MacArthur, Douglas, $d 1880-1964

Reason: Now defunct AACR2 Rule 21.6C2: If responsibility is shared among more than three persons or corporate bodies and principal responsibility is not attributed to any one, two or three, enter under the title. Make an added entry under the heading for the first person . . . named . . . in the item.

RDA CHANGE applied in this case: The main entry, or the authorized access point, is *the first named person, not the title* in the case of more than *three authors*. This is a major departure from AACR2. By RDA guidelines, *any or none* of the other authors may be traced. This decision is up to the cataloger.

Title Page 4. The Beauty of the Beast: Poems from the Animal Kingdom. Selected by Jack Prelutsky. Illustrated by Meilo So.

M.E. 245 04 The beauty of the beast. Poems from the animal kingdom
A.E. 700 1b Prelutsky, Jack, $e compiler
A.E. 700 1b So, Meilo, $e illustrator

Reason: AACR2 Rule 21.7B1: Collections of works by different persons . . . enter it under its *title* . . . make added entries under the headings for the compilers or editors if there are not more than three. RDA: The same, but if there are more than three editors, you *may* trace all of them.

A collection of poems by multiple authors receives a title main entry.

Title Page 5. Nightmares! Poems to Trouble Your Sleep, by Jack Prelutsky. Illustrated by Arnold Lobel.

M.E. 100 1b Prelutsky, Jack, $e author
A.E. 245 10 Nightmares! Poems to trouble your sleep
A.E. 700 1b Lobel, Arnold, $e illustrator

Reason: AACR2 Rule 21.4A1: Enter a work . . . by one personal author under the heading for that person.

A collection of poems by one author receives a personal main entry for the author.

Title Page 6. Georgia O'Keeffe: One Hundred Flowers. Edited by Nicholas Callaway

M.E. 100 1b O'Keeffe, Georgia, 1887-1986, $e artist
A.E. 245 10 Georgia O'Keeffe, one hundred flowers
A.E. 246 10 One hundred flowers
A.E. 246 13 100 flowers
A.E. 600 10 O'Keeffe, Georgia, 1887-1986
A.E. 700 1b Callaway, Nicholas, $e editor

Reason: AACR2 Rule 21.17 A (Art work without text, or very little text). The artist is the main entry. In this case most of the book consists of reproductions of O'Keeffe's art.

Title Page 7. Will You Be Mine? A Nursery Rhyme Romance. Compiled and Illustrated by Phyllis Limbacher Tildes

M.E.: 100 1b Tildes, Phyllis Limbacher, $e author
A.E.: 245 10 Will you be mine?
A.E. 730 0b Mother Goose

Reason: The nursery rhymes are from Mother Goose, but that name is not in the title. A uniform title added entry must be created to make this accessible by the commonly known name for nursery rhymes, or Mother Goose.

CHAPTER 6, CREATING AUTHORIZED FORMS OF NAMES

Test Your Knowledge

Multiple Choice

1. C
2. A
3. B

4. C
5. A
6. B
7. A
8. C
9. A
10. C

Forms of Entry

1. Nixon, Richard M. (Richard Milhous), 1913-1994
2. Hopper, Grace Murray
3. Clinton, Hillary Rodham
4. Perlman, Itzhak, 1945-
5. Obama, Barack
6. American Idol (Television program)
7. Kennedy, Edward M. (Edward Moore), 1932-2009
8. Cooper, Bradley
9. Lin, Maya Ying
10. Zaharias, Babe Didrikson, 1911-1956

CHAPTER 7, CREATING MARC 21 RECORDS

Test Your Knowledge

1. False. Correct answer: Machine Readable Cataloging.
2. False. It is quite possible for a school librarian to have a firm understanding of the tags used most often in MARC records for school materials.
3. False. The second indicator for "The" is "4," standing for "t, h, e," and a blank space.
4. False. In a title main entry we do not trace the title. It is automatically traced because there is no 100 or author field above it. It should look like this: 245 04 The big yellow dog. This is one of the conventions that is difficult to explain in a computer environment, because it relates to the days of catalog cards.
5. True.
6. True.
7. False. If subfield $d has a holding symbol in it, that library modified the original DLC record.
8. False. A second subfield "4" means Cover title, not spine title.
9. False. If the first indicator is "0," the series is not repeated in the 830 field.
10. True.
11. True.

12. False. A personal name subject heading goes in a 600 field.
13. True.
14. False. Fiction is a form subdivision and should be preceded by $v, not $x.
15. B 710.
16. False. In an author/title added entry, the title subfield ($t) cannot have an initial article, which in this case is "The." There are no nonfiling indicators, so it would be indexed under "The," which is incorrect.
17. True.
18. 100 1b Mandela, Nelson, $d 1918-2013
19. 100 0b Avi, $d 1937-
20. 700 1b Sendak, Maurice, $e illustrator
21. 600 10 Wilder, Laura Ingalls, 1867-1957 $x Homes $y Missouri
22. 600 10 Roosevelt, Franklin D. $q Franklin Delano, $d 1882-1945 $x Press relations
23. 650 b0 Presidents $z United States $v Portraits
24. 651 b0 France $x History $y Revolution, 1789-1799
25. 650 b0 German language $v Dictionaries

CHAPTER 8, CATALOGING BOOKS

Test Your Knowledge

Quotations

1. Your users don't really expect you to do perfect cataloging but they probably expect to find library books in the catalog and on the shelf, and not in your office.—Kathryn L. Corcoran, Library Services Director, Munson-Williams-Proctor Arts Institute.
2. I've got to stop being such a snob about leather-bound books, he reminded himself. E-books do have their moments.—Dan Brown, *Inferno*

CHAPTER 9, CATALOGING NONPRINT AND ELECTRONIC MATERIALS

Test Your Knowledge

Quotations

1. The importance of images and visual media in contemporary culture is changing what it means to be literate in the 21st century. Today's society is highly visual, and visual imagery is no longer supplemental to other forms of information.—ACRL Visual Literacy Competency Standards for Higher Education
2. Film can be an interesting way for teachers to connect sometimes theoretical or abstract course concepts to a world outside the classroom.—Author unknown

CHAPTER 10, CATALOGING BOOKS IN SERIES

Test Your Knowledge

Quotation

Many people, myself among them, feel better at the mere sight of a book.—Jane Smiley

CHAPTER 11, USING *SEARS LIST OF SUBJECT HEADINGS*

Test Your Knowledge

Subject Headings

1. **1. Robins. 2. Birds.** If you look up Birds in Sears, it authorizes you to make specific headings for any type of Bird. The wording is: SA (for See Also) types of birds, e.g., Canaries, to be added as needed. Sometimes it helps to assign both the general and specific, which is what I have done here.
2. **Children -- Health and hygiene.** If you look up Children and follow the subdivisions all the way through alphabetically, you'll find -- Health and hygiene. If you look up Health, you'll find authorization for "groups" with the subdivision Health and hygiene, for example, Women -- Health and hygiene. "Children" represents a "group"; hence you use the subdivision -- Health and hygiene.
3. **Los Angeles (Calif.) -- Race relations.** Look up Chicago (Ill.) in Sears. Any subdivisions found at the "key heading" of Chicago (Ill.) may be used with any city. You must include the name of the state in parentheses after the name of the city. Do not use postal abbreviations such as IL or MN.
4. **American drama -- Collections.** See the section on Literary Form Headings.
5. **China -- History -- 1912-1949.** Look up China in Sears. You'll find a historical breakdown at the name of the country. Choose the one that most closely matches your book. See the section on History of Countries.
6. **Pesticides -- Bibliography.** Pesticides is an authorized subject heading in Sears. Bibliography is a form subdivision that may be applied as needed. See the section on Form Subdivisions.
7. **Grant, Ulysses S. (Ulysses Simpson), 1822-1885 -- Homes.** The subdivision Homes is an authorized subdivision to be used with any president's name. See the section on Key Headings for Presidents.
8. **1. Ojibwa Indians -- Medical care AND 2. Native Americans -- Medical care.** This is the same concept as the first item in this exercise. It is acceptable to assign both a general and a specific subject heading to a specific topic.
9. **Swahili language -- Grammar.** Look up English language. Here you will find all the subdivisions that may be used with any language. You must in-

clude the word "language," such as French language -- Grammar. So it's not
Swahili -- Grammar. See the section on English language as a Key Heading.

10. **United States -- History -- 1755-1763, French and Indian War -- Fiction.**
Look up United States -- History, find the correct subdivision for the French
and Indian War, then add -- Fiction. See the section on Fiction as Subdivision.

11. **Gates, Bill, 1955- .** Correct form of the name per the LC Name Authority
File. No -- Biography. See the section on Biography.

12. **No subject heading.** See the section on Literary Form Headings.

13. **Elderly -- Home care.** Look up Aged. It says USE Elderly. Look up Elderly.
Look at the authorized subdivisions under Elderly. One of them is -- Home care.

14. **Mountaineering.** This is the authorized subject heading for mountain climbing. No -- DVD or anything similar indicating the media type. See the section on Nonbook Materials.

15. **Smallpox.** Authorized under Headings to Be Added by the Cataloger.

16. **Short stories.** See the section on Short Stories.

17. **Vietnam War, 1961-1975 -- Conscientious objectors.** "Key Headings." Use
the Key Heading World War, 1939-1945. Look at the subdivisions under
that subject heading in Sears. Any of those apply to any war. -- Conscientious
objectors is authorized as a subdivision. See the section on Key Headings.

18. **Arizona -- Economic conditions.** Start at Economic conditions in Sears and
read the SA "names of countries, cities, areas, etc." with the subdivision Economic conditions. Or start at the Key Heading for states, Ohio. You'll find
-- Economic conditions in the authorized subdivisions.

Multiple Choice

19. C
20. B
21. A
22. A
23. C
24. B

MARC Coding

25. 650 b0 Predatory animals
26. 651 b0 Great Britain $x History $y Henry, VIII, 1509-1547 $v Fiction In this
case, "Henry, VIII, 1509-1547" is a historical era, not a person's name.
27. 600 10 Zuckerberg, Mark, $d 1984-
28. 650 b0 Penguins $v Juvenile films
29. 650 b0 African Americans $x Civil rights $z Alabama $z Montgomery $x
History $y 20th century
30. 650 b1 Poisonous snakes

CHAPTER 12, USING *ABRIDGED DEWEY*
DECIMAL CLASSIFICATION

Test Your Knowledge

1. 921 Ga
2. 636.003
3. 728.0944
4. 373.794
5. Bibliography of substance abuse, classified in substance abuse with a standard subdivision for bibliography
6. False
7. 590.75; 590. 7 (Education, research, related topics) and 590 (animals).
8. Bibliography of substance abuse classified in Bibliography
9. 917.88
10. 799.29775

CHAPTER 13, BUILDING DEWEY NUMBERS
IN THREE MAJOR AREAS

Test Your Knowledge

400s

1. 463. It is printed this way in Abridged Dewey 15th ed., p. 568. In other editions: "Add to base number 46 notation 01-8 from Table 4, e.g., grammar of Spanish language 465." Here you are asked for a Spanish dictionary. 3 is the number to add onto 46.
2. 475. It is printed this way in Abridged Dewey 15th ed., p. 570. 47 is the base number for Latin language. 5 is for grammar.
3. 496.3. In Abridged Dewey 15th ed., you must start in the Relative Index by looking up Swahili. Here it says 496. Turn to p. 575, where you will find 496 African languages. There is nothing about Swahili here, but that is not important. The Relative Index told you Swahili belongs here. Add the "3" to mean dictionaries.
4. 495.73. In Abridged Dewey 15th ed., p. 575, you will find Korean as 495.7. Add the "3" for dictionaries.
5. 491.75. In Abridged Dewey 15th ed., p. 572, you will find Russian and related East Slavic languages with the following note after .71-.75: "Add to base number 491.7 notation 1-5 from Table 4, e.g., grammar of Russian 491.75."
6. 492.43. In Abridged Dewey 15th ed., p. 574, you will find Hebrew. Add the "3" for dictionaries.

800s

1. 822 St. See the explanation at Adding to Base Numbers in Literature.
2. 812.008. See the explanation at Collections, Single Country.
3. 811 Sa. See the explanation at Adding to Base Numbers in Literature.
4. 895.61. Same explanation as at number 1, but for poetry rather than drama.
5. 839.72008. See the explanation at Collections, Single Country.
6. 808.8. This is the number for more than one country, more than one genre.
7. 891.81008. See the explanation at Collections, Single Country.
8. 869.08. See the explanation at Collections, One Country, Several Types of Literature.

900s

1. 941.085
2. 968.8303
3. 973
4. 940.53
5. 973.925
6. 976.4
7. 917.8
8. 915.104
9. 956.7044
10. 912.417

Glossary

AACR2R. *Anglo-American Cataloguing Rules, Second Edition*, Revised (2002), 2005 Update is a cataloging code used internationally. It was first published in 1967 as AACR and was succeeded by RDA, which was first made available in 2010. Many of the rules in AACR2 are also in RDA. The rules cover the description of and the provision of access points for many types of library materials.

Access point. An entry point into a catalog. In card catalogs, there were few access points for each cataloged item because each one required a separate card. In today's online public access catalogs, almost any word in the record can be an access point.

Added entry. Access point in a bibliographic record that is not the main entry. Called a Secondary Access point in RDA.

Analytic. A way to access *part* of a total work.

Annotated Card Program (AC). Former name for the current CYAC Program (CYACP), the Children's and Young Adults' Cataloging Program, at the Library of Congress. This office supplied cataloging data for MARC records specific to juvenile literature.

Area tables. Table 2 in the Dewey Decimal Classification, a systematic listing of numbers that, when added to DDC numbers, extend the initial concept to include a particular geographic area.

Authority control. A way of ensuring consistency in the forms of names and subjects used in the catalog and of linkages among them. Forms and linkages are recorded in a Name Authority File, particularly the one maintained by the Library of Congress.

Authorized Access Point. RDA terminology for the AACR2 term "main entry." The main or primary access point representing the work being cataloged.

Attributes. FRBR terminology. Entities have certain characteristics, or attributes.

Base numbers. Numbers used as the basis for the construction of a Dewey Decimal Classification number not specifically included in the schedules.

Biannual. Twice a year (the same as semi-annual).

Bibframe. A potential replacement for MARC coding that will integrate with the new RDA/FRBR relationships model.

Bibliography. A list of citations to works constructed according to a selected citation style, such as APA or MLA.

Biennial. Every two years.

Biography. A work about an individual (biography) or groups of individuals (collective biography).

BISAC Subject Headings. Book Industry Standard and Communications terms, a standard used by bookstores to categorize books based on topical content.

Book catalog. The earliest form of library catalog. Entries were made in the order that books arrived in the library.

Broader term (BT). A hierarchical designation in the *Sears List of Subject Headings*. At any particular term within the alphabetical listing of Sears, it may list other terms that are broader in concept.

Call number. Another name for a classification number, used when books were retrieved from closed shelves, or "called for" by a library user.

Card catalog. A library catalog that used a filing system of 3-by-5-inch cards to represent each cataloged item in a library. Each card provided a different access point to the item.

Cataloging in Publication (CIP). A catalog record created at the Library of Congress before a book is published. CIP information is later published in the completed book, usually on the back of the title page.

CE-MARC. Curriculum Enhanced MARC, referring to certain fields in the descriptive record that are useful to students and teachers, such as the Summary note, Reading level notes, and Study program notes.

Chief Source of Information. AACR2 terminology. When cataloging an item, it is the first place you look for information to use. For a book, it is the title page; for a motion picture, it is the title screen.

Children's and Young Adults' Cataloging Program (CYACP). A part of the Children's Literature Section of the Library of Congress, this program provides summaries and subject access points in cataloging for books written for the K–12 audience.

Choice of entry. From AACR2R Chapter 21, Choice of Access Points. Guide to deciding what names associated with the cataloged item will serve as access points in the catalog record. One access point will be the main entry; any others are added entries.

Collation. The former term for the Physical Description Area in the catalog record.

Controlled language or vocabulary. A predetermined set of terms to be used for subject headings or other vocabulary lists where consistency is necessary.

Corporate author. A group rather than an individual deemed responsible for the content of a cataloged item. These can be companies, colleges, organizations, governmental jurisdictions, and other groups.

Copy cataloging. Using a previously existing catalog record as the foundation for a new record.

Copyright date. The first date on which the content of an item is fixed in a tangible form and the owner is given exclusive rights to offer copies for sale.

Cross-reference. Leads the catalog user from one part of the catalog to another related part.

Cutter number. Named for Charles A. Cutter, this alphanumeric system is used in the second line of a Dewey classification number to subarrange by main entry multiple books on the same topic.

Delimiter. In MARC coding, a character marking the beginning or end of a unit of data and preceding a subfield code. Its form is variable. Often seen are these: # and $.

***Dewey Decimal Classification* (System).** Classification scheme conceived by Melvil Dewey as an alternative to fixed shelving. It allows for new concepts to be integrated with existing concepts through the use of ten classes (categories) of knowledge.

Dictionary catalog. Card catalog in which all access points, be they authors, subjects, or titles, were interfiled according to specified filing rules.

Divided catalog. Card catalog in which access points were filed according to type: author, subject, or title. Sometimes two types were interfiled, and the third type was filed in a separate catalog.

Downloadable audiobook. The text of a book being read aloud, transferred to the listener's device via an electronic download.

Downloadable e-book. Text of a book in readable form, transferred to a reading device via an electronic download.

Entities. FRBR terminology. The FRBR conceptual framework consists of three separate entities (parts) of a bibliographic record.

Et al. Latin for "and others." Used in AACR2 in the statement of responsibility when there are more than three individuals performing a function.

Expression. FRBR terminology. The intellectual or artistic realization of a Work. The second of the four Primary Entities.

Fixed location. Items shelved in a static position rather than relative to the other items around it and to its subject matter.

Form of entry. How the name will be represented in the access point. Established forms of entry are available online from the Library of Congress Authorities.

***Functional Requirements for Bibliographic Records* (FRBR).** A conceptual model for bibliographic control based on entities and relationships developed by the International Federation of Library Associations (IFLA). Pronounced "fer-ber."

General material designator (GMD). Indicator of class of material to which an item belongs. This designation was used in records for nonprint materials under AACR2, with the term appearing in brackets following the title of the item. The GMD is not part of RDA and is not used in current cataloging.

Genre subject headings. Terms in MARC field 655 that convey what an item is rather than what it is about.

Holding symbol. Identifying alpha (and occasionally alphanumeric) code used to represent individual libraries. Used in catalogs that show the holdings of more than one library.

Indicator. The first two character positions at the beginning of each data field that has varying numbers of characters (vs. the fixed field). Used as a shortened way of designating or defining something about the field.

Infinite hospitality. The characteristic of being able to include ever-increasing numbers of concepts or subjects in a classification scheme.

Interface. The design on the screen that allows the user to interact with a catalog or database.

International Standard Bibliographic Description (ISBD). An internationally agreed on standard punctuation format for recording and displaying bibliographic information in a standard catalog record.

International Standard Book Number (ISBN). A ten- or thirteen-digit coding system for identifying books.

Interpolate. To insert something new between preexisting items. Library items classified by subject area always have room for interpolation of new items.

Item. FRBR terminology. The fourth of the four Primary Entities. The actual physical copy of a particular Manifestation.

Key headings. Terms that act as a pattern or template to follow in formulating specific headings needed but not printed in Sears.

Keywords. Natural language words used as access points in a catalog record. The opposite of controlled language, such as in Sears.

Leader. The first field of a MARC record, a fixed field, with only twenty-four characters. It consists of data elements providing information for the automation system that is processing the record.

Leaf. AACR2 definition: a page printed on one side.

Library hand. An accepted way to handwrite the bibliographic information on cards, used by catalogers before printed cards.

Library of Congress. The largest library in the United States. Located in Washington, D.C., where it serves the research needs of Congress and the public. Supported by federal appropriations.

Library of Congress Control Number. System of numbering catalog records emanating from the Library of Congress. Formerly called Library of Congress Card Number.

Library of Congress Authorities. Authority file that lists established name and subject headings used by catalogers to maintain consistency in forms of access points.

Library of Congress Classification. A classification system begun in the late nineteenth century to organize and arrange the book collections of the Library of Congress. Serves as an alternative to the Dewey Decimal Classification for academic and large public libraries.

Library of Congress Program for Cooperative Cataloging Policy Statements. Service that explains and interprets RDA. Available free at the *RDA Toolkit* website. Formerly known as the Library of Congress Rule Interpretations and most recently as Library of Congress Policy Statements.

***Library of Congress Subject Headings* (LCSH).** Collection of terms that serves as an alternative to Sears subject headings. Used in academic and most public libraries. Can be accessed through the Library of Congress Authorities website or as a free pdf at LC's website. Until 2012 libraries had to purchase it in a red-colored, multivolume set from the Library of Congress.

Main entry. One of multiple access points to a bibliographic record, designated as the primary one under AACR2. Most of the time it is a personal name. Sometimes it is a title. In RDA it is synonymous with the Authorized Access Point.

Manifestation. FRBR terminology. The third of the four Primary Entities. Physical embodiment of an Expression of the Work. The manifestation level data comprises most of a bibliographic record.

MARC 21. Machine Readable Cataloging. A format for encoding bibliographic records, composed of codes and content designators.

Metadata. Bibliographic data for any cataloged item, placed in a "container" known as the MARC format.

Mnemonic. Acting as a memory device. The Dewey Decimal System has mnemonic features that contribute to its consistency and ease of use.

Monograph. A book designed to start and finish in a finite number of volumes, or a single publication. The opposite of a serial.

Narrower term (NT). Term used in Sears and LC subject headings as a way to designate authorized terms narrower in scope than the one under consideration.

Nonfiling characters. Articles (A, An and The) at the beginning of titles, coded so that they are eliminated from the indexing in an online catalog.

Notation. In classification systems, symbolizes the subject of each class and its place in the sequence of the classification scheme.

OCLC. Online Computer Library Center. Based in Dublin, Ohio, its headquarters houses the mainframe computer holding millions of machine readable catalog records, shared by libraries internationally.

OPAC. Online Public Access Catalog.

Original cataloging. Cataloging not based on previously existing catalog copy.

Page. AACR2 definition: a leaf printed on both sides.

Parallel title. A title in a language different from that of the title proper, appearing on the title page but not grammatically linked to another part of the description.

Paris Principles. A statement of cataloging principles approved by the International Conference on Cataloguing Principles in 1961. It has served as a basis for international standardization of cataloging practices since that time.

Personal main entry. AACR2 terminology. An individual's name serving as the primary access point in the bibliographic record.

Playaway. A listening device and the audio recording that is housed on it in electronic format.

Preferred Source of Information. RDA terminology. When cataloging an item, it is the first place you look for information to use. For a book, it is the title page; for a motion picture, it is the title screen.

Prescribed punctuation. As part of ISBD, punctuation to be used within and between each defined Area of a catalog record.

Primary Access Point. RDA terminology for the AACR2 term "main entry."

Primary Entities. Comprises Group 1 of the three groups in a FRBR-conceptualized bibliographic record. There are four Primary Entities making up the main sections of a bibliographic record: the Work, the Expression, the Manifestation, and the Item.

Prime mark. Punctuation mark used in a Dewey Decimal Classification number as a conceptual breaking point in a long number. A classification number may be shortened by removing numerals to the right of the prime mark.

Provider-neutral. Characteristic of generic catalog records for e-books in which producer/distributor and type of device needed to read the book are not included.

RDA. *Resource Description and Access*. The cataloging code adopted by the Library of Congress on March 31, 2013.

RDA Toolkit. Electronic publication of RDA, available for subscription online.

Related term (RT). Used in Sears and LC subject headings as a way to designate terms bearing some relationship in meaning to the word under consideration.

Relationships. FRBR terminology for defined connections between and among entities.

Relative Index. Alphabetical index to the DDC schedules.

Relative location. Position of items shelved relative to their subject area and relative to the other items already shelved. The opposite of fixed location.

Reprint. A reproduction of a bibliographic item printed previously, usually, but not always, with no alteration from the first printing.

Resource discovery. The ability to find needed material. Supporting resource discovery is RDA's stated purpose for the catalog. This statement compares to Cutter's first and second objectives for the catalog, both of which focus on the catalog as a finding tool.

Responsibility Entities. Comprises Group 2 of the three groups in a FRBR-conceptualized bibliographic record. These are the people or corporate bodies that had something to do with the intellectual or creative product.

SA (See also). In Sears, designation that alerts the cataloger to use specific terms that cannot all be listed in Sears because of space constraints.

Schedules. The main numeric classification scheme in the Dewey Decimal System.

Sears List of Subject Headings. A controlled vocabulary used in bibliographic records in smaller public and school libraries.

Secondary Access Point. RDA terminology. Entry point in the catalog record that is not the main or Authorized Access Point.

See also cross-reference. Reference that leads the user from a subject heading or personal name that is authorized to another subject or name that is related and also authorized.

See cross-reference. Reference that leads the user from an unauthorized name or subject heading to those that are authorized.

Semi-annual. Twice a year (the same as biannual).

Serial. A publication that comes out at regular or irregular intervals, retaining the same title with each item.

Shelflist file. File kept in the cataloging department with cards arranged in shelf, or classification, order.

Sine loco [S.l.]. Abbreviation formerly used in catalog records when the place of publication was not known, in this format: [S.l.]

Standard subdivisions. Table 1 in the Dewey Decimal Classification. Notations defining recurring forms and approaches that may be used to further define any subject number in the schedules.

Statement of responsibility. A transcription of authorship and other contributions as stated on the title page or in certain defined locations on nonprint media.

Stereotyped plates. Metal copy of typeset image used to print, proposed as a way to preserve and store early catalog records.

Study program. Notation in the notes area of bibliographic records to indicate motivational reading or other related reading programs to help users choose reading-level-specific books.

Subfield code. Code in MARC to indicate parts of a field, such as the dates of an author's birth and death, which in the 100 field are marked by subfield "d."

Subject Entities. Group 3 of the three groups in a FRBR-conceptualized bibliographic record. These are subject headings categorized as Content, Object, Event, and Place.

Subject headings. A controlled language from which to assign subject access points to cataloged items. Sears and Library of Congress are the two used most. The opposite of keywords.

Subject headings subdivisions. Additions to subject headings that in effect narrow and focus a broad subject. Through the use of subdivisions, we can indicate, for example, specific time periods in U.S. history.

Surrogate. A substitute, as a catalog record is a surrogate for the item it describes or represents.

Syndetic structure. A linking structure of subject headings authority lists, such as Sears and Library of Congress. See, See also, BT, NT, and RT are all part of the syndetic structure.

Tags. Field identifiers in MARC, three characters in length, each with specific meaning and use protocols.

Title main entry. The primary access point to a bibliographic record when a personal or corporate main entry is not allowed by the cataloging rules.

Trace. To provide an access point in the catalog.

Truncate. To shorten by cutting off. Dewey Decimal numbers can be truncated at concept segments of the number.

Uniform title. A title assigned to a work that has appeared under more than one title. This is done as part of authority control and allows the user to retrieve the item no matter the form under which the title has been published.

Union catalog. Catalog that shows the holdings of more than one library. It can be a regional public library system's catalog or something as large as the OCLC database.

Unpaged. Designation in the bibliographic description for a book (usually a picture storybook) indicating that the pages do not have page numbers printed on them.

Used for (UF). A notation for handling synonyms in subject headings. Indicates that one term is not used, and another synonymous term is used instead.

Variant title. Forms of the title found in places other than the preferred source of information, such as on the spine.

Verso. The back side of a leaf in a book, or the left-hand page in an open book. CIP information is usually printed on the verso of the title page.

WebDewey. Dewey Decimal Classification system available online from OCLC.

WEMI. In FRBR, Acronym for Work, Expression, Manifestation and Item, the four primary entities.

Work. RDA terminology. The first of the four Primary Entities. The idea of the story, not the physical item.

WorldCat. The OCLC database in which millions of bibliographic records are available to subscribing libraries for cataloging purposes and also, to some extent, to the general public.

Bibliography

Adamich, T. (2006). CE –MARC: The educator's library "receipt." *Knowledge Quest, 35*(1), 64–68.

Ambrosius, A. (2012, January 13). *Libraries rethinking the Dewey Decimal System.* Retrieved from: http://sussex.patch.com/groups/editors-picks/p/libraries-ditching-or-doctoring-the-dewey-decimal-system.

American Library Association, Association for Library Collections and Technical Services. (2007). *Differences between, changes within: Guidelines on when to create a new record.* Chicago: ALCTS/ALA.

Anglo American Cataloguing Rules (2nd ed.). (2005). Chicago: American Library Association.

Annual report of the trustees of the public library of the City of Boston, 1898. (1899a). Boston: Municipal Printing Office.

Annual report of the trustees of the public library of the City of Boston, 1899. (1899b). Boston: Municipal Printing Office.

Bealle, J. (2011). Dewey decimal classification. In S. S. Intner, J. F. Fountain, & J.Weihs (Eds.), *Cataloging correctly for kids* (5th ed.) (pp. 135–147). Chicago: American Library Association.

BiblioCommons. (2013). *Search that is as intuitive as it is intelligent.* Retrieved from: http://www.bibliocommons.com/products/bibliocore/for-users/search.

Bowman, J. H. (2005). *Essential Dewey.* New York: Neal-Schuman.

Bulletin of Bibliography (1923). *11*(10), 180.

Chan, L. M. (2007). *Cataloging and classification: An introduction.* Lanham, MD: Scarecrow Press.

Children's subject headings (CSH) list. (n.d.). Retrieved from: http://www.loc.gov/aba/cyac/childsubjhead.html.

Culbertson, B., Mandelstam, Y., & Prager, G. (2011, September). *Provider-neutral e-monograph MARC record guide.* Washington, DC: Program for Cooperative Cataloging.

Cutter, C. A. (1869). The new catalogue of the Harvard College Library. *North American Review, 108*(January), 96–129.

Department of the Interior, Bureau of Education. (1876). *Public libraries in the United States of America: Their history, condition, and management. Special report. Part II. Rules for a printed dictionary catalogue, by Charles A. Cutter.* Washington, DC: GPO.

Dewey, M. (2004). *Abridged Dewey decimal classification and relative index* (14th ed.). Albany, NY: Forest Press.

Dewey, M. (2012). *Abridged Dewey decimal classification and relative index* (15th ed.). Dublin, OH: OCLC.

DVD region code. (2012, September 20). Retrieved from: http://en.wikipedia.org/wiki/DVD_region_code.

Ferro, F., & Lushington, N. (1998). *How to use the library: A reference and assignment guide for students.* Westport, CT: Greenwood.

Flynn, E. A. (2013). Open access metadata catalogers and vendors: The future of cataloging records. *Journal of Academic Librarianship, 39*(1), 29–31.

Follett Software Company. (n.d.-a). *Ask Ms. MARC.* Retrieved from: http://www.follettsoftware.com/askmsmarc.cfm.

Follett Software Company. (n.d.-b). *Tag of the month.* Retrieved from: http://www.follettsoftware.com/tagofthemonth.cfm.

Fred Kilgour. (n.d.). In *Wikipedia.* Retrieved February 25, 2012, from: http://en.wikipedia.org/wiki/Fred_Kilgour.

Gross, M. (2006). *Studying children's questions: Imposed and self-generated information seeking at school.* Lanham, MD: Scarecrow Press.

Hart, A. (2010). *The RDA primer: A guide for the occasional cataloger.* Santa Barbara, CA: Linworth.

Heine, C., & O'Connor, D. (2014). *Teaching information fluency: How to teach students to be efficient, ethical, and critical information consumers.* Lanham, MD: Scarecrow Press.

History of the card catalog. (2011, June 8). In *LIS Wiki.* Retrieved from: http://liswiki.org/wiki/History_of_the_card_catalog.

HLWIKI International. (2013). *Resource description and access (RDA).* Retrieved from: http://hlwiki.slais.ubc.ca/index.php/Resource_Description_and_Access_%28RDA%29.

How one pioneer profoundly influenced modern librarianship. (n.d.). Retrieved from: http://www.oclc.org/dewey/resources/biography/.

Hufford, J. R. (1991). The pragmatic basis of catalog codes: Has the user been ignored? *Cataloging & Classification Quarterly, 14*(1), 27–38. In V. L. P Blake. (2002). Forging the Anglo-American Cataloging Alliance: Descriptive cataloging, 1830–1908. *Cataloging & Classification Quarterly, 35*(1/2), 3–22.

International Historic Films. (2012). *What is NTSC and PAL standard?* Retrieved from: http://ihffilm.com/videostandard.html.

Intner, S. S., Fountain, J. F., & Weihs, J. (Eds.). (2011). *Cataloging correctly for kids: An introduction to the tools* (5th ed). Chicago: American Library Association.

Jewett, C. C. (1853). *Smithsonian report on the construction of catalogues of libraries and their publication by means of separate stereotyped titles with rules and examples* (2nd ed.). Washington, DC: Smithsonian Institution.

Kaplan, A. (2006). Do I have to make a new record? Deciding when you have a new edition and when you have a second copy. *Library Media Connection, 24*(5), 28–29.

Kua, E. (2004). Non-western languages and literature in the Dewey Decimal Classification scheme. *Libri, 54*, 256–265.

Lake Placid Club demolition undertaken at Mirror Lake facility (1993, February 16). *Watertown Daily Times* (online in Newsbank).

LC training for RDA: Resource description and access. (2012). *Module 2: Describing carriers and identifying works.* Retrieved from: http://www.loc.gov/catworkshop/RDA%20training%20 materials/LC%20RDA%20Training/LC%20RDA%20course%20table.html.

Library catalog. (n.d.). In *Wikipedia.* Retrieved December 9, 2013 from: http://en.wikipedia .org/wiki/Library_catalog.

Library of Congress control number. (n.d.-a). In *Wikipedia.* Retrieved from: http://en.wikipedia .org/wiki/Library_of_Congress_Control_Number.

Library of Congress control number. (n.d.-b). Retrieved from: http://www.oclc.org/bibformats/ es/0xx/010.shtm.

Library of Congress (LC) RDA training materials. (n.d.). Retrieved from: http://www.loc.gov/ catworkshop/RDA training materials/LC RDA Training/LC RDA course table.html.

MARC code lists for organizations. (n.d.). Retrieved from: http://www.loc.gov/marc/organi zations/orgshome.html.

MARC standards. (n.d.). Retrieved from: http://www.loc.gov/marc/.

MARC 21 format standards for bibliographic data. (n.d.). Retrieved from: http://www.loc.gov/ marc/bibliographic/ecbdhome.html.

MARC 21 reference materials. Part VII: A summary of commonly used MARC 21 fields. (n.d.). Retrieved from: http://www.loc.gov/marc/umb/um07to10.html.

McCoppin, R. (2011, February 19). Dewey's days numbered? Some suburban libraries shelve old classification system, which still has its defenders. *Chicago Tribune.* News Section, 1.1.

McCroskey, M., & Turvey, M. R. (2003). What is CIP and how does it benefit the school library media specialist? *Knowledge Quest, 32*(2), 45–46.

McCroskey, M., & Turvey, M. R. (2013). *Using CIP to create the local catalog record: The nuts and bolts.* Retrieved from: http://www.ala.org/aasl/aaslarchive/pubsarchive/kqarchives/ added/ciptutor.

Miller, Joseph. (2011). Sears list of subject headings. In S. S. Intner, J. F. Fountain, & J. Weihs (Eds.), *Cataloging correctly for kids* (5th ed.) (pp. 129–134). Chicago: American Library Association.

Millions of Harvard Library catalog records publicly available. (2012, April 24). Retrieved from: http://archive.is/sSaex.

Nicholson, J. (n.d.). *RDA in MARC.* Retrieved from: http://www.llaonline.org/ne/lla2011/ RDApreconference.pdf.

Olson, N. B. (2008). *Cataloging of audiovisual materials and other special materials: A manual based on AACR2 and MARC 21* (5th ed.). Westport, CT: Libraries Unlimited.

Prescott, S. (2001). If you knew Dewey . . . Melvil Dewey. *School Library Journal, 47*(8), 50–53.

Purpose of the CIP program. (n.d.). Retrieved from: http://www.loc.gov/publish/cip/about/.

Robinson, J. (2009, September 7). Two types of series books. In *Booklights* [blog]. PBS. http:// www.pbs.org/parents/booklights/archives/series/.

Rules for descriptive cataloging in the Library of Congress. (1949). Washington, DC: Library of Congress, Descriptive Cataloging Division.

Satija, M. P., & Haynes, E. (2008). *User's guide to Sears list of subject headings.* Lanham, MD: Scarecrow.

Schiff, A. L. (2011). *Changes From AACR2 to RDA: A comparison of examples.* Retrieved from: http://faculty.washington.edu/aschiff/BCLAPresentationWithNotes-RevMay2011.pdf.

Sears, M. E. (2010). *Sears list of subject headings* (20th ed.). New York: Wilson.

Sharp, H. A. (1935). *Cataloguing, a textbook for use in libraries.* London: Grafton.

Simpson, C. (2011). *Copyright catechism II: Practical answers to everyday school dilemmas.* Santa Barbara, CA: Linworth.

Spicher, K. M. (1996). The development of the MARC Format. *Cataloging & Classification Quarterly, 21*(3–4), 75–90.

Tarulli, L. (2012). *The library catalogue as social space.* Santa Barbara, CA: Libraries Unlimited.

Taylor, A. G., & Joudrey, D. N. (2009). *The organization of information* (3rd ed.). Westport, CT: Libraries Unlimited.

University of Florida, George A. Smathers Libraries. (2013, December 10). *Creative Commons CC0.* Retrieved from http://www.uflib.ufl.edu/catmet/creativecommons.html.

Van Orden, P., & Strong, S. (2007). *Children's books: A practical guide to selection.* New York: Neal-Schuman.

Weihs, J., & Intner, S. S. (2009). *Beginning cataloging.* Santa Barbara, CA: Libraries Unlimited.

Wiegand, W. (1996). *Irrepressible reformer: A biography of Melvil Dewey.* Chicago: American Library Association.

Working Group on the International Standard Bibliographic Description. (1974). *ISBD(M): International Standard Bibliographic Description for monographic publications* (1st standard ed.). London: IFLA Committee on Cataloguing.

WorldCat rights and responsibilities for the OCLC cooperative. (2013). Frequently asked questions. (n.d.) Retrieved from: http://rlin21.rlg.org/worldcat/recorduse/policy/questions/default.htm.

Index

name headings
  authorized form of, 30, 75–76
  changing an authorized form of, 79
  commonly known form of, 77–78
  consistency of, 78–79
  corporate, 100
  forename, 78, 94, 103
  fullest form of, 77–78, 86
  geographic, 85
  given, 78, 94
  parentheses and, 77
  pseudonymous, *See* pseudonyms
natural language indexing, 200
new record, when to create, 132
nonfiling indicators, 94, 96, 98, 104, 113, 124, 128, 283
notes area, 109, 116–117, 123, 139, 147–149
notes fields, order of, 98, 116
NTSC video standard, 143, 145–146, 148, 151

OCLC, 10–12, 30–32, 93, 132, 222, 224, 283
  statistics page of, 11
On the Construction of Catalogues of Libraries (Jewett), 7
ONIX program, 39–40
OPACs
  authority control and, 75–76, 87
  display interface and, 17–20, 71
  display similar to card in, 17–20
  entry points in, 5
  search interface of, 4
open entry and series, 190
original cataloging, 75, 110, 283
  Creative Commons and, 32

page, definition of, 121
Panizzi, Antonio, 6–7
parallel titles, 130, 132
Paris Principles, 9, 283
performer note tag 511 (MARC record), 143, 147, 148, 151, 156, 160–161, 164, 169, 171, 172, 176

photographer as added entry, 67–68
photographer as main entry, 67–68
physical description area, 97, 109
  audiobooks, downloadable, 172, 176
  books, 111, 115, 119, 120–121, 125, 127, 129, 131, 163
  CDs, 156, 160, 161, 163
  DVDs, 143, 145–146, 151
  eBooks, downloadable, 173, 177, 179
  Playaways, 164
  RDA changes in, 116, 119, 121, 125, 129, 131, 145–146
place of publication, 114, 120, 160
  CIP and, 35, 38
  CDs, 157
  RDA changes in, 114, 257
plates, 97, 119, 120–121
Playaways, 139, 162–165, 284
poetry, classification of in DDC, 229, 241–242, 244
preferred source of information, 49, 77, 113, 284
  CDs, 153
  DVDs, 142
presidents, classification of, 246–247
pre-paging, 120
primary access point, 48, 284
provider-neutral catalog records, 199, 279, 284
pseudonyms, 76, 78, 80, 81, 83
publication date vs. copyright date, 115
publication, distribution area tags 260 and 264 (MARC record), 97, 114–115, 119, 120, 157, 158, 160, 167, 190

RDA record, identifying, 257
RDA changes from AACR2
  added entry, 48
  author called creator, 112
  copyright symbol, 152
  dates of birth of authors, 86
  distinguishing between identical names, 86
  edition statement, 96, 113
  et al., 59, 130, 257
  GMD, 142, 157, 282

About the Author

Marie Kelsey, PhD, professor emerita, College of St. Scholastica, Duluth, Minnesota, recently completed a forty-year career in librarianship, twenty-seven years of which were devoted to cataloging and technical services in academic libraries. She is also a licensed K–12 librarian and retired director of the Educational Media and Technology program at St. Scholastica.

Dr. Kelsey earned her master's degree in English at Bemidji State University and her master's and PhD degrees in Library Science from the University of Wisconsin, Madison. She has authored several articles on cataloging and other aspects of school librarianship. In 2006, her book *Ulysses S. Grant: A Bibliography* (Praeger, 2005) was named one of five best bibliographies of the year in history by the Reference & User Services Association (ALA) History Section's Bibliography and Indexes Committee.